HISTORY

OF THE

POLITICAL AND MILITARY

TRANSACTIONS IN INDIA

DURING THE ADMINISTRATION

OF THE

MARQUESS OF HASTINGS

1813-1823

HISTORY
OF THE
POLITICAL AND MILITARY
TRANSACTIONS IN INDIA
DURING THE ADMINISTRATION
OF THE
MARQUESS OF HASTINGS
1813-1823.

BY HENRY T. PRINSEP

IN TWO VOLUMES-VOL. II.

Published by

Gyan Publishing House
5, Ansari Road
Daryaganj, New Delhi-110002
Phone: 011-47034999, 9811692060
E-mail: books@gyanbooks.com

Distribution Network
gyanbooks.com
India, USA, Canada, UK, Australia

ISBN: 978-93-6280-048-0 (Set)
978-93-6280-981-0 (HB)
First Published, 1825

2nd Impression 2024

Printed at: Gyan Press, Delhi.

HISTORY OF THE POLITICAL AND MILITARY TRANSACTIONS IN INDIA DURING THE ADMINISTRATION OF THE MARQUESS OF HASTINGS 1813-1823, (VOL. II.)
Author: HENRY T. PRINSEP

HISTORY

OF THE

POLITICAL AND MILITARY TRANSACTIONS

IN INDIA.

HISTORY

OF THE

POLITICAL AND MILITARY

TRANSACTIONS IN INDIA

DURING THE ADMINISTRATION

OF THE

MARQUESS OF HASTINGS

1813—1823.

BY HENRY T. PRINSEP,

OF THE BENGAL CIVIL SERVICE.

ENLARGED FROM THE NARRATIVE PUBLISHED IN 1820.

Res poscere videtur,—ut non modo casus eventusque rerum, qui plerique fortuiti sunt, sed ratio etiam causæque noscantur. TACITUS.

IN TWO VOLUMES.—VOL II.

LONDON:

KINGSBURY, PARBURY, & ALLEN,

LEADENHALL STREET.

1825.

CONTENTS

OF THE

SECOND VOLUME.

CHAPTER XIII.

GENERAL PREPARATIONS.

1817, JUNE TO NOVEMBER.

CHAPTER XIV.

PINDAREES. POONA. NAGPOOR.

1817, OCTOBER TO DECEMBER.

b 2

CHAPTER XV.

NAGPOOR. HINDOOSTAN.

1817, DECEMBER.

CHAPTER XVI.

HOLKUR. HINDOOSTAN.

1817–18, DECEMBER, JANUARY, FEBRUARY.

CHAPTER XVII.

POONA.

1817–18, NOVEMBER TO APRIL.

CHAPTER XVIII.

HINDOOSTAN. KANDES.

1818. FEBRUARY, MARCH.

CHAPTER XIX.

NAGPOOR. DUKHUN.

1818. FEBRUARY TO MAY.

CHAPTER XX.

NAGPOOR. PESHWA, &c.

1818, MAY, JUNE, JULY.

CHAPTER XXI.

NAGPOOR—ASEERGURH.

JULY 1818, TO APRIL 1819.

CHAPTER XXII.

POLITICAL REVIEW.

CHAPTER XXIII.

POLITICAL REVIEW.

CHAPTER XXIV.

FINANCIAL REVIEW.

A Map of the SEAT of WAR in INDIA.
1817-18.

HISTORY, &c.

CHAPTER XIII.

GENERAL PREPARATIONS.

1817, JUNE TO NOVEMBER.

Treaty of Poona executed—cessions adjusted—Vakeels dismissed—advantages to Gykwar—increase of subsidiary force—consequent cessions and exchange of territory—GovernorGeneral's plans—Hindoostan—Dukhun—Madras army—how disposed—delays in Dukhun—Lord Hastings leaves the Presidency—Political operations—their scale enlarged on Lord Hastings' sole responsibility—he takes the field—crosses the Jumna—General Donkin moves from Agra—negotiation with Sindheea—terms proposed —demand of Hindia and Aseergurh—reasons—treaty signed and ratified—consequent general order—its execution—Treaty with Ameer Khan—and Keroulee chief—Jaloun—Sâgur—Bhopâl.

THE rainy season of 1817 was spent in preparations for a great military effort against the Pindarees, and whatever powers of central India might support them; and in arrangements for

VOL. II.   B

giving immediate effect to the several stipulations of the treaty of Poona, particularly those relating to the territorial cessions of the Pêshwa.

Less difficulty or evasion was experienced, in obtaining the punctual execution of the treaty, than might have been expected from the known personal character of that prince : but our continued possession of his three forts of Singurh, Rygurh, and Poorundur, to which, from their strength and vicinity to Poona, he was known to attach a high value, was a powerful motive for alacrity ; since, without the unequivocal display of good faith on his part, he could scarcely have hoped for their restoration. The formal orders for the delivery of the forts and territories of Goozerat and the northern Konkan, together with those for Koosigul and Darwar, were obtained by the 18th of June ; and as, with exception of the killadar of Darwar, none of the subordinate officers made any demur to implicit obedience, the whole of these districts were in our hands before the end of July, and the sole point remaining to be settled was, the value at which the Konkan should be taken, whence the extent of the further cessions to the south was to be regulated. It had been agreed to rate the Konkan at what the Pêshwa's accounts of the average for the past twenty years might show to have been the actual receipts from it, clear of all deductions, and with an allowance for the expense of collection. On reference to these, instead of their exhibiting a product of more than eleven lakh of rupees, the rate Mr. Elphinstone had been willing to allow, the net value was not found to exceed seven lakh; so that, to make up the thirty-four lakh of rupees, a territory producing thirteen would, under the treaty, have been demandable in the Carnatic, instead of nine, as at first assumed. In consideration of his former offer to accept nine, the Resident, though he saw no reason why he should not draw the actual advantage, in the same manner as he must have abided the loss, still thought it right to act with some indulgence, and not to press with too much severity. Accordingly, he limited his present demand to eleven lakh, notwithstanding which, many obstacles and delays were thrown in the way of the assignment of specific territory. The Resident, seeing this, made a written demand of Ranee Bednore, Soondoor, and some other districts, estimated to yield that amount : but, while this matter was under discussion, receiving intimation of an arrangement on foot with Futteh Singh Gykwar, to obtain Ahmedabad for the Company, he so far modified the demand as to take the four and a half lakh of rupees rent, payable for the Pêshwa's moiety of that place by the Gykwar, instead of an equal cession towards the Carnatic, leaving six and a half lakh only to be made good from that quarter. On this basis, an agreement was finally concluded in August ; Darwar and Koosigul being taken at eighty-four thousand rupees, and the Pêshwa's territories, south and eastward of the Wurda, to make up the remaining five lakh and sixty-six thousand rupees.

The other articles of the treaty had previously been executed. The resident vakeels of foreign states received their formal dismissal, at the time the first orders for surrender were delivered. Bajee Rao himself, after admitting Mr. Elphinstone to an audience, at which he seemed very sullen and dejected, quitted Poona on the 18th of June, on the pretence of his annual pilgrimage to Pundurpoor, leaving all minor arrangements to be settled by his ministers. The vakeels of the other Mahratta powers, though dismissed, were many of them natives of the Pêshwa's territories, and had, therefore, claims to be allowed a continued residence there, notwithstanding their dismissal from public employ. Hence, it was impossible to prevent the continuance of their intrigues ; and, even if they had themselves been removed, other unacknowledged instruments and emissaries were at hand in abundance. Nevertheless, there was this advantage in the strictness of the 4th article of the treaty, that besides abolishing the formal character of the communications that pass-

ed between the Pêshwa and other powers, it imposed the necessity of concealing the instruments
and existence, as well as the nature of the intrigues afloat ; for it would thenceforward be a
sufficient ground of complaint, that communications were passing, without waiting for proof of
a hostile purpose, before they could be noticed.
Thus, intrigue became much more hazardous to
Bajee Rao ; though he was not of a disposition to
be deterred by such hazards. This, however, was
not the only object contemplated at the time of
imposing this humiliation. It was conceived to
be the most public and effectual mode of pro-
claiming to the other princes of India, the new
condition, in which the former head of the Mahratta empire was to be considered as having placed
himself. The case was not one in which feelings
of tenderness towards the pride of Bajee Rao
were entitled to much weight : but, since it was
of importance to eradicate in him the disposition
to regard himself as the rallying point of the
Mahratta nation, and, if possible, to remove this
dangerous notion from others, the public dismissal
of vakeels was thought to be a most effectual
means of promoting the end, and in this view it
was desirable to require it on this occasion.

The treaty of Poona, independently of its advantageous compromise of all past claims of the
Pêshwa on the Gykwar family, for an annual pay-

ment of four lakh of rupees, gave the latter a most
profitable lease of Ahmedabad, and remitted in
perpetuity all tribute or compensation for military
service, extinguishing thereby all pretensions of
feudal superiority. These benefits, which together were reckoned considerably to exceed twenty
lakh of rupees a-year in value, were about to be accorded to the Gykwar, for no other merit or claim
on his part, except the murder of his minister and
representative, for which deed this might be considered as a just atonement exacted from a prince,
who had by his conduct identified himself with
the actual perpetrator of the crime. The Bombay Government, thinking the moment of our
having made such considerable acquisitions for this
ally favourable for urging separate objects of
mutual advantage to the two states, determined,
at the time of imparting the above benefits, to
attempt to procure Futteh Singh's consent to provide funds for an increase of the subsidiary force,
and thus to bear a more just proportion of the general charge incurred in the defence of Goozerât,
than had hitherto been contributed by the Gykwar.
The proposed addition to the subsidiary force was
one thousand infantry and two regiments of cavalry for the Goozerât force. The troops subsidized
at present consisted only of three thousand infantry, with no regular cavalry of any kind. With
a frontier so exposed, as that of the Gykwar, on

the east, the north, and the west, such a force was obviously a very insufficient protection. Indeed, its acknowledged inadequacy obliged us always to keep a further body of our own troops in the neighbourhood; many of whom, particularly a regiment of dragoons, (the King's 17th,) were constantly acting with the subsidiary force, without any demand upon the Gykwar for the expense of a reinforcement so necessary to its efficiency, though he derived the whole advantage. Under these circumstances, and in consideration of the very flourishing condition into which the affairs of the principality had been brought since the establishment of our influence, as well as of the many advantages at different times secured for the family, the Bombay government thought itself warranted in asking an increase of subsidy on this occasion, sufficient to make the force kept up strong enough to act independently in support of our interests in that quarter. It was resolved, at the same time, to urge a further reduction and reform of the irregular and inefficient, though very chargeable military establishment maintained by the Gykwar himself. The Supreme Government signified its entire approval of the proposition, if Futteh Singh's assent should be obtained.

The provision for this additional subsidy, most desired by the Bombay Government, was the moiety

of the Katteewâr tribute, realised by its own
agency for the Gykwar. The other half of this
tribute had been enjoyed by the Pêshwa, and
was included in the cessions of the treaty of
Poona; consequently, it was an object to exclude
all foreign influence from that part of the country.
To this, however, Futteh Singh showed a decided
repugnance; but the advantages of the farm, just
obtained of Ahmedabad, were tendered by him in
lieu of it, and ultimately accepted, with some further rents of inferior importance, to complete the
sum required for the increase of subsidy. A further arrangement was afterwards made for the
exchange of the interest in Ahmedabad, held by
the Gykwar, independently of the farm, for three
pergunnahs of our own, situated inconveniently
near to Brodera. These were Dubhoee, Buhadur-
poor, and Saolee, yielding altogether near three
lakh, an amount which was expected to exceed
the value of the interest accepted in exchange.
Other advantages also had accrued to us from the
treaty of Poona, affording the means of advantageous exchanges; and the opportunity was
taken of improving our frontier, and consolidating our scattered possessions in Goozerât, so as to
avoid the frequent collision of a divided authority,
which existed under the former relations with the
court of Brodera. The negotiation was conducted on the principle of equal exchange: but such

are the habitual delays of a Mahratta durbar, and such the pertinacity with which it seeks to drive the hardest bargain possible, that the treaty was not concluded until the 6th of November, 1817, and much further matter yet remained to be ad-·justed; insomuch, that the agreement was not forwarded for the final ratification of the Governor-general, until the November following. The mutual transfers then amounted to five lakh and seventy-eight thousand, eight hundred and forty-eight rupees : amongst them, in addition to what have above been mentioned, the British government ceded its moiety of the town of Pitlawud for the Gykwar's moiety of Oomrut, by which, and other similar exchanges, the possessions of both were consolidated and improved. The hitherto indefinite frontier of our immediate territories in Goozerât was fixed by these arrangements. The pergunnahs of Gogo, Bhaonugur, and Sehoree, are the most southernly ; thence a line through Rampoor to Patree on the lesser Rin, and eastward from Patree through Vurungam, Ahmedabad, and Kuppurwunj, to Bala-Sinore and Beerpoor on the Myhee, forms our western and northern boundary ; the Myhee is our boundary to the east.

The only other changes consequent upon the treaty of Poona, which are of sufficient importance to require notice, were those which arose out of

the cession of the Pêshwa's rights in Hindoostan
and Bundelkhund. But, as the settlement of
these fell in with the preparations and general
plan of the ensuing campaign, it is better to leave
each separate case to find its place amongst the
transactions that brought us into contact with
the party whom it concerned. The cession of
these rights by the Pêshwa, just at this time,
gave us a great advantage in the subsequent operations : had they remained vested in Bajee Rao,
as they would have done in the event of no rupture having occurred with him, and the expectation of thus acquiring the disposal of them could
not have been anticipated, the peaceable settlement of central India would have been embarrassed and impeded by long and intricate disputes,
and clogged at every step by endless intrigue and
irritating discussion. The disposal of these benefits was desirable, rather as a means of effecting
other objects by their exchange, than with a view
to appropriate the whole to ourselves, as was
abundantly verified by the actual result. We shall
now proceed to explain the general plan of operations, devised for the execution of the Supreme
Government's determination to suppress and ex-
tinguish for ever the existing mischief of predatory associations.

The plan of Lord Hastings embraced the whole

circle of the reserved possessions of Sindheea and
Holkur, including likewise a great part of Rajpootana. Within these limits, it was his intention, if possible, wholly to confine the campaign,
by surrounding them with a cordon of efficient
corps, which should converge simultaneously
towards a common centre; making provision,
however, for the possible event of the enemy's
passing this barrier, and by no means neglecting
the defence of our own territories. On the side
of Hindoostan, it was his Lordship's intention to
have four divisions in the field, each of sufficient
strength to act independently under any circumstances; besides two corps of observation, to
guard the most exposed part of our frontier, in
case the enemy should find the opportunity of
undertaking an offensive enterprise. The points
at which the several corps were ordered to collect
were, Kalinjur in Bundelkhund, for the left division, the command of which was given to Major-
general Marshall, some point on the Jumna mid-
way between Kalpee and Etâwa for the centre
division, Agra for the right under Major-general
Donkin, and Rewaree for the reserve under Sir
David Ochterlony. The two corps of observation
were to be stationed, one about Rewa, to the
south of Mirzapoor and Bunarus, under Brigadier-
general Hardyman, and the other further east-

ward, in the southern extremity of Buhar*, under Brigadier-general Toone. On the side of the Dukhun, his Lordship expected to have in the field at least four substantive corps and a reserve, each of strength enough to act independently. In Goozerat a corps was also to be formed, to penetrate in a north-easterly direction, and complete the cordon of the intended area of operations.

It was his Lordship's design to assume the personal direction of the different movements, and to fix his head-quarters with the centre division of the Bengal army, appointed to rendezvous between Kalpee and Etâwa ; and it was deemed necessary, with a view to ensure a due consistency of action on the side of the Dukhun, to request the Commander-in-Chief of the Madras Presidency to take the personal command of the troops between the Nerbudda and Kishna ; and to regulate the disposition of the forces to be there collected, so as to fall in with his Lordship's projects on the side of Hindoostan. Sir Thomas Hislop accordingly took the field, under the Governor-

---

* Beyond Buhar to the east, the Bengal southern and western frontier was considered to be sufficiently guarded by the troops already in position at Midnapoor and Cuttack ; but, on the defection of the Nagpoor Raja, a reinforcement was sent from the Presidency, in which a squadron of dragoons was included.

general's orders, on the 21st of June; and was vested with full political powers, in addition to his military command. Colonel Sir John Malcolm, an officer of the Madras Establishment, of high name and merit, had returned to India in the beginning of 1817 ; and, happening to come to Bengal to wait upon the Governor-general, just at the time when the plan of operations for the ensuing season was under deliberation, he was thought a fit person to be employed as the political agent on the part of the Governor-general, to aid Sir Thomas Hislop in that capacity; but with a commission to act separately with the concurrence of Sir Thomas Hislop, whenever circumstances might require it. This officer was in consequence made acquainted with the whole of the plans in contemplation, and returned to the headquarters of the Madras army early in July, carrying with him the commissions of Brigadier-general for himself and Colonels Doveton, Smith, Floyer, and Pritzler. Sir John Malcolm immediately set out on a tour to the several native courts, in order to concert measures with the respective British residents ; while Sir Thomas Hislop was engaged in making the military dispositions for the approaching campaign.

Lord Hastings was extremely desirous of having two corps at least upon the Nerbudda by the close of the rains, if possible ; wishing rather to fall upon the Pindarees; while their power of rapid movement would be cramped by the swollen state of the rivers. Colonel Adams, with the Nagpoor subsidiary force, was already at Hoshungabad : the other force was to be assembled at Hindia, lower down the river. A movement northwards from both these points, in combination with an advance of the left division of the Bengal force from Bundelkhund, in the direction of Sâgur, would effectually drive the Pindarees from their usual haunts which lay immediately above the ghâts into Malwa.

The troops under Sir Thomas Hislop's command, exclusive of the reserve, (which was ordered to collect in advance of Adoni, and placed under Brigadier-general Pritzler's direction,) amounted to four battalions of European, and thirty-one and a half of N. I., eight regiments of N. C., a squadron of dragoons, two of horse artillery, and seven and a half companies of foot artillery. Besides the above, there were six battalions of the Nizam's reformed infantry, and four thousand horse, under European officers : also four thousand Siladar horse, raised for the campaign by the Raja of Mysoor, under the stipulations of the treaty contracted with him ; and the troops of Sulabut Khan, a powerful jageerdar of the Nizam, settled under our guarantee at Ellichpoor in Berar. The following was the dis-

position made of these extensive means: Colonel
Adams was already at Hoshungabad with the
Nagpoor subsidiary force ; which was constituted
the fifth division of the army of the Dukhun.
To Hindia Sir Thomas Hislop intended to proceed in person, with a division, to be called the
first, composed of a squadron of dragoons and two
regiments of N. C., one European and six native
battalions of infantry, with field artillery but no
battering train. A brigade of the Nizam's infantry, the Mysoor horse, and Sulabut Khan's
troops, were, with a few regulars, to be formed
into a separate division, the third, to proceed in
advance, under the command of Sir John Malcolm. Colonel Doveton's force was constituted
the second division, and appointed to manœuvre
in Berar, in support of Sir Thomas Hislop, and
for the security of the Nizam's territories. Colonel Smith's force was destined to form the
fourth division, and to operate in Kandês to the
south of the Sâtpoora range of hills, which divides
the valleys of the Taptee and Nerbudda, keeping
in communication with Colonel Doveton on one
side, and with the Goozerat force on the other.
Sufficient provision was thought to be made for
the doubtful disposition of Bajee Rao and the
Poona Mahrattas, as well as for the Nizam's weakness and the turbulence of the Putans of Hyderabad, by leaving three native battalions, reinforced

by half the Bombay European regiment *, at the former place, and a force similar in every respect at the latter; both under the support of the reserve assembling in advance of Adoni, and capable of being further supported by the divisions of Brigadier-generals Smith and Doveton, who were purposely held back from the most advanced line of operation, that they might be available in either direction.   At Nagpoor the force was smaller ; consisting of only two weak Madras battalions, and three troops of Bengal cavalry. There was certainly no hostile appearance in the conduct of our allies, at the time the above military dispositions were made.   Nevertheless Mr. Elphinstone leaned to the opinion, that the irritated feelings of Bajee Rao, while the humiliations put upon him by the treaty of Poona were fresh in his memory, rendered it unsafe to carry the subsidiary force to a distance from the capital.   But he yielded to the more confident judgment of Sir John Malcolm, who, on his arrival at Poona on the 5th of August, finding the Pêshwa still absent, went out by dâk, a

* This corps was to be sent up from the Bombay presidency, and the other half of it was intended to be posted at Ahmednugur.   The regiment, however, arrived so opportunely at Poona, that the whole was engaged in the operations at that city, and the detachment was of course never forwarded to Ahmednugur.

distance of ninety miles, to meet him; and, after having been received with great attention at two audiences, returned with the avowed conviction, that his Highness could not be meditating any fresh hostility. He urged also the advance of Colonel Smith to the north at an early period, as of material importance to the success of the general plan.

The arrival of the Madras forward divisions at the points assigned to them was delayed by a continuance of heavy rain beyond the usual season, as well as by an attack of illness, from which Sir Thomas Hislop recovered with difficulty, and some other untoward circumstances: hence the first division, instead of arriving at Hindia by the beginning of October, as was intended, did not reach that point until the 10th of November. The operations on the side of Hindoostan were, in some degree, retarded in consequence. It is necessary to mention them more in detail.

The Marquess of Hastings embarked a second time on the voyage up the Ganges on the 8th of July, 1817. He arrived at Cawnpoor in September; having stopped nowhere on the route, except for a very few days at the city of Patna, whither a complimentary deputation had come down from Katmandoo, to which it was thought politic to show every possible attention. In consequence of the delay on the side of the Dukhun, the Bengal troops were not put in motion till the middle of October ; the 10th of that month being fixed upon for the rendezvous of the Bundelkhund army, and the 20th for that of the centre and Agra columns. The Rewaree force was intended to act as a reserve, and was therefore not required to be so early in motion.

In the interval, the political operations had commenced. The Supreme Government were authorized, by instructions recently received from England, to undertake active measures for the suppression of the predatory hordes, to the extent of dislodging the Pindarees from their haunts in Malwa and Sâgur, and likewise to make such arrangements with the chiefs in the neighbourhood, or those to whom we might restore the lands recovered from the Pindarees, as should secure us against their re-establishment in that part of the country. The Marquess of Hastings had himself always been of opinion, that, without a complete reform of the condition of Central India, that is to say, without so altering the relations of the several princes and associations one to another, as to remove all inducement to predatory and ambitious adventure, on the extensive scale on which it was now prosecuted, no partial measures, howsoever brilliant or successful on our part, and distressing to the adventurers for the time, could prevent the speedy recurrence of the

evil, and probably in a more formidable shape.
His Lordship saw plainly, that with mere temporary expedients, the work would be left to be
done over again ; and that there could be no security for the future in any plan that did not settle,
or provide the means of settling, every one's pretensions to dominion, so as to leave a broad line
of demarcation between the chief of a regular
government and the leader of lawless banditti.
The whole of Central India was at present the
arena of a general scramble for sovereignty. It
was requisite, at length, to fix who should be
acknowledged as the lawful possessors now and
from this time forth. His mind was fully convinced, that without doing this, and without binding the recognised possessors in such a league, as
should, on one hand, check their disposition to en-
croach on each other, by the prospect of certain
loss of the stake each possessed, and, on the
other, should unite them all by a sense of common
interest against a common depredator, little would
be done towards the eradication of the prevailing
habits of predatory adventure, which were the
grand object of anxiety and alarm. He did not
despair of being able to form such a combination,
by offering the general guarantee and protection
of the British government ; though it was evident, that nothing short of that inflexible rigour
of control and irresistible power of enforcing obe-

dience to its award, which the British government
alone could exercise, could possibly impose a due
degree of restraint on the passions and ambition
of a host of greedy pretenders, aspiring by right
of birth, or of the sword, to the territorial sove-
reignties of this wide expanse.

His Lordship hoped, that the principal chiefs,
Sindheea and Holkur, would voluntarily second
the design upon a proper invitation, for both had
reason by this time to know, that the fortunes of
their families were on the wane ; and though the
invitation promised to gratify no ambitious views
of aggrandisement, at any rate it would rivet
their dominion over their remaining territories,
and ensure to their families the entire inheritance,
instead of a dilapidated succession, fast decreasing,
day after day, by waste and usurpation, similar
to what had been witnessed for the last ten years.
The great officers of both families, who had already tasted of these usurpations, and probably
expected further advantage from the confusion,
were the persons from whom the most serious opposition to the plan was to be feared ; but even
they might be won over by the proffered guarantee of their past gains against the caprice of a
master and the fickleness of fortune ; and then,
in fact, the needy and desperate alone would
heartily oppose the execution of the design.   To
Ameer Khan it was resolved to offer such a gua-

rantee immediately ; his actual independence of
Holkur might fairly be assumed, from his whole
conduct since Juswunt Rao's death. Sindheea's
sirdars, on the contrary, could not be separately
treated with, unless the temper of that prince
should be declaredly inimical.

Such was the outline of the policy which Lord
Hastings determined to observe towards the Mahratta powers of Central India. In furtherance of
it, he did not hesitate boldly to assume the principle, that in the operations against the Pindarees,
no one could be suffered to be neutral; but all
should be required to join in the league for their
suppression, under conditions, securing their active co-operation, as well in the present measures
of cure, as in the ulterior preventive efforts
against the future rise of these or similar associations into dangerous importance. The independent principalities, like Bhopâl and some of the
Rajpoot states, were likewise to be included in
the league, on the condition of a moderate tribute,
sufficient to defray the expense of our general
protection of all ; but in all cases where Sindheea
or Holkur could establish the right to a separate
tribute, that also was to be confirmed to them
under British guarantee. The orders for the
simultaneous execution of this extensive plan of
concert throughout every part of India, were
issued towards the end of September. It had

been originally intended to wait till the armies
were in the field ; but the discussions respecting
the march of part of Sir Thomas Hislop's army
by the route of Sindheea's territory of Boorhanpoor, rendered it necessary that the communication of our designs should not be longer delayed ;
suspense in respect to them being always more
prejudicial than a direct knowledge of the worst
that is to happen.

The negotiations with Holkur, Ameer Khan,
Jypoor, Joudhpoor, Oodeepoor, and the other
Rajpoot states *, were intrusted to Mr. Metcalfe,
the resident at Dehlee. Captain Close, the resident at the durbar of Sindheea, was appointed to
conduct the negotiations at Gwalior. The revision of our relations with the Bundeela chiefs,
who owed tribute or allegiance to the Pêshwa,
viz. those of J'hansee, Sumthur, Jaloun, Dutteea,
and Tehree, and the settlement with Bunaeek
Rao, who, on behalf of Rukhma Baee, widow of
the late occupant, administered the affairs of
Sâgur†, were confided to the political agent in

* Kota, Boondee, Banswara, Bikaneer, and Jesselmeer.
There was also a late dependent of the Pêshwa's, the Keroulee Chief, with whom engagements were to be made at this
residency.

† The Jaloumnan, Nana Govind Rao, was the hereditary
chief of Sâgur (vide p. 239, vol. i. for an explanation of the
nature of this claim of inheritance); but as it was a principle
with us not to disturb occupancy, unless the occupant should

Bundelkhund, Mr. Wauchope. The Resident at Nagpoor was directed to tender to the acceptance of Nuzur Mohummed, of Bhopâl, the terms which had been proposed to his father in 1814-15; and to require him, in case of his acceding to them, to forward without delay a written paper containing the several stipulations, preparatory to the advance of Colonel Adams through his territories. Nuzurgurh was named as the fort to be required of him for a depôt. The arrangements of detail were left to Sir Thomas Hislop and Sir John Malcolm, whose arrival on the Nerbudda was then shortly expected.

In communicating the course he was about to adopt to the council at Fort William, the Marquess of Hastings briefly declared his reasons for deviating from the more limited views that seemed to be entertained in England; and at the same time expressed a confident hope, that the enlarged plan he had laid down for the secure and permanent attainment of his object, would meet with the assent of the most considerable princes of Central India. " It was his boast," he said, " to have an earnest desire to accomplish every thing by pacific means, and to be able to declare with sincerity, that the exclusive object of his present

range himself on the side of the enemy, Bunaeek Rao was to be permitted to engage for what he held of Sâgur, notwithstanding the abstract right of Govind Rao.

preparations was to get rid of the greatest pest that society ever experienced." He did not hesitate to take upon himself the undivided responsibility of acting without the full sanction of the home authorities; for he felt confident the result would justify his determination in the eyes of those authorities, and of the British nation at large.

On the morning of the 16th of October, the Governor-general took the field in person, and on the 20th reached the rendezvous of the centre division of the grand army, which was appointed to assemble at Sekundra on the Jumna. The next day the force was reviewed. It consisted of two battalions of European and seven battalions of native infantry, five squadrons of European dragoons, and eight of native cavalry, besides two troops of a newly-raised corps, mounted on dromedaries. There were also three troops of horse-artillery, together with a light and heavy train, and every equipment for a siege, in case it should be found necessary to undertake any enterprize of that nature. The number of fighting men of the regular army attached to this division exceeded twelve thousand five hundred. On the 26th of October, this force crossed the Jumna on a bridge of boats constructed for the purpose, and thence proceeded in its march direct upon Gwalior, by the route of Jaloun and Seonda.—

The right division under Major-general Donkin, in strength about four thousand infantry and three thousand cavalry, including an irregular corps, moved simultaneously in the same direction from Agra. The time of movement was so calculated, that the centre division should arrive at Seonda on the Sindh on the same day that General Donkin reached the Chumbul at Dholpoor Baree; after which both forces would advance on Gwalior, or prosecute other operations, according as circumstances might require. Their approach accelerated and fixed Sindheea's determination to agree to the terms, upon which his co-operation in the campaign had been demanded. Yet he did not sign the treaty till the 5th of November, when the two armies were, respectively, within but one march of the point assigned to them on his frontier. It will be necessary to give at some length the particulars of the negotiation.

In the month of September, the Resident first mentioned in durbar the march of our troops from the Dukhun to the Nerbudda by the route of Boorhanpoor, and applied, as a matter of mere form, for orders to his Highness' officers on the route to allow a free passage, and to afford every aid and facility due to us as friends and allies. At this period, the military at Gwalior were more tumultuous than ordinary, having actually beset the quarters of the chief with the clamorous demand of immediate payment of arrears, and held

him in personal restraint. The talk of Bajee
Rao's positive determination to break with the
English was general through the camp; and the
wish for Sindheea to join him in hostility was evidently the prevailing sentiment, insomuch that it
was greatly feared he would be driven to this
course. It seemed very doubtful, however, what
line of conduct it was the real intention of Sindheea to adopt. The reply of the durbar to the
application for passes contained an assurance, that
his Highness had not given up the intention of
himself taking measures against the Pindarees ;
and a hope was expressed, that, on hearing this,
the march of the troops might be stopped, till it
was seen what could be done. This being declared impossible, after what had occurred in the
last two years, the passports were prepared and
despatched on the 1st of October.

The knowledge of our preparations on both
sides of India augmented the ferment and confusion amongst the troops of Sindheea, and completely distracted the mind of the chief. In the
hope of allaying this in some degree, it was resolved, as above noticed, not to defer the communication of our views and designs to the durbar,
until the military preparations should be more
advanced. Accordingly, between the 10th and
15th of October, the Governor-general's views
were completely unfolded to his Highness, by the
presentation of a note prepared and sent for the

express purpose from head-quarters. This exposé, after remonstrating with Sindheea for having harboured the freebooters, that during two successive years had ravaged our territories, and for having fed us with empty promises of punishing the perpetrators of these enormities, while, both before and since, he was in constant correspondence with them, and was even supposed to share the booty, went on to combat the plea he had advanced, of inability to control their acts. Admitting it as a personal exoneration of his Highness, it was nevertheless declared to constitute a virtual dissolution of the treaties, concluded with him under a different impression respecting the efficiency of his government; more especially to annul those stipulations, which left his Highness free and independent in his dealings with all feudatories and dependents in Malwa, Mewur, and Marwar, and prohibited our interference in their affairs. Of course, the moment he ceased to have the power of restraining the hostility of such dependents, when directed against ourselves, the restriction upon our taking measures for the purpose could no longer be suffered to have a binding effect. The note professed, that the British government sought no objects of private advantage, but merely the suppression of the Pindarees, and the final and total extinction of such associations; and asserted, that to this object its plans would be exclusively directed: and his Highness' hearty co-operation was demanded, in the mode which the Resident would explain. It was further notified, that any harbouring of the Pindarees, or reception of them into his ranks, or any encouragement of others in such conduct, would be regarded as an act of unequivocal hostility. A hint was thrown out, that, if his Highness could not control the acts of any of his more immediate subjects or officers than the Pindarees, the British government was willing to engage to lend its aid for the purpose of enforcing obedience. But, if they should assist or give asylum to the freebooters, it would be indispensable that they should be dealt with as enemies to both governments.

Captain Close was instructed, in case Sindheea agreed to the propositions of the above note, to submit to him the following terms of concert. His troops to be at our disposal entirely, and either to be stationary, or to be employed, at our option, with a British superintending officer attached to each division. Funds to be provided for the punctual payment of the force to be employed, and which was fixed at five thousand horse, by assignment for three years of the stipends receivable from us under the treaty of November 1805, and of the tributes demandable from Joudhpoor, Boondee, and Kota. Doulut Rao himself was not to move from Gwalior, or such other station as might be indicated; but this and some other points of less moment were not to be made matter of direct stipulation, lest they should have too humiliating an appearance. It was thought indispensable to require some security for the good faith with which Sindheea might enter into the above stipulations. The demand of the two forts of Hindia and Aseergurh, to be retained during the war, was accordingly resolved upon. The only material difficulty experienced in the negotiation, was, in procuring the cession of Aseergurh. Objections were, indeed, started to the assignment of the stipends and tributes, on the ground, that the former had been already assigned to individuals, and that of the latter, there were arrears due, for which it was desired to obtain our guarantee. These points were, however, given up comparatively without difficulty : but with respect to the stipulation for the surrender of Aseergurh, which was considered one of the strongest forts in India, and the key of the Dukhun, the greatest repugnance was evinced. The discussions were brought, in the end, to the single point, who should bear the expense of its reduction, in case of the Kiladar's resistance, and to whom the fort should belong, if captured under such circumstances. At first, the ground of pride had been taken, and the humiliation of the cession was objected; but this was got over by the Resident's agreeing to allow his Highness' flag to fly, and a nominal garrison and Kiladar to remain in ostensible possession, if our troops were admitted in such numbers, as to amount to a substantial occupation. At length it was settled, that, should the Kiladar resist, the property of the fort should not be lost to Sindheea, unless his collusion should be clearly detected. But a firmer stand was made upon the other point, viz. who should bear the expense of reducing it in that case; for Captain Close, having reason to suspect that orders had early been issued to the Kiladar to resist at all hazards, was urgent to throw the burthen of the consequences of such treachery upon the guilty party. The expense of taking Aseer, if resistance should be offered, was finally made chargeable upon the stipends and tributes to be ceded; which was, in fact, nearly equivalent to a concession of the point on our part; this fund having already been placed beyond Sindheea's control by the other stipulations. For although we had engaged, at the end of the three years, to render an account of the appropriation of this money, and repay any balance that might remain beyond the actual expense of the five thousand horse, still we were to have the ordering of the expenditure; and as it would be our interest to see that the whole fund was employed in this way, for the horse would be efficient in proportion as their pay was liberal, it was evident Sindheea could not expect that any part would be left unappropriated. Thus, it mattered little to him what further charges were thrown upon it.

With respect to Hindia, a place of little strength, though of consequence from its commanding some of the best fords and passes of the Nerbudda, no difficulty whatever was made ; and it was surrendered by the Kiladar on the first summons. The subsequent occurrences in the Dukhun prevented the Governor-general from alloting a force to the immediate reduction of Aseergurh. But the course of events showed, that he had not misjudged the importance of its possession, for both the Pêshwa and Bhoosla flew to it, as a last refuge ; and had it been in our hands agreeably to the stipulation to that effect in the treaty of Gwalior, the final issue of the war would have been much accelerated. After the rise of the Mahrattas in arms, it was well known that Sindheea's commander would not surrender the place without a siege ; hence it was resolved to delay presenting the order, until the means of enforcing it were at hand. It was well, however, to have the right of demanding so important a fortress, when circumstances might render it expedient in any possible turn the war might take. The public declaration of Sindheea's assent to our occupation of it was moreover advantageous, inasmuch as it marked his entire acquiescence in our plans, and abandonment of the cause of those, who were prepared to offer opposition. Some such security was, doubtless, necessary ; for we were already possessed of proof of

Sindheea's intrigues with Bajee Rao and the Pindarees ; besides which, a secret correspondence between him and the court of Katmandoo had very recently been detected*. But a much more substantial security for Sindheea's conduct than the surrender of any number of forts could give, was to be found in the proximity and disposition of our armies. Had he delayed the signature of the treaty another day, orders had been issued to the Resident to advance his demand, by requiring the perpetual cession of the Rajpoot tributes, together with the district of Ajmeer, in addition to the other stipulations. He affixed his signature on the very day these orders arrived, and thereby avoided these fresh demands.

* Accident led to this discovery. A full-size impression of Sindheea's seal happened to drop from the turban of one of his emissaries, while in the act of crossing the Ganges at Bithoor. Suspicion was of course excited, and he was stopped along with his companion. On searching them, letters, written with the design of stirring up the Goorkhas to make common cause with the rest of the independent powers of India, were found neatly pasted between the leaves of a Sanscrit book of the Vedas, which one of them, travelling in the character of a student, was carrying with him. Several sealed and some open letters from the chief himself were found upon them. The former were sent by his Lordship to be presented to his Highness in full durbar, unopened and without comment; in order that he might not suppose us to be ignorant of the intrigues and machinations afoot, and might be cautious not to provoke our vengeance by any overt act of hostility.

On the 6th of November, the day after the treaty was executed, it was ratified by the Governor-general, and the circumstance was communicated to the army under Lord Hastings' command, in the following short but expressive general order.

" The Governor-general has great pleasure in announcing to the army, that the Maha Raja, Doulut Rao Sindheea, has signed a treaty, by which his Highness engages to afford every facilitation to the British troops, in their pursuit of the Pindarees through his dominions, and to co-operate actively towards the extinction of those brutal freebooters. In consequence, the troops and country of his Highness are to be regarded as those of an ally.

" The generous confidence and animated zeal of the army may experience a shade of disappointment, in the diminished prospect of serious exertion ; but the Governor-general is convinced, that the reflection of every officer and soldier in this army will satisfy him, that the carrying every desired point by equity and moderation is the proudest triumph for the British character."

Officers were immediately appointed to proceed to Sindheea's several corps. Major Bunce of the king's 24th dragoons, was sent to Bahadur-gurh, Baptiste's head-quarters; but Baptiste had gone off to Gwalior before his arrival, and the second

in command said he could not receive the major
without express orders from his superior. Major
Ludlow was ordered to Ajmeer, where Bapoo
Sindheea was stationed; and Captain Caulfield to
Juswunt Rao Bhâo's camp at Jawud; but neither
the state of that part of the country, nor that of
the troops of this chief, were such as to allow of
his joining for some time; as will hereafter be
more particularly mentioned.

Although Sindheea was thus compelled to sign
the treaty, it was not to be expected, that he would
heartily join in the cause; and he endeavoured for
some time to evade its stipulations, by every
means in his power. For the first six weeks or
two months afterwards, no effort whatever was
made by him to furnish the five thousand auxiliary horse stipulated for; nor was any disposition
shown to give us effectual co-operation. He was
evidently on the watch for some insight into the
probable result of what was passing with the other
Mahratta powers, all of whom brought matters to
the extremity of open war, in the course of November and December. Bajee Rao took the lead
by attacking the Residency and British troops at
Poona, on the very day of the signature of the
treaty at Gwalior. As long as the other Mahratta chiefs continued in this disposition, it was of
course necessary to maintain towards Sindheea the
same attitude which had compelled him to accept

our terms; for, until some decided blow should be struck, no efficient restraint but the certainty of immediate attack could be placed on his natural desire to set aside the engagements he had entered into. This had been fully contemplated: and his acceptance of our conditions was valued more for the effect it was expected to have, in paralyzing his underhand or open efforts against us, by exhibiting him to the world as one who had deserted the cause of our enemies, than from any hope of benefit from his co-operation. As soon as our success in other quarters should have confirmed Doulut Rao in his resolution to abide by his engagements, the treaty was so drawn, as to give us every advantage we could have desired at his hands, as will be abundantly evident in the sequel.

Ameer Khan followed the example of Sindheea; and an agent, whom he had sent to Dehlee to negotiate, signed the treaty proposed to him by the Resident there, on the 9th of November. The terms were a guarantee on our part to himself and family of all territories Ameer Khan might be in the actual tenure of, under grants from Holkur; the Putan army immediately to be disbanded, and the artillery to be given up for an equitable compensation: other articles secured the aid of Ameer Khan for the suppression of the Pindarees. In the negotiations respecting this treaty, it was agreed, that the compensation for the artillery, which was fixed at five lakh of rupees, should be paid down in advance, to enable Ameer Khan to disband his army, which he could not effect without money. The son and heir of this chief was to come to Dehlee, and reside there as an hostage for his father's fidelity; and, on his arrival, two lakh of rupees were to be paid, the remaining three lakh to be afterwards remitted, as soon as the Resident was satisfied that Ameer Khan was diligently employed in the work of disbanding his troops. It was also settled, that territories belonging to any of the Rajpoot states, and forcibly occupied by him, should be given up on our requisition.

This treaty was ratified by the Governor-general, on the 15th of November. A month had been fixed as the period for the counter ratification to be procured from Ameer Khan; but, before the expiration of that period, the rise of the Pêshwa and Bhoosla in arms to oppose our measures had occurred, and there was time within the month for him to learn the event of their first efforts against us. This chief had, therefore, all the advantage of waiting to see the probable issue of affairs in other quarters, and he availed himself of this advantage to the utmost; insomuch, that it was for some time doubtful whether or not he would abide by the act of his envoy. His own

interest and inclination undoubtedly prompted
him to secure to himself independent dominion, as
soon as possible; but this was offered him at the
price of the sacrifice of his army; and his control
over that army was not such as to enable him to
disregard its feeling, which, until the ill-success of
Bajee Rao and Apa Saheb became known, was too
decidedly hostile to the British propositions, for
him to venture to declare himself in opposition to
it. In the end, finding himself placed between
General Donkin's force, and that assembled at
Rewaree, under the command of Major-general
Sir David Ochterlony, he felt both the necessity
of coming to a decision, and the advantage of
choosing his side, while the proximity of our divisions gave him the means of setting the feelings of
his own retainers at defiance. He accordingly
ratified the treaty in the course of December,
and thenceforth entered heartily into the cause,
adopting readily all our plans, and abiding by our
suggestions.

The Keroulee chief, Raja Manikpal, who
usually resided at Hindoun, and was formerly a
dependant of the Pêshwa, signed a treaty, by
which he placed himself under our protection,
and lent us the use of his means, on the same
day with Ameer Khan. The tribute he owed
the Pêshwa being only twenty-five thousand ru-

pees per annum, was remitted in this case, in consequence of our past experience of his favourable sentiments.

On the 8th of October, Govind Rao, the Nana of Jaloun, had signed a treaty, whereby the Pêshwa's right of tribute and of military service, transferred to us by the treaty of Poona, was commuted for the cession of Mahoba, a pergunnah of forty-three villages that jutted into our Bundelkhund frontier, and four other villages on the banks of the Jumna. Bunaeek Rao of Sâgur rejected the offer made to negotiate with him, in order to fix the relative situation he was to hold towards the British government, now that it had acquired the Pêshwa's feudal superiority over that principality. The Nuwab of Bhopâl, on the contrary, accepted at once, and with eagerness, the terms offered to him, and proved himself to the extent of his ability a staunch and zealous ally ; by which conduct he ultimately reaped abundant advantages, while Bunaeek Rao brought on his own ruin.

The circumstances that attended the opening of the campaign against the Pindarees, and the crisis brought on by the sudden rise of Bajee Rao and Apa Saheb in open hostility, have been specially reserved for a separate chapter.

CHAPTER XIV.

PINDAREES.—POONA.—NAGPOOR.

1817, October to December.

Pindarees during rains—General Marshall from Bundelkhund—A Pindaree enterprise—frustrated—Operations on
the Nerbudda—Sir Thomas Hislop's retrogade movement
—Operations in Malwa—Sir Thomas Hislop recalled
thither—Poona affairs—reduction of Soondoor demanded
—and effected—Fresh levies of troops—Sepahees tam-
pered with—Kandês—Critical situation of brigade—it
moves to Kirkee—Moro Dikshut—Brigadier-general
Smith on the frontier—Precautions—Pêshwa's demands
—Residency attacked and burnt—Battle of Poona—Moro
Dikshut killed—Cruelties of Mahrattas—Brigadier-general Smith's move on Poona—Attacks Bajee Rao's camp—
City surrendered—Nagpoor—Retrospect from July—Raja
irresolute—Receives titles from Poona—and is publicly
invested—Precautions of defence—British position—attacked—pressed—and partly carried—Charge of Captain
Fitzgerald—restores the day—Defeat of the enemy—re-
flections—Loss on both sides—Influence of these events
—Charge of treachery weighed.

THE Pindarees cantoned for the rains of 1817
in three bodies, under Cheetoo, Kureem Khan,

and Wâsil Mohummed.   The durra of the former
occupied the position furthest to the west, and
shifted its ground several times in the season,
from about Ashta and Ichawur westward to the
Kalee-Sindh.   Kureem, who had resumed the
command of his durra from Namdar Khan, his
lieutenant, lay about Bairsea, due north of Bhopâl.   Wâsil Mohummed, brother and successor to
Dost Mohummed, deceased, was at Garspoor,
westward of Sâgur.   It was generally known
throughout the durras, that the English meditated offensive operations against them in the
approaching season.   Kureem was therefore particularly active in recruiting his durra, and raising
fresh infantry, with a view to enable him to meet
the emergency.   He was desirous also of concerting a general plan of defence with the leaders
of the other durras; and a meeting was accordingly appointed on the 15th of September for
that purpose.   The ill-will that subsisted between
Cheetoo and this chief was, however, too rancorous to allow of any cordiality between them.
At the same time, though the chiefs received
general assurances of support in the hour of need
from all quarters, there was no one of the native
princes yet willing openly to take their part, or
to incur the responsibility of admitting their
families into any forts capable of affording them
protection.   Thus the rainy season passed with-

out their having been able to disencumber themselves of their families and baggage, or to fix upon any consistent plan of action for the campaign. Sheikh Dulloo, the most adventurous of all the chiefs, declared his intention of joining Trimbukjee at Choolee-Muheshwur, ánd seeking his fortune in another expedition to the Dukhun. The rest were distracted, and inclined to wait the issue of the expected rise of the Mahrattas in support of their cause. The spirits of Kureem's durra were damped by a destructive fire that accidentally broke out in their cantonment on the 17th of September, and consumed the greater part of their valuables. In the present temper of their minds, this was regarded as an omen of ill-fortune.

Meantime, the left division of the grand army from Hindoostan, consisting of two strong brigades of infantry and a regiment and irregular corps of cavalry, assembled on the 10th of October at Kalinjur, under the command of Major-general Marshall. It immediately advanced on Punna in Bundelkhund, and thence continued its march to Hutta on the way to Sâgur, where it arrived on the 28th of October. While this army was on the advance to the south, a bold enterprise was attempted from the durra of Wâsil Mahommed at Garspoor, whence an active *luhbur* was sent out in a north-easterly direction to plunder our own provinces of Bundelkhund. It penetrated by the Heerapoor ghât to the westward of General Marshall's route, and ravaged the territories of some Bundeela chiefs as far north as Mow, near Raneepoor. From this town the party was beaten off; but as they were thought to have thence taken a direction eastward, some alarm was felt at Banda, the civil station of Bundelkhund, which was at this time totally without protection, all the troops of the province having marched to the south with General Marshall. The Marquess of Hastings hearing of this bold enterprise on the 1st of November, when he was at Jaloun with his division, detached two squadrons of the 7th N. C. with the dromedary corps and two light companies to proceed with all expedition, under the command of Major Cumming of the 7th N. C., so as to cover Banda, in case of that station being threatened. The marauders got intelligence of this detachment, and retired again to the south-west without doing further mischief in Bundelkhund. Major Cumming was, however, reinforced, and ordered to remain with his detachment about Kyta, in order to cover our frontier on that side, and more effectually to keep open the communication between General Marshall and the centre division under his Lordship's personal command.

During this diversion, the left division continued its advance from Hutta to Rylee, where it arrived on the 10th of November, and thence opened a communication with Colonel Adams at Hoshungabad. Wâsil Mahommed retired from Garspoor westward to Gunj Basouda, as this division advanced. On the same day that General Marshall arrived at Rylee, Lieutenant-general Sir Thomas Hislop reached Hurda, and took the command of the first division of the army of the Dukhun. Brigadier-general Sir John Malcolm had arrived in the valley of the Nerbudda some time before. Every thing was therefore now in readiness for the combined movement, that had been concerted to drive the Pindarees out of Malwa. In expectation of it, the Goozerât force had by this time advanced to Dohud or Dwahud, to intercept their escape westward; and Lord Hastings having concluded the treaty with Sindheea, moved his own division to a position that should prevent their penetrating to the north or east; while he ordered General Donkin to advance from Dholpoor in a southwesterly direction, so as to guard the left bank of the Chumbul, and cut off any retreat on that side. It had been planned, that one of Sir Thomas Hislop's divisions should penetrate into Malwa by marching straight upon Ashta, while another moved by Oonchôd, further to the west; that

Colonel Adams should at the same time move upon Ressein, while General Marshall marched from Rylee westward on Sâgur and Ratgurh.

The execution of this plan was, however, interrupted by intelligence which had reached Sir Thomas Hislop of the Pêshwa's having risen in arms. After some deliberation as to the course to be adopted in this perplexity, the Lieutenant-general resolved to send forward Sir John Malcolm with the third division, reinforced by a brigade of regular troops, while he himself returned by the Boorhanpoor route towards the Dukhun, to support the divisions of Brigadier-generals Doveton, Smith, and Pritzler, the two latter of which had previously been directed on Poona. In furtherance of this determination, Sir Thomas Hislop thought it advisable to employ himself in the first instance in summoning Aseergurh, the orders for the surrender of which had recently been forwarded to him, and in laying siege to it in case of resistance. This opinion was founded on the assumption of our interests in the Dukhun being more seriously endangered than they were. It is true, that recent communications from Mr. Jenkins had described the Raja of Nagpoor as likely to follow the example of Bajee Rao; which obliged Sir Thomas to detain a brigade of Colonel Adam's force to the south of the Nerbudda, and to order a battalion of it, with three additional troops of cavalry to hold themselves in readiness to march on Nagpoor, as a reinforcement to the troops there; nor was it long before the Resident was obliged to avail himself of their active services. However, even in the worst event, the entire force of Brigadier-general Doveton was applicable in this direction, without the necessity of holding back a second division for the purpose, to the prejudice of other parts of the general plan.

Sir Thomas Hislop, with the first division of the army of the Dukhun, began to retrace his steps towards Boorhanpoor on the 19th of November: Sir John Malcolm having previously been despatched with the third and Colonel Adams with the fifth division, to prosecute alone the operations against the Pindarees. The former crossed the Nerbudda on the 16th of November, the latter on the 14th. A movement had been combined with General Marshall, so as to bring the three armies respectively to Ashta, Ressein, and Ratgurh, all on the same day, which was fixed for the 22d of November. These points having been reached without fail, three other points, Tullain, Bairsea, and Gunj Basouda, were then designated and occupied respectively by the three divisions on the 26th of November. The freebooters were by these operations driven entirely out of their usual haunts: and, as the divisions advanced, their agents were expelled from the several towns and villages, which were taken possession of or restored, according as there appeared to be claimants with a valid title or not. All that belonged to Sindheea or Bhopâl were immediately delivered over to the agents of these chiefs in attendance with the divisions. The Pindarees had hitherto retired in masses, with all their property and families, carefully keeping beyond the reach of a surprise. The durras had not yet joined, but they had converged in their retreat. After this, however, Kureem and Wâsil Mahommed effected a junction about Seronj, and retired together on the high road leading by Nya-Suraee to Gwalior. Cheetoo moved westward, towards Holkur's army, which had by this time taken the field.

During these movements, the Marquess of Hastings, on the 14th of November, received advice of the state of affairs at Poona, and the certainty of a rupture with the Pêshwa. Apprehending the possibility of Sir Thomas Hislop's suspending his advance into Malwa in consequence of the intelligence, his Lordship immediately issued the most distinct and positive instructions for his adherence to the original plan of the campaign, thinking Brigadier-generals Smith and Pritzler strong enough to operate against Bajee Rao, while Brigadier-general Doveton's position in Berar would overawe or enable him to act against the Nagpoor Raja, in case of his defection also. He declared it to be, at all events, of vital importance to the success of the general plan, that the first division should advance to the support of Sir John Malcolm, who might else be opposed by an accumulation of force, with which he would scarcely be competent to cope. These instructions were enforced in several subsequent communications, particularly one of the 21st of November from Erich. They reached the head-quarters of the Madras army, when they had already retrograded as far as Charwa. On receiving them, the Lieutenant-general immediately retraced his steps ; and on the 26th of November again began his march to the north, with intent to move by Oonchôd direct upon Oojein, to which point he ordered Sir John Malcolm to look for his support.

But ere we pursue further the narrative of occurrences in Hindoostan, it will be necessary to give some account of the important events that had taken place in the interval at Poona and Nagpoor.

After the execution of the treaty of Poona, Bajee Rao had retired, and still continued, on different pretences, to absent himself from his capital, whither he did not return till the end of September. His ministers had, in the interim, been very urgent for the performance of an old

promise we had given, to reduce for him the rebellious feudatory of Soondoor.   It was a case
of disputed succession, in which Bajee Rao had
declared for Juswunt Rao Gorepara, to the prejudice of Sheeo Rao, the present occupant.   The
place being surrounded on every side by our own
territories, we had been induced to offer our services for its reduction, in preference to allowing
Bajee Rao to carry his own military rabble into
the neighbourhood.   But as yet the Madras Presidency had not found a convenient time for ful-
filling this promise; and the court of Poona was
always particularly urgent in pressing it, at moments of the greatest inconvenience.   The object
at the present juncture was evidently to throw
obstacles in the way of the formidable assemblage
of troops making in the north.   Mr. Elphinstone,
sensible that our ally had a plausible pretext for
complaining of our dilatoriness in this instance,
more especially as he was paying to the competitor, whom he favoured and recognised, a compensation of ten thousand rupees a-year, suggested
to Sir Thomas Hislop the propriety of employing
in this service a part of the reserve then collecting
about Adoni.   The presence of Colonel Munro in
the neighbourhood, where he had been sent as
commissioner, to take charge of the districts lately
ceded by the Pêshwa, afforded to the Lieutenant-
general the opportunity of availing himself of his

services, without embarrassing Brigadier-general Pritzler's operations with the rest of the reserve. Orders were accordingly issued to Colonel Munro to undertake the enterprise; and he was shortly afterwards vested with a separate command of the reserve, and the rank of Brigadier-general, under orders from the Marquess of Hastings. The place was surrendered by Sheeo Rao Gorepara, on Colonel Munro's approach towards the end of October; the British government agreeing to assign to Sheeo Rao a provision about equal to what Juswunt Rao his competitor had been receiving. The latter, however, becoming involved in the subsequent measures of the Poona Court, Soondoor was ultimately restored to its former occupant.

During the whole of October, Bajee Rao continued to collect troops from all parts, and to call upon his jageerdars to do the same. The reason assigned for this conduct to Mr. Elphinstone, at the first conference to which he was admitted, which however did not take place before the 14th of October, was his desire to co-operate in the objects of the present campaign to the utmost extent of his means. This pretence was too shallow to disguise his real designs, which were manifested by his altered conduct towards the jageerdars, to all of whom he was now studiously attentive, exerting himself with great address in gaining their attachment. Even Rasteea, whose family had been entirely ruined not long before, and Apa Dêsaee Nipaneekur, a third of whose jageer had lately been confiscated, together with the Vinshorkur, who had himself much to expect from our success in Hindoostan, were completely won over by this conduct. The Pêshwa's intention of heading the hostile league against our supremacy was evident from numberless other circumstances ; particularly from the discovery of several profligate efforts to seduce the sepahees of the brigade, as well as those of Major Ford's battalions, to desert their colours. The native officers and men of the regular corps were generally proof against his solicitations, and acquainted their officers with the attempts made to tamper with them. But in Major Ford's battalions there was a larger proportion of Mahrattas, and it was natural enough that these should be won over on such an occasion.

Towards the latter end of October, there was an immense collection of Mahratta troops at Poona, the jageerdars having exerted themselves to bring forward all they could muster, and the prince himself having made extensive levies. Gokla was the adviser and principal commander in this crisis. The Mahrattas fixed their several encampments close round the cantonment of the brigade, the site of which had been chosen judiciously enough with a view to the defence of the city against external attack ; but it was particularly open to surprise, and otherwise much exposed, when threatened by an enemy both within and without. In proportion as the accumulation of the Mahratta soldiery on every side became greater, the situation of the brigade grew more and more alarming. Each corps as it came in encroached upon the ground of its cantonment, and the horsemen rode blustering and prancing about, in the manner usual with Indian troops when their designs are hostile. Colonel Burr, the officer in command at Poona, had a strong brigade of three battalions ; but the European regiment had not yet joined from Bombay, nor was it expected till the 2d of November. Mr. Elphinstone, though fully aware of the Pêshwa's determination to push matters to an open rupture, was nevertheless very unwilling to be the first to resort to measures of actual or apparent hostility. He therefore refrained from authorising the brigade to take up a stronger position, until it became obviously unsafe to allow of its remaining longer in the present one. He had remonstrated, but to no purpose, against the concentration of troops at the capital, and against the temper they displayed : Bajee Rao distinctly refused to send away any part of his force. On the 31st of October, appearances were so menacing, that the Resident resolved to move the brigade to Kirkee, where the ground was peculiarly advantageous. The stores were consequently sent off on that day, and the brigade followed on the next. Letters had in the mean time been dispatched, to expedite the arrival of the European detachment, which also, by a forced march, came into Kirkee on the 1st of November.

A brief description of the ground about Poona will be necessary to the clear understanding of the ensuing operations. The city of Poona is situated on the right bank of the Moota-Moola river, which runs from west to east, taking its name from two streams which unite to the north-west of the town. Just at the point of confluence stood the British Residency, separated from the city by the Moota, while the Moola came down with a sweep from the north. This latter river was fordable opposite to the Residency; and about a mile up the stream there was a good bridge over it, above which the river took a semi-circular reach to the north. At the western extremity of the semicircle lies the village of Kirkee, between which and the river to the east is an admirable position for a brigade to occupy, protected by the river in the rear and on the left, and supported on the right flank by the village. The original cantonment was on the right bank of the Moota-Moola, to the east of the city, and close upon it, so that both the city and the Moota lay between the brigade and the Residency. By moving the troops to Kirkee, the Residency lay on the contrary between them and the enemy, forming an advanced position towards the city. Major Ford's battalions were cantoned at Dhapoora, a few miles distant to the west.

After the removal of the troops to Kirkee, nothing but war was talked of. Moro Dikshut, who seems to have conceived an attachment to Major Ford very uncommon between Europeans and natives, sent for that officer, and endeavoured to persuade him to accept his protection and assurance of safety. His master, he said, was bent upon an open rupture, and expected that the greater part of our native troops would come over to him, or at all events, that the numbers he had collected must overwhelm the brigade. He advised Major Ford, therefore, as a friend, to consult his own safety in such an extremity : adding, moreover, that he had exerted himself to the utmost to dissuade his prince from the course he was pursuing, but to no purpose, the counsels of Gokla and of the war party having prevailed ; that a sense of duty would oblige him to side against us, though much against his inclination ; and that he was desirous of manifesting his friendship for Major Ford, by providing for his personal security. When this officer explained what he considered his own duty to require of him in such circumstances, and expressed his resolution to abide the result, whatever it might be, Moro Dik-shut took a very affectionate leave, commending his family to the Major's care, if the event should be adverse to the cause he had espoused, and as-suring him of every personal attention and assist-ance that he could bestow in the opposite case.

Brigadier-General Smith had proceeded north-wards towards Byzapoor, on the borders of Kan-dês, early in the month of October ; and his ab-sence, by depriving the brigade at Poona of the support it usually derived from the vicinity of the main body at Seroor, which lies about thirty miles only to the north-west of the capital, naturally raised the hopes and courage of the enemy. On hearing of the hostile indications at Poona, a light battalion was ordered back to Seroor ; and, to-wards the end of October, the Brigadier-general himself concentrated his force at a place called Phool-tamba, on the Godavuree. He had arranged with Mr. Elphinstone, that, if he did not hear daily from Poona, he was to consider the commu-nication as cut off, and immediately to march to the south. But, unless in the last extremity, his force was not to be diverted from the part assigned to it in the general operations towards Hindoo-stan.

After the movement of the brigade to Kirkee, every day produced more decisive symptoms of approaching hostilities. An officer on his way to

Bombay was attacked and plundered, and escaped with difficulty, severely wounded. This occurred only two miles from Poona ; while the Mahrattas were continually riding round the cantonment, and abusing our men and officers as they lay at their posts. The Resident, therefore, thought it advisable to increase the strength of his force as much as possible, by calling in the light battalion that had been ordered back to Seroor, together with a corps of one thousand auxiliary horse, that had been forming there under Lieutenant Swanston. Still, however, he resolved to remain at the Residency to the latest moment, in order not to be the first to declare war, or to assume the appearance of hostility. The light battalion left Seroor on the 5th of November, and moved half way to Poona. The news of its approach was conveyed to Bajee Rao in the forenoon of the 5th ; and his army was immediately put in motion. A battalion of Gokla's at the same time moved round to the west, and took up a position directly between the Residency and the brigade at Kirkee, with the intention of cutting off the communication between the two. Mr. Elphinstone sent to demand the reason of this hostile proceeding, and of the general movement of the troops. Upon this, an intimate at the palace of the Pêshwa, named Wittojee Naeek, came on his part to say, that intelligence had been received of troops being on their way to Poona, as well from Seroor as from General Smith's army ; that Bajee Rao had twice before been the dupe of his own irresolution, but was now determined to be beforehand in his demands. These were explained to be, that the Europeans lately arrived at Poona should be sent back to Bombay ; that the brigade should be reduced to its usual strength, and be cantoned at such place as Bajee Rao might select. To these demands a categorical and immediate answer was required, on the tenor of which the question of peace or war would depend. Mr. Elphinstone replied, that he could not admit his Highness' right to make any such demands : at all events, it was out of his power to grant them, the extent of the force to be stationed at Poona having been fixed by superior authority. With respect to the categorical answer required, he could only say, that, if his Highness joined his army, he should proceed to the brigade ; and if his Highness' troops advanced towards the brigade, they would assuredly be attacked : for, though he was most anxious to avoid a rupture, he did not fear the issue. Wittojee Naeek returned with this reply. He was no sooner gone, than the Pêshwa, either upon a preconcerted signal, or more probably without waiting the answer, mounted his horse, and joined his army at the Parbutee Hill, which lies a little to the south-west of Poona. His troops immediately advanced on the Residency.

Mr. Elphinstone and the gentlemen attached to his suite had barely time to mount their horses, and retire by the ford of the Moola, under cover of the Resident's honorary guard, ere the enemy arrived and took possession of the houses, from which there had not been time to remove a single article. The whole were plundered, and afterwards burnt; whereby much valuable property was destroyed, and, amongst other things, all Mr. Elphinstone's books and papers, a loss more irreparable than all the rest. The Resident's party made good its retreat along the left bank of the Moola, skirmishing with some horse that followed, and under the fire of Gokla's battalion from the opposite side of the river. At the bridge they crossed and joined the brigade, which had previously turned out and advanced from Kirkee at Mr. Elphinstone's requisition, as soon as the hostile approach of the enemy had been observed.

The position at Kirkee was admirably adapted to purposes of defence; but it had been concerted between the Resident and Colonel Burr, that the brigade should advance and fight its battle in the plain between Kirkee and the city. The plan was highly judicious; for it was uncertain how far the fidelity of the sepahees had been proof against the late attempts to seduce them, and it was desirable, therefore, to risk something for the sake of inspiring them with additional confidence in them-

selves and their cause : whereas, to coop them up
in a defensive position, exposed to the taunts and
insults of the Mahratta cavalry, would have had a
most disheartening effect, and must have operated
to increase the number of desertions, by giving to
the enemy the advantage of the show of superiority. As it was, seventy men went over from
Major Ford's battalion, and were followed after
the action by one hundred and fifty from the irregular horse, notwithstanding the success of the
day. Besides the above reason, the enemy were
well provided with artillery, which would have
enabled them to give great annoyance to the position, and to wear out the spirits of the men by a
succession of casualties, and by the fatigue of continual alerts from day to day, before General
Smith should arrive, which at the shortest could
not be in less time than a week. Moreover, although the Mahrattas were at present in the confidence of a great numerical superiority, an advance
to the attack; in despite of their numbers, would
confound them by its boldness, as much as it
contributed to raise the spirits of our own people.
At the same time, if we could obtain but a partial success in the plain, it would completely
dishearten the enemy, and prevent his afterwards
attempting any thing against the position ; an object which was well worth some risk on our part.

　　Wherefore, leaving the post of Kirkee, in

charge of part of the 2d battalion of the 6th
Bombay N. I., Colonel Burr advanced with the
remainder of his force, consisting of the Bombay
European regiment, under Major Wilson, the 2d
battalion of the 1st, and 1st battalion of the 7th
Bombay N. I. His line was formed with the
Europeans in the centre, the 2d battalion of the
1st to the right, and the 1st battalion of the 7th
on the left. A detachment of the battalion left
in Kirkee, together with the Resident's escort,
which had joined along with himself during the
advance, were held in reserve to keep in check
any parties of horse that might get round the
flanks of the line. In this order, the brigade
marched into action. Major Ford, who, with his
two battalions, occupied a separate cantonment at
Dhapoora, a short distance to the west, marched
in immediately to take his share in the danger ;
but the Vinshor jageerdar had been posted with
a large body of horse to intercept him ; so that
he was obliged to fight his way to the ground in
squares, and did not reach the right of the line
till the troops were hotly engaged.

The fighting commenced a few minutes after
Mr. Elphinstone had joined the brigade by the
Kirkee bridge. The enemy showed immense
bodies of horse on our front, and opened a heavy
cannonade from many guns, but chiefly from a
distance. The fire was returned from the four

six-pounders of the brigade, two of which were placed on each flank of the Europeans. In the mean time, the Mahrattas attempted to push bodies of horse round our flanks, in which manœuvre they partly succeeded. A spirited charge was then made in close column by one of Gokla's battalions, raised and commanded by Major Pinto, a Portuguese. It was directed against the left of our line, where the 1st battalion of the 7th was posted. The enemy's battalion was driven back after a short contest, with the loss of its immediate commander and many men : but the 1st battalion of the 7th, in its eagerness to follow up the success, for the purpose of capturing the guns of the repulsed battalion, became separated from the general line of the brigade, and Gokla, perceiving this, ordered down a body of his best horse to charge it while yet in the confusion of the pursuit. Moro Dikshut also led a party of horse, under his command, to the charge at the same time. Our battalion was in considerable danger, the horse having got round both its flanks; but Colonel Burr, hastening to the spot with a part of the European regiment, while the two guns on its left were served with great effect, was enabled to restore the day, bring back the battalion into line, and afterwards form it *en-potence* (at right angles with the line), in order to check any further ill consequence from the enemy's out-flanking us. Major Ford had by this time brought up his battalions on the right, which, being formed in square, had a similar effect on that flank.

In the above charge, Moro Dikshut was killed by a grape-shot from the guns on the left of the Europeans, which struck him after he had led on his party into the space intervening between the 1st battalion of the 7th and the rest of the line. He fell, respected by both parties. He had been stimulated to extraordinary exertion on this day, by an insinuation made in the presence of his prince, apparently with his countenance, that his general opposition to a rupture with the English was the result of personal cowardice. This taunt induced him to solicit the honour of guarding the *Juree Putka*, or standard of the Mahratta empire, in the fight, and it was under his charge when he fell.

Except in the above instance, the Mahrattas never came to close quarters. They continued, however, to fire on our line as it advanced, occasioning some further casualties, but keeping always at a respectful distance. At night-fall, the troops returned to Kirkee, and were not afterwards molested. Our loss in this action was, eighteen killed and fifty-seven wounded; amongst the latter was Lieutenant Falconer, of the 2d battalion of the 1st Bombay N. I. The enemy

left about five hundred on the field. The light
battalion and irregular horse came in from Seroor
without opposition, on the morning of the following day ; and Bajee Rao, though he drew up his
troops in order of battle, refrained from giving us
further molestation, but encamped his army on
the ground of the old cantonment.

No sooner was the die cast, than the Mahrattas proceeded to give a ferocious character to
their hostility, in order to widen the breach, and
prevent any speedy reconciliation. Two officers,
Captain Vaughan and his brother, who happened
to be travelling with a small escort, were surrounded at Tulleegâm, on the Bombay road ;
and having been induced to surrender by the offer
of quarter, were both inhumanly hanged. The
Pêshwa afterwards disavowed altogether this act
of barbarity ; and it is probable enough that he
had no share in the transaction. Ensign Ennis
of the Bombay engineers, who was taking a sur-
vey about fifty miles from Poona, was likewise
intercepted and shot by Bheels. Two other officers, Lieutenants Morieson and Hunter, of the
Madras cavalry, were marching towards Poona,
from the Nizam's dominions, utterly unconscious
of the rupture, until they came within twenty
miles of the city. Gokla then sent out a party of
Arabs to bring them in. On the first alarm, they
took post in a Choultree, and made a resolute

defence with the havildar's party they had for
escort; but were at last overpowered, and carried prisoners into Poona. Their lives were
spared, but they were sent immediately under a
guard to the Konkan, and shifted from fort to
fort, until re-captured three months afterwards
at Wusota. So close was their confinement, that
the bursting of a shell over their prison gave the
first intimation of approaching deliverance, while
the besiegers were equally in ignorance of their
fate. The feeling of exasperation, with which
the Mahrattas entered into the war, was yet more
strongly evinced by their conduct to the women
and dependents of the brigade, whom they found
in and about the old cantonment. Most of these
were mutilated, and sent into Kirkee in that
state; and many were put to death with studied
cruelty.

While this was passing at Poona, General Smith,
finding the communication intercepted, was already
on his way to the south. On the 8th of November
he arrived at Ahmednugur, having yet been little
harassed on the march. Between this place and
Seroor, parties of cavalry kept hovering about
him; but it was not till he had passed the latter
place likewise, that the enemy gave him any serious annoyance. He had no regular cavalry with
him, the 2d of the Madras establishment not
having yet joined. The only horse with the divi-

sion were about five hundred of the auxiliaries,
lately raised under the treaty of Poona, and commanded by Captain Spiller. The Mahrattas appeared in such numbers, as to surround the Brigadier-general on every side ; and, though there
was some skirmishing between them and Captain
Spiller, in the course of which the latter succeeded in dispersing a much larger body than his
own, and was wounded on the occasion, still the
enemy found an opportunity of breaking in upon
the line of march and carrying off a part of the
baggage.

On the 13th, the division arrived at Poona ; and
the next day was fixed for the attack of the Pêshwa's camp. It was delayed, however, in consequence of some doubts entertained, respecting the
practicability of fording the river at the place intended. On the morning of the 16th, Colonel
Milne, of the King's 65th, was sent with a strong
brigade to ford the Moota-Moola, a little below
the old cantonment, in order to occupy a village
on the east of the enemy's position, whence an
attack was to be made at daybreak next morning,
while General Smith advanced against his left.
The Pêshwa's army turned out to oppose the passage of the river ; but it was effected in good
order, under a heavy cannonade, which was answered from eight guns attached to Colonel
Milne's force. Our loss in this affair was about

sixty men and an officer. Colonel Milne then took up his ground for the night on the enemy's right flank. Before daylight next morning, the combined attack was commenced as agreed upon ; but the camp was found deserted, the enemy having retired quietly in the night, leaving his tents standing. His rear-guard moved off as General Smith approached, and was cannonaded from a distance. He carried away all his guns, except one of enormous size, called Maha-Kalee, which was too unwieldy for speedy transport, though mounted on a carriage that made it serviceable in the previous cannonade. The city surrendered in the course of the day, and was occupied by our troops, who were with difficulty prevented by General Smith's exertions from committing excesses, in revenge for what their families had suffered from the hands of the Mahrattas. On the 19th, General Smith prepared for the pursuit of Bajee Rao, having been joined on the preceding day by the 2d Madras cavalry, under Lieutenant-colonel Colebrooke. On the same day, a detachment was sent out to capture the enemy's artillery, which was ascertained to have been left with a considerable part of his baggage in a position under cover of the fort of Singurh. The enterprise was conducted by Captain Turner of the light battalion, and was completely successful: eighteen guns, with all their tumbrils and ammunition, and a large quantity of baggage, fell into our hands on this occasion.

The flight of the Pêshwa, and General Smith's unremitting pursuit, were productive of nothing of importance during the remainder of the month of November, nor indeed until the commencement of the new year. Wherefore, instead of proceeding with the narrative of operations in this quarter, it will be more perspicuous to relate here the occurrences at Nagpoor and in Hindoostan, during the two last months of 1817.

Pending the discussions with Bajee Rao, which ended in the treaty of Poona concluded in June, Apa Saheb lent himself openly to the intrigues and counsels of those, who wished him to make common cause with the Pêshwa. On hearing of his submission, the Nagpoor Raja began to have some personal apprehension of the consequences of the display of such a bias, and accordingly thought it necessary to put on the appearance of a line of conduct directly the reverse. Nurayun Rao was ostensibly reinstated in favour, and occasionally employed in communications with the British Resident. In the course of July, the discussions respecting the reform of the contingent were likewise brought to a settlement; the Bhoosla agreeing to a proposition, that certain of his jageerdars should furnish a definite number of their best horse, none to be paid at a lower rate

than twenty rupees, and the whole to be under
one well-paid commandant, with two British
officers to be attached to the contingent, empowered to inspect and to exercise a general
superintendence.

In this favourable disposition the Raja continued till the end of October ; indeed, on the
21st of that month, Mr. Jenkins wrote, that
although his Highness was still in active communication with Poona, he, the Resident, did not
anticipate a change of conduct for the worse.
But no sooner were the hostile designs of Bajee
Rao towards the English made known unequi-
vocally at Nagpoor, than he came at once to the
resolution of making common cause with the
head of the Mahratta nation. Towards the middle of November this change became manifest,
and, in consequence, the Resident requested, that
a brigade of Colonel Adams's division might
be halted to the south of the Nerbudda, and hold
itself in readiness to detach a battalion with three
troops of cavalry to reinforce the brigade at Nagpoor, . which had suffered much from sickness.
Things remained in this posture for some time,
Apa Saheb continuing his military preparations.
The news of the result of the action at Poona on
the 5th of November occasioned no remission
of these hostile demonstrations ; nor was any
stronger effect produced by the subsequent intel-

ligence of General Smith's arrival at that city,
with the main body of the subsidiary force. Apa
Saheb, however, long hesitated as to the course
he should pursue ; giving ear alternately to the
counsels of those who urged his adherence to the
British alliance, and of those who stimulated him
to the opposite line of policy, and represented it
as an act of imperative duty to aid in the restoration of the Mahratta empire to its pristine splendour and power. His inclination shifted from
one side to the other, according to the prevalence
of sober judgment and the cooler calculations of
prudence and experience, or of the delusion of
his imagination by the phantom of ideal great-
ness, presented to his mind as the sure result of
daring enterprise, by the young and thoughtless
among his courtiers, at moments when his brain
was already intoxicated with the fumes of a
deleterious *hooka*. In the public communications
between the Raja and the Resident, there was
never a word that betrayed any inimical feeling :
on the contrary, the Mahratta Moonshee attached
to the Residency was sent for on the first arrival
of intelligence of the Pêshwa's defection, and,
in his presence, Apa Saheb inveighed in the
strongest terms against the treachery and want
of faith evinced by Bajee Rao, in his conduct
towards the English at Poona.

On the night of the 24th of November, Mr.

Jenkins received a note from Ramchundur Wâgh, informing him that a *Khilât* (dress of honour) had arrived for the Raja from Poona, and that his Highness intended next day to go in state to his camp, in order to be formally invested with it, and to assume the *Juree Putka*,* or golden streamer, the emblem of imperial command, which, with the title of *Sènaputtee*, general, had been conferred on him by the Pêshwa. Mr. Jenkins was invited to assist at the ceremony ; but he remonstrated against the acceptance of the *Khilât*, or of any titles from a power now at open war with the British, and refused to give the sanction of his presence to such an act. Remonstrance was, however, of no avail : Apa Saheb went in state to his army on the 25th, and was formally invested with the *Khilât* and other insignia. His troops immediately took up positions very threatening to the safety of the Residency ; and the indications of approaching hostility were so strong, as to induce Mr. Jenkins to call in the brigade from its cantonment about three miles westward of the city, and to post it in the best attitude for defence of the Residency against any sudden attack. This was done on

* Putka is literally a girdle, and the standard consisted of a swallow-tailed pennon on a spear, with the girdle fastened by the middle in a common knot about a foot below the bottom of the flag.

the evening of the 25th of November. Throughout the 26th, the symptoms of an intended attack grew stronger every hour. The Raja's infantry and large masses of cavalry, in bodies called *goles*, of various strength and number, began to show themselves on all sides; and every gun that could be got ready was wheeled out of the arsenal and brought to bear directly upon some part of our position. But there was yet no official message or communication from the Raja. The best defensive dispositions were made, that the nature of the ground and the limited time would allow. The force at Nagpoor consisted of two Madras battalions of N. I., the first of the 20th, and the first of the 24th, both reduced considerably by sickness. There were also two companies forming the Resident's escort, three troops of the 6th Bengal cavalry, and a detachment of the Madras artillery, with four 6-pounders. Lieutenant-colonel Scott, of the 1st battalion of the 24th N. I., commanded the whole; and the following was his plan of defence.

The Residency lies to the west of the city of Nagpoor, and is separated from it by a small ridge running north and south, having two hills at its extremities, called the Seetabuldee hills, about three hundred and thirty yards apart. That to the north was the higher, though much the smaller of the two; upon it were posted three hundred men of he 24th N. I., with one of the 6-pounders, under the command of Captain Sadler. The 20th and the escort were stationed on the larger hill, with the rest of the 24th and of he artillery ; and the three troops of cavalry in the grounds of the Residency, together with some light infantry to keep off the hovering parties of the enemy's horse, but under orders not to advance into the plain against them. The women and valuables were lodged at the Residency.

At sunset of the 26th of November, as our picquets were placing, they were fired upon by the Raja's Arab infantry. Immediately afterwards, his artillery opened on the position, and was answered by ours from the hills. Our men were much exposed, particularly those on the smaller hill, the summit of which was not broad enough for the brow to afford any protection. There was also a *bazar* to the north-east of this hill, that approached close to its foot; here the Raja's Arab infantry were posted, and kept up a very galling fire from under cover of the huts and houses, which cut up our people most severely. The firing did not cease with the daylight, but continued with little intermission till about two o'clock of the morning, by which time we had sustained a heavy loss, particularly on the smaller hill, where some assaults had been attempted that were repulsed with great difficulty. Captain Sadler, the officer in command there, was killed ; and Captain Charlesworth likewise, the next in com-

mand, was wounded in the defence of this important point.

After two o'clock there was an intermission of
the enemy's fire for some hours, with only now
and then an occasional shot. Our troops availed
themselves of the opportunity to strengthen their
position and make up fresh cartridges. This was
an awful moment for those who were at leisure, to
calculate upon the prospects of the morrow. It
was evident, that what had passed was only the
prelude of a more serious contest, when day should
reappear. We had already suffered much ; and
if the attack were renewed with tolerable perseverance by a constant succession of troops, it was
quite manifest that our battalions, however well
they might behave, must in the end be overpowered. The numbers of the assailants would allow,
and, indeed, suggest this mode of acting ; and
this seemed to be their design, as far as could be
judged from their previous conduct.

From the unavoidable haste with which the
position on the Seetabuldee hills had been occupied, as well as the want of entrenching tools in
sufficient abundance, no artificial defences had
been added to the natural strength of the ground.
This omission was now remedied in the best manner the time would allow, by placing along the
exposed brow of the hills, especially of the smaller
one, sacks of flour and wheat, and any thing else
capable of affording cover to the men. It was

also deemed proper to confine the defence of the latter to the summit, many men having been lost from being placed in exposed situations on the declivity. The men of the 24th were also relieved early in the morning by a detachment from the 20th, and by the escort, to whom was intrusted the defence of this important post, the key of the whole position.

At daybreak, the fire recommenced with more fury than before, additional guns having been brought to bear during the night. The enemy fought too with increasing confidence, and closed upon us during the forenoon. The Arabs in the Raja's service were particularly conspicuous for their courage and resolution; and to them the assault of the smaller hill had been allotted. *Goles* of horse also showed themselves to the west and north, as well as to the south of the residency grounds, so as to oblige Captain Fitzgerald, who commanded the cavalry, to retire further within them, in order to prevent any sudden *coup-de-main* in that quarter.

About ten o'clock in the morning, an accident, which happened to the screw of the gun on the smaller hill, created some confusion, and rendered it for a few minutes unserviceable. The Arabs saw their opportunity, and rushed forward with loud cries to storm the hill. Our men were disconcerted, and the smallness of the total force having made it impossible to hold a support in readiness for such an extremity, the hill was carried before the gun and the wounded could be brought off: the latter were all put to the sword. The Arabs immediately turned the gun against our post on the larger hill, and with it and two more guns of their own, which they brought up, opened a most destructive fire on the whole of our remaining position. The first shot from the captured gun killed two officers, Doctor Neven, the surgeon, and Lieutenant Clarke of the 20th ; the second, a round of grape, was fatal to the Resident's first assistant, Mr. George Sotheby *,

* At the moment of receiving the wound, Mr. Sotheby was addressing the men of the escort, who had escaped from the smaller hill, and endeavouring to rally them and revive their spirits. A pistol he had in his girdle was struck on the handle by a grape shot, that forced the muzzle into his body, and inflicted a desperate wound, of which he died in the course of a few hours.

This gentleman was originally of the Bombay Civil Service, but had been tempted by early ambition to try his fortune in the college of Bengal, where his successful studies obtained him the highest possible distinction, and secured him employment under the Supreme Government. He thenceforward attached himself to the political line, and his abilities in this department had already been conspicuous on many occasions ; nor was there any one of the junior officers of the department, whose reputation stood so deservedly high, or whose services were more justly valued by the Governor-general. He was on the eve of rising to a station that must soon have led to fame and fortune; but after the and totally disabled four men besides. The fire from the smaller hill was so destructive, as greatly to distress the troops on the larger, which it completely commanded. The Arabs too, flushed with their late success, were seen advancing in great numbers along the ridge, as if with the design of attacking that remaining point : while the attention of our small party was divided between them on one side, and the main body of the enemy in the plain to the south, who were also closing fast. The prospect was most discouraging ; and, to add to the difficulty of the crisis, an alarm had spread amongst the followers

rugged part of his career had been surmounted, was unfortunately thus cut off, when just on the point of reaching the summit of his hopes and expectations. The loss of a man of merit, from whom the state has received good service, is a subject of public regret at all times ; but the interest felt is enhanced in a tenfold degree, when the individual is yet the object of public hope, and is suddenly snatched away, ere it has been fully realised. Independently of any private sympathy for the deceased, the death of one so generally known and esteemed as George Sotheby, considering the circumstances under which it occurred, could not have been passed over with the bare mention of his name among the list of slain. The compiler of this work is, however, proud to acknowledge, that this notice is equally a tribute paid to private friendship ; for he long enjoyed the intimacy of the deceased, and had personal experience of his worth. He was in his thirtieth year when his death occurred in the manner related.

and families of the Sepahees, whose lines were to
the west of the smaller hill, now occupied by the
Arabs ; and the shrieks of the women and children contributed not a little to damp the courage
of the native troops. They would scarcely have
sustained a general assault, which the enemy
seemed evidently to meditate.

Just at this critical moment, the spirits of all
were raised to the highest pitch of enthusiasm, by
observing a most successful and unexpected
charge of the cavalry upon an immense *gole* of
the enemy's horse. Captain Fitzgerald had kept
himself in reserve within the residency grounds,
until the enemy, accumulating on all sides, and
closing every instant more and more, brought at
last a couple of light guns to bear upon him, the
fire of which occasioned several casualties in his
line. Seeing now that the case was one of absolute extremity, he resolved to charge the gole
that most immediately threatened him, in order,
if possible, to capture these guns. The residency grounds were bounded on that side by a
dry nulla, which the charge had to cross. Captain Fitzgerald himself led the column ; and as
soon as thirty or forty men had got over, advanced at once upon the enemy. They retired
before him as he pushed forwards, until, having
passed to some distance beyond the guns, and
seeing that the Mahrattas were making a demon-

stration of surrounding his small party, he commanded a halt. In the mean time, the rest of
the cavalry had also crossed the nulla, and followed the advance, but had very judiciously
stopped short on reaching the abandoned guns.
These were immediately turned upon the enemy
by the men of the regiment, all of whom had been
trained to the use of artillery, as a part of their
ordinary discipline. Their well-directed fire kept
the Mahrattas at a distance, while two other guns
that had also been brought in advance were similarly captured. The latter were instantly spiked;
but the cavalry retired with the former, dragging
them back into the residency grounds, and firing
as they retreated.

The sight of what was passing on the plain
below damped the courage of the assailants, in
proportion as it elevated the spirits of our men.
The firing was now recommenced from the larger
hill with loud huzzas, and every one was watching the opportunity to recover the smaller one
from the Arabs. An opportunity was very soon
offered by the explosion of a tumbril on the spot,
which created a similar confusion to that of which
the enemy had lately taken advantage. The circumstance was no sooner observed, than a party
from the larger hill, headed by several officers,
who darted forwards without any particular orders, rushed to the attack, and drove the Arabs

from the post at the point of the bayonet, recovering
our own gun as well as capturing the two others
brought up by the enemy. Amongst the rest,
Captain Lloyd of the Resident's escort distinguished himself on this occasion, as did Lieutenant
Grant, the adjutant of the twenty-fourth, who,
though twice wounded, was amongst the foremost
of the party, and received a third and mortal
wound in the assault. The tide of success had
now turned, and Apa Saheb's troops gave way on
every side. The Arabs, however, still remained
in force about their bazar to the north-east of our
position, until a brilliant charge was made upon
them by Cornet Smith with a troop of the cavalry,
which succeeded in dispersing them, and in capturing two more guns. Our troops now moved
down from the hills, and drove the enemy from
all the surrounding houses and villages, securing
all the guns not previously carried off.

Thus, about noon of the 27th, terminated the
most trying contest that our native army had
ever been engaged in. Its fatigues and anxieties
continued without intermission for eighteen hours.
Under Providence, the success of this action must
be chiefly attributed to the bottom of the troops,
and to the cool decision in the hour of danger
which particularly marked the conduct of the
officers engaged. The former quality is entirely

distinct from any strength of limb or of mus-
cular power requisite to the long endurance of
fatigue. It is purely a virtue of the mind, and
consists in a buoyant disposition, that never will
abandon itself to despair. The natives of India
are of themselves rather prone to throw up the
game as lost upon the slightest reverse; and the
history of its wars, particularly that of the battles
of Aurung-Zeeb, affords abundant instances of the
ruin of a good cause, by yielding to this habitual
despondency. If the character of the native sepahee
is so different in our service, it is because he acts
rather upon his officer's judgment than his own;
and so long as he observes him coolly giving his
orders, sees hope in implicit obedience, and never
will despair while this ground of confidence remains. The conduct of the British officers engaged at Nagpoor afforded a triumphant display
of that collected judgment under extreme peril,
which, to the glory of the nation, is its peculiar
characteristic. The well-timed charge of Captain
Fitzgerald stands conspicuous amongst the many
brilliant exploits achieved in the campaign. It
was generally allowed to have given the turn to
the tide of success on this day; and, consequently,
to have mainly contributed to the salvation of our
interests within the Nagpoor dominions: to say
nothing of the effect on public opinion, that would

have been felt throughout India, even to Nipâl, had Apa Saheb succeeded in cutting off this brigade.

The number of the combatants on either side was immensely disproportionate. Altogether, on our side, there were not more than fifteen hundred fighting men, including the cavalry and artillery: whereas the Bhoosla Raja had upwards of ten thousand infantry in the field, and at least an equal number of horse. His chief reliance, however, was placed in a body of between three and four thousand Arabs, who behaved with great bravery on this, and, indeed, on all subsequent occasions. Our loss in killed and wounded amounted by the returns to three hundred and thirty-three, being more than one-fifth of those engaged, a most unusual proportion for the victorious party. Amongst these were four officers * killed, and seven severely wounded, besides Mr. Sotheby above mentioned. The loss on the Raja's side was never precisely ascertained; but it must have been very severe. His army was so disheartened after the action, that it could not be persuaded to

* Captain Sadler and Lieutenant Grant of the 24th Madras Native infantry, Lieutenant Clarke of the 20th, and Doctor Neven, assistant surgeon, killed. Captains Charlesworth, Lloyd, and Pew, wounded severely; also Lieutenants Thullier and Bayley, with Cornets Smith and Hearsay of the cavalry, and several others slightly.

renew the attack, notwithstanding that a Sepahèe of the escort, who deserted immediately after, represented in strong colours the exhausted condition of our troops, and their want of ammunition for many more rounds, in order to excite them to a second trial.

The result of this action proved the wisdom of the resolution of the commanding officer at Poona to advance and meet the enemy, in preference to abiding his attack. ˉ At Nagpoor, indeed, there was no choice; but the much greater hazard of the contest there proves the superior advantage of numbers, when acting on the offensive, against the same odds of skill and discipline.

It has been thought necessary to be thus particular in the account of these two affairs, because they formed two of the most glorious triumphs of the war, and because the effect, produced by their issue, gave the Mahrattas a distrust of themselves, highly favourable to the early accomplishment of Lord Hastings' views. Both the Pêshwa and the Bhoosla evidently reckoned with certainty on their ability to overwhelm the small force stationed at their respective capitals, and were astonished to find their utmost means baffled by mere detachments. In proportion as their estimate of their own strength had before been sanguine, they now gave way to despondency; and though Bajee Rao was sensible that he had too long practised the

arts of duplicity, to be admitted to a reconciliation
on any terms that would leave him in the exercise of dominion, he never afterwards attempted
any enterprise that showed the smallest confidence
in his means, nor ever rose above the character of
a heartless and desperate fugitive. Apa Saheb
had yet something to hope from the known clemency and moderation of the English. As soon,
therefore, as he despaired of the cause he had
espoused, he resolved to establish a claim to forgiveness by the promptitude of his submission.
Immediately after the action of the 26th and
27th, he sent vakeels to express his sorrow, and
to disavow having himself authorised the attack.
The Baees, or women of the Raja's family, also
interceded for him ; but Mr. Jenkins refused to
treat at all, while his army continued in force.

Bajee Rao and Apa Saheb have been accused of
treachery, as well as of a breach of hospitality and
of the laws of nations, in thus attacking the residents, who, in their capacity of ambassadors,
might be deemed entitled to a sacred inviolability.
There is, however, this palliative to be found for
their conduct ; that the Residents had each of
them an army under his direction, expressly de-
signed for his support against the intrigues or
violence of the court at which he resided. Thus
armed, they of course lost much of the sacred
character of heralds. If justice required, as

doubtless it did, that they should at least have had the option of retiring unmolested, this option, or something equivalent to it, was afforded to Mr. Elphinstone ; and if it was not tendered to Mr. Jenkins, it was merely because, when the matter was discussed in the Raja's council, it was decided to be useless to make an offer, which the attitude he had already assumed showed that the Resident had no thought of accepting. With respect to the treachery of secret previous preparation, if we allow to a native power the abstract right of shaking off our alliance under any circumstances, we must concede to him this further step, as indispensable to its exercise. For, as it is an article of all our subsidiary alliances, that a military force shall be stationed at the capital, it is to be presumed that open preparations for war would always be anticipated, and the design frustrated by the immediate employment of the force against the person of the prince. Wherefore, if there was any treachery in the conduct of these Mahratta chiefs, it was not so much in the manner, as in the act itself of their defection ; for it is in the essence of our contracts of alliance, that, although accepted by the native power for the sake probably of some present advantage, or to get rid of some temporary evil of yet harder endurance, the benefit on our side is intended to be permanent ; for which purpose, we stipulate for the perpetual continuance of the engagement, and the native power binds itself to this stipulation. Thus, it is as much an act of treachery in our ally to attempt to baulk us of our advantage, by shaking us off after having got for himself the benefit stipulated for and contemplated, as it would be on our part to leave him to be in the first instance overwhelmed, after having engaged to assist him out of his difficulties. In this view, the defection of both these princes was decidedly treacherous, inasmuch as both, with a full knowledge of the terms on which alone our aid would be granted, bound themselves personally and voluntarily to adhere to them in perpetuity, and neither had any plea whatever of any default in executing the stipulations on our part, to urge in justification of his breach in the performance of his own part of the engagement.

CHAPTER XV.

NAGPOOR.—HINDOOSTAN.

1817, DECEMBER.

Reinforcements to Nagpoor—Colonel Gahan—Major Pitman
—Brigadier-general Doveton—Brigadier-general Hardyman—Terms proposed to the Raja—He temporizes—and
surrenders—His camp attacked—and carried—Fort of
Nagpoor occupied by Arabs—Besieged and assaulted without success—Arabs capitulate—Reasons for the Raja's
reinstation—Terms—Dissent of Governor-general—Re-
tracted—British acquisitions—Reflections—Hindoostan—
Pindarees—Suspicious conduct of regular powers—Effect
on Lord Hastings' plans—Cholera morbus—its virulence
—and symptoms—Centre division arrives at Erich—
Moves back to the Sindh—Movements in pursuit of Pindarees—Affair at Bicheetal—Wife of Kureem captured—
Escape through Huraotee—Distress—Exploit of a Havildar—Consequent military dispositions.

THE Bhoosla Raja's defection and attack on the
British Residency did not remain long unpunish-
ed. Troops poured into Nagpoor from every
quarter : some in consequence of the provisional
requisition of the Resident, others under orders
from Sir Thomas Hislop or the Marquess of Has-

tings himself. The first reinforcement that arrived was that under Lieutenant-colonel Gahan, which had on the first alarm been ordered down from the valley of the Nerbudda. It consisted of a strong battalion of Bengal infantry, 1st battalion of the 22d, the remaining three troops of the 6th Bengal cavalry and two gallopers. This detachment arrived on the 29th of November, and gave entire confidence to the troops in position on the Seetabuldee hills, which till then had been under very considerable apprehension of a second attack, and of the ultimate failure of their stores and ammunition. Mr. Jenkins had on the preceding day agreed to a suspension of arms, at the Raja's request, in order to allow time for this reinforcement to join without molestation; holding out, however, to Apa Saheb the necessity of disbanding or separating himself from his army, as an indispensable preliminary to a restoration of peace on any terms.

Major Pitman, who brought up the second reinforcement, was at Omraotee on the frontier of Berar, when he received a hasty note despatched by Mr. Jenkins on the night of the 25th of November, while the issue of the attack was yet doubtful. He immediately forwarded the note to Brigadier-general Doveton, who was then at Jafurabad, and set off himself with two battalions and a few of the Nizam's reformed cavalry, hastening his march in the hope of arriving at the scene of danger in time to afford relief. He reached Nagpoor on the 5th of December. Brigadier-general Doveton followed with the whole second division of the army of the Dukhun, and entered that city with the light troops in advance on the 12th of December. The rest of the division came up two days afterwards. This officer rightly judged the re-establishment of affairs at Nagpoor to be an object of superior importance to the occupation or probably the reduction of Aseergurh, which was the duty originally assigned to him in the general plan of operations. Indeed, it was of the utmost consequence that the Bhoosla should be crushed as early as possible, in order that other potentates might be deterred, by the rapid and exemplary punishment of his defection, from following in the same career.

In addition to the formidable force thus collected at Nagpoor, the Marquess of Hastings, immediately on hearing of the attack made upon the brigade there stationed, ordered down Brigadier-general Hardyman with the corps of observation under his command, in Rewa. This officer, not receiving the order until the 6th of December, did not reach the neighbourhood until every thing had been already adjusted by General Doveton. His force was, however, of use in reducing Jubulpoor, where it gallantly routed a considerable body of

troops opposed to it in the field, and in occupying
the Bhoosla territory to the north and in the
valley of the Nerbudda; and its further advance
was countermanded, to allow of its being so employed.   In the mean time, Brigadier-general
Doveton, having allowed his troops a day to
recover from the fatigue of their long and harassing marches, had proceeded to enforce upon
Apa Saheb the acceptance of such terms as
should break his military power, and reduce him
for the future to a state of entire dependence on
the British government.

On the morning of the 15th of December, Mr.
Jenkins offered to the Raja the following terms
of submission, as the only means of saving his
army from attack, and himself from absolute
ruin.   The Raja to acknowledge, that by his defection he had placed his territories at the mercy
of the British government, which was consequently absolved from all ties towards himself,
and free to dispose of them at pleasure; to give
up all his artillery, leaving it to the discretion of
the British authorities to restore such as they
might think proper; to disband the Arabs and
other mercenary troops, who were to march off
in the directions assigned, leaving the city and
fort of Nagpoor to our occupation.   Apa Saheb
himself was required to come in and reside at the
British Residency, as a hostage for the per-

formance of these conditions, and four o'clock of the next morning was fixed as the limit of time for his acceptance of them ; by which hour, if he did not submit, it was declared that he would be attacked without further ceremony. He was, however, given to understand that, upon accepting the above terms, the former relations would be restored, and no greater sacrifice required than a territorial cession sufficient to meet the charges of the subsidiary force, and due provision for our future exercise of so much internal control, as might be necessary to secure us against a repetition of similar conduct on the part of the Raja.

Nurayun Pundit, who, since the breaking out of hostilities, had been the constant mediator between Apa Saheb and the British representative, came several times in the course of the 15th to temporize and to solicit a longer respite. But Mr. Jenkins insisted on the acceptance of the terms by the next morning at the latest, though he extended the period to seven o'clock. In the evening of the 15th, General Doveton beat to arms and approached the Seetabuldee position, where he bivouacked for the night. At six o'clock in the morning, Nurayun came again to say, that the Arabs and other troops would not allow his master to come in, and that a longer time would be indispensable to settle with them,

and to withdraw them from the artillery which
was to be given up.   The acceptance of the conditions was promised, but a respite of two or
three days was solicited.   The period allowed for
Apa Saheb to come in was now extended till nine
A. M.; with the understanding, that, by submission in this particular, he might obtain a
farther extension for the execution of the other
terms prescribed.   When the time expired, nothing had been done.   Brigadier-general Doveton
accordingly advanced his army, in order of battle,
to a position close upon the Raja's camp on the
south of the city, from which he had previously
determined to make the attack.   Apa Saheb now
gave way entirely to his personal fears, and,
mounting his horse, rode off with his ministers,
Nagoopunt and Ramchundur Wâgh, and a few
other attendants, straight to the Residency, where
he delivered himself up to Mr. Jenkins.   Notice was
immediately sent to Brigadier-general Doveton,
who halted upon receiving the information.   The
time for the surrender of the artillery and disbanding the army was then brought into discussion; the Resident insisting on the instant
execution of the former point, in order to prevent
any clandestine removal of the guns, while the
Raja pressed for a further delay.   It was arranged that the artillery should be abandoned,
and the troops withdrawn to a distance by twelve

o'clock of the same day; and Ramchundur Wâgh was sent to expedite the requisite arrangements for the purpose. He returned a little before twelve, reporting every thing to be in readiness; whereupon a couple of *hurkaras* were sent to the Brigadier-general, in order that he might detach a party to take possession of the guns said to be so abandoned. On questioning them more closely, General Doveton suspected that some deception was intended; and accordingly, instead of sending a party, he resolved to advance his whole line. He did so by open column of companies from the right of battalions. The guides led him to the arsenal south of the city, where thirty-six guns were found and taken possession of without resistance; a Lascar, however, was on the point of applying the match to one of them, when his arms were seized. The General, leaving Colonel Scott with a brigade from his left in possession of these guns, continued his advance towards the Sukur-Duree gardens, where he knew there were other batteries. The moment that the troops debouched from behind some trees separating the Sukur-Duree from Nagpoor, a heavy fire was opened upon their front and right flank; no time was therefore lost in forming into line for the attack. The cavalry and horse artillery on the extreme right, under Colonel Gahan, made a detour round the Sukur-

Duree garden, and, after carrying a battery that opposed them in that quarter, came in flank of the main position of the enemy; while Colonel M‘Leod's division advanced to the attack in front under a heavy cannonade. The enemy was formed in a retiring angle; and after Colonel M‘Leod had carried the right of his position, where his strength of infantry was the greatest, the guns on his left still kept playing on our reserve, under cover chiefly of his cavalry. Colonel Gahan charged and drove them off, continuing the pursuit to some distance; but the guns were not silenced, until stormed shortly afterwards by a party from the reserve. By half-past one, seventy-five guns, mortars and howitzers of different calibre and descriptions, were in our hands. The enemy's camp was also taken, with forty elephants, belonging for the most part to the Raja, and all his camp equipage. The troops had on this occasion to advance upwards of one thousand yards in face of a powerful artillery; consequently the acquisition was not made without loss. Of the Europeans thirty-nine, and of the natives one hundred and two, were killed or wounded; but fortunately no officer was amongst the number.

Mun-Bhut and Gunput Rao were the Sirdars who instigated this resistance. Treachery on the part of the Raja was not suspected; though it is not improbable that Ramchundur Wâgh may have connived at the abstraction of many of the guns, under the notion that Brigadier-general Doveton would have been satisfied with the capture of those left at the arsenal. Such a trick is so perfectly consistent with the half-measure policy pursued throughout by Apa Saheb, as to leave it by no means clear, that he did not participate in the guilt of the blood unnecessarily shed on this occasion. But the point was never made the subject of a special investigation.

Mun-Bhut Rao, with the Arab infantry, fled into the city, and occupied the fort, a place of considerable strength, within which were the Raja's palaces and other strong buildings. Two days were spent in endeavouring to persuade them to evacuate it and retire, on which terms they were promised a safe conduct to the Nagpoor frontier. Their arrears were also paid up in the course of this negotiation; yet in the end they refused to evacuate. The siege of the fort was accordingly commenced. By the 20th, a howitzer battery was erected at the foot of the larger of the Seetabuldee hills, and, on the 21st, the mound of a tank that lay between it and the fort, not two hundred and fifty yards from the western (Jooma) gate, was seized, for the purpose of being converted into a breaching battery. All the captured guns that were thought to be of

sufficient calibre were brought into this position;
and though it was soon found, that their fire had
little effect in comparison with our own 18-
pounders, yet on the 23d of December, the gate
was considered to be sufficiently injured, to make
an assault practicable. Accordingly, a storm was
attempted on the morning of the 24th; and four
companies of the Bengal battalion, the 1st of the
22d, headed by a company of the Royal Scots,
and accompanied by the sappers and miners, advanced to the Jooma gate, in the hope of establishing themselves there, if not of carrying the
place. At the same time, Colonel Scott led an
attack on the Toolsee-bâgh, a garden on the
south of the city, and between it and the river
Nâg, while Major Pitman advanced to co-operate
with a detachment of the Nizam's infantry. The
breached gate was found to be so commanded
from inner walls, as to have all the effect of a
retrenchment; and the storming party, after
losing many men in attempting to penetrate or
establish themselves, was in the end obliged to
retire. On this failure, Colonel Scott and Major
Pitman were also recalled. Our loss was ninety
killed, and one hundred and seventy-nine wounded.
Lieutenant Bell, of the Royal Scots, was amongst
the former, and Lieutenants Cameron and Cowell
in the number of the latter.

Brigadier-general Doveton now saw that the

place could not be taken without a more efficient battering train; he therefore resolved to wait the arrival of that attached to his own force from Akola, before he ventured to renew his operations. The Arabs, however, feeling that they had already done enough for their honour, and that, being entirely without hope of support, their ultimate reduction was almost inevitable, resolved to make the best advantage of their successful resistance, by offering to evacuate on terms. They accordingly proposed to march out with their families, baggage, private property, and arms. The proposition was immediately accepted, as time was a principal consideration with us: and the garrison evacuated the fort on the 30th of December, and was escorted beyond the Nagpoor frontier by a detachment formed for the purpose. Mun-Bhut surrendered himself to the Resident on the same day.

The military operations against the Bhoosla state were thus happily brought to a final conclusion, within little more than a month from the commencement of hostilities by the Raja. Nothing now remained, but to make such a settlement of the Nagpoor government, and of the relations of the state with the British, as should give us complete security for the future, and some indemnification also for the past. There were many important considerations involved in the choice of the course to be now adopted, which rendered it desirable that the views of the Governor-general should first be ascertained. But the communication had hitherto been so completely cut off, that no instruction as to the treatment of Apa Saheb, in the event of his submission, had yet been received. The Raja still continued at the Residency: and, as he was impatient to return to the palace, upon which the British flag was now flying, there seemed to be no ground for his further detention. The case, therefore, appeared to require the Resident to act upon his own responsibility, and come to some agreement, or at least lay the foundation for a final settlement without further delay. Mr. Jenkins had seen no cause to be dissatisfied with the conduct of the Raja since he had voluntarily surrendered himself; on the contrary, he regarded the circumstance of the abandonment of so many guns at the arsenal, as well as the subsequent payment of the arrears due to the Arabs as soon as demanded, as clear proofs that he had exerted himself both sincerely and sedulously to execute the conditions demanded of him; so that, although he had not come in within the prescribed time in the first instance, nor surrendered the whole of the guns, nor quietly disbanded the troops, nor given up the city and fort, agreeably to the letter of the stipulations, still, as his personal surrender had been received when he did come in, and as the failure of performance in other respects arose from causes apparently beyond his control, the Resident did not consider his claim to be reinstated, with the limitations and sacrifices he had been led to expect on his submission, to be at all weakened by subsequent events. Yet, while he felt the necessity of permitting the fallen prince to resume his station, he was no less sensible of the impossibility of placing further confidence in one, who had proved himself to be so inveterately addicted to intrigue, and so complete a Mahratta at heart. His military power had fortunately been annihilated; but the resources of the Nagpoor territory, if left to Apa Saheb's uncontrolled disposal, presented means of further mischief, which there could be little doubt he would avail himself of, unless checked with a strong hand. In preparing the definitive treaty for the Raja's acceptance, Mr. Jenkins, therefore, resolved to assume and act upon the principle, of reducing the head of the Bhoosla state to the condition of a mere pageant, and giving the British government a control over every branch of internal as well as of external administration, to the extent of imposing a ministry of its own selection, though composed of native subjects of the Raja. The forts of the country were, according to this plan, to be open to the discretionary introduction of British garrisons; and, for securing the subordination of the capital, the Seetabuldee hills were to be fortified.

In fact, we were to have complete military occupation of the whole country ; and, after his recent experience of the character of the ruling prince, the Resident could not consider any less security as either solid or permanent. In addition to the powers of general control, territory equal to the full charge of the subsidiary force (about twenty-four lakh of rupees) was to be ceded in perpetuity, in lieu of the present annual payment of seven and a half lakh, which only provided for the extraordinary field charges of the troops. The districts proposed to be demanded were, those held by the Raja, north of the Nerbudda, including Sir-Gooja, Jushpoor, Sohagpoor, and Sumbhulpoor to the east; all the valley to the south of the river, and as far as Chupara, between Jubulpoor and Nagpoor; together with Mooltaya, Bytool, Gawilgurh, and all the Raja's remaining possessions in Berar.

Mr. Jenkins had drawn up a treaty on the above basis, and was on the point of submitting it to the Raja's acceptance, preparatory to his reinstallation ; when, on the 2d of January, he received the instructions issued by the Marquess of Hastings, on first hearing of the defection of the Bhoosla prince. These instructions peremptorily forbad any personal reconciliation whatsoever, directing the young grandson of Ragoojee, by the daughter married to Gooja Apa, to be placed on the guddee, and affairs to be confided to the conduct of a regency of our own selection. The deposition of Apa Saheb was considered to be indispensable, both as a punishment for his defection at so critical a period, and from a conviction, that he could no longer be trusted even with the semblance of authority. The powerful motives that had swayed the mind of Mr. Jenkins, were wholly unknown to his Lordship at this time: consequently, when indistinct accounts of the recent occurrences at Nagpoor, subsequent to the arrival of General Doveton at that city, were received by his Lordship from different quarters, before the official reports of the negotiations came to hand, the veto against the reinstallation of Apa Saheb was twice repeated, under the supposition of his reiterated default in the performance of his engagements; unless the British government should have been already too far committed to retract with honour.

In consequence of the receipt of these instructions, Mr. Jenkins delayed to submit to the Raja his own draft of the definitive treaty, substituting a provisional engagement, which stipulated, that he should retain the guddee until the pleasure of the Governor-general should be known; but with a proviso for an eventual settlement on the basis above set forth, in case the Marquess of Hastings should confirm his restoration. The Resident

confidently expected this confirmation, as soon
as all the circumstances should have been made
known ; and in this he judged rightly. For the
Governor-general, on receiving the ample details
contained in the official despatches, which, however, were a long time on the road, became sensible of the necessity of replacing Apa Saheb, not
so much with a view to the immediate and advantageous settlement of affairs in that quarter, as
from respect to the moral obligation to do so,
under the circumstances of his surrender. As a
matter of policy, it may be right to mention, that
the Baees along with the infant grandson of Ragoojee, who was nine or ten years old, and had
already the title of Bala-Saheb, had, with Goojur
Apa his father, been sent off against their will to
Chanda, before General Doveton's arrival. This
could not have been prevented at the time ; neither would it have been possible to have secured
the person of the young prince, in the event of
the most complete success of our arms, after all
the reinforcements had come up. To have proclaimed the boy would, therefore, have only had
the effect of occasioning his instant death ; after
which we should have had a long and harassing
war to wage against the actual sovereign, unaid-
ed by any party in the state, or any head round
which the malcontents might rally.

Convinced by the representation of these difficulties, Lord Hastings in the-end approved of the
propositions submitted by Mr. Jenkins, and directed the treaty to be concluded on the basis
above described, which was done in the ensuing
month of February. However, when the specific
cessions demanded came to be discussed, along
with the other provisions for the control of the
Raja's internal administration, Apa Saheb pressed,
with apparent earnestness, that the whole country
should be taken under British rule, with a reservation of one-fourth of the revenues for his personal expenses, under a guarantee that this proportion should not fall short of fifteen lakh of
rupees. For such an income, he offered to for-
swear his independence and abandon the cares of
government altogether, and to range himself in
the same class with the Nuwabs of the Carnatic
and of Bengal. But the offer being saddled with
other expensive provisions for creditors and relations of the Raja, and the possession of the country by the British government being on other
grounds not desirable, it was not thought fit to
entertain it. By the arrangement actually concluded, we obtained the cession of territory
that stood in the Bhoosla accounts as yielding
a net revenue of 22,47,200 rupees, after de-
ducting alienations and demands of all kinds.
The ceded country was fertile, and, with the

exception of the jungul tract south of Buhar, well watered by the Nerbudda and its tributary streams. Through the exertions of the troops commanded by General Hardyman, who defeated the Sooba of Jubulpoor in a brilliant affair on the 19th of December, as before stated, and of the reserve brigade of the subsidiary force under Lieutenant-colonel M'Morine, which was equally successful against Sudoo-Baba of Sirinugur on the 15th of January, the whole had been brought under subjection before the end of the latter month, except the forts of Chouragurh and Mundela; and the considerable resources it afforded were made available to the operations of the current season.

It is impossible to close the account of this portion of the transactions at Nagpoor, without remarking on the extreme weakness and irresolution betrayed throughout by Apa Saheb. He might perhaps be excused for not concerting the time of his defection with the Pêshwa, so that both attacks should have been made the same day; for the character of Bajee Rao warranted the precaution of waiting to see him actually committed, before his ally should stir a step. But, after the resolution to join the confederacy was once formed, and after collecting an overwhelming force, which he assured himself must overpower the brigade at Nagpoor, his long hesitation before the

attack was authorised, his disavowal of it after
the failure, and his paltry attempt to throw on
Mun-Bhut the whole responsibility, in the hope
thus to escape himself, were acts of the most decided pusillanimity. He never seems to have
known his own mind from first to last, but betrayed the greatest weakness and want of judgment, in so soon abandoning the cause he had
espoused, before it was by any means desperate ;
and particularly in not renewing the attack after
the first repulse, when he knew our troops must
be exhausted. Instead of doing so, he remained
idle at Nagpoor, till the arrival of General Doveton with an overpowering force, without making
any effort whatever to obstruct that officer's march,
or to cut off either of the detachments which preceded him. He must have felt, and indeed was
explicitly told, that he could be admitted to no
reconciliation that would leave him political independence or the reality of power : but sovereignty
on any terms, though but a mere shadow, was
too dearly prized in possession, to allow him fairly
to commit it to the hazardous chance of a pro-
tracted struggle for the substance. No country
was ever better adapted to desultory warfare than
the Bhoosla territory ; the whole is a continued
tract of mountains, ravines, and junguls, forming
altogether as difficult a theatre of war as any in
existence. Subsequent experience has proved the

facility, with which, had he retired with his army unbroken, he might have prolonged the contest indefinitely; and, by giving occupation to a large proportion of our military force, have prevented that concentration of means for the destruction of his confederate, the Pêshwa, which was afterwards so successfully directed to that object. However, there can be no doubt, that both must have fallen in the end; but a great difference might have been made in the time, the charge, and the trouble, it would have cost us to effect our purpose. It was the peculiar merit of Lord Hastings' plan of operations, to have placed such means at command, as should make the cause of the Mahrattas desperate under any combination of circumstances; and the further we trace the detail of events in their order of occurrence, the more reason shall we find to admire the forecast, which so disposed those means, that not one adverse circumstance or occasion of danger arose, without its remedy and corrective being found ready at hand. This will be particularly observable as we proceed with the narrative of the transactions on the side of Hindoostan, to which quarter it is time again to turn our attention.

The march of the three divisions of Malcolm, Adams, and Marshall, to Tullain, Bairsea, and Basouda, and the advance of the last named to Seronj, had completely driven the Pindarees out of their haunts in Malwa by the end of November. As above related, the durras of Kureem and Wâsil Mohummed retreated northward by Nya-Seraee on the main road to Gwalior; while Cheetoo moved off in a westerly direction, as well to avail himself of the support he expected from the army of Holkur, which was already assembled in force, as to fall back on the position of Juswunt Rao Bhâo, one of Sindheea's commanders, from whom he had obtained assurances of protection, and of a refuge for his family in the strong fort of Kumulner.

The disposition of Holkur's military began, at this time, to assume a decidedly hostile character. The march of the main body of the Pindarees towards Gwalior, and the uniform conduct of Sindheea's captains, as well as the reluctance of the chief himself to execute the conditions of the treaty of concert he had lately signed under compulsion, seemed to indicate a similar bias in that durbar. It was also doubtful, whether Ameer Khan would ratify the engagements of his agent at Dehlee. Connecting all these appearances, therefore, with the open resort of the Pêshwa and of the Bhoosla to arms, there was certainly ground to apprehend the worst from the aspect of affairs at the close of the month of November. The Goorkhas of Nipâl too were collecting their forces, and known to be in close communication with the

powers of Hindoostan ; so that the slightest reverse, in the temper of men's minds at the time,
would soon have been magnified into a disaster,
capable of involving the whole of India in one general combustion. The success at Nagpoor, however, confounded all their calculations, and operated powerfully to destroy the vain illusions of
the ill-disposed. Ameer Khan ratified the treaty
of his agent on the first receipt of the intelligence;
communicating to Sir David Ochterlony the circumstances of the battle, and using many expressions of wonder and admiration at the conduct of
the troops engaged, with whose numbers he was
perfectly acquainted. But the spirit which had
been excited, was not every where so soon al-
layed; and in Hindoostan, as well as in the
Dukhun, there were moments, when the firmness
and decision of those intrusted with the chief direction of affairs were distinctly called forth into
action. The sudden developement of the extent
of combination, which had been organizing against
us, might have induced many to contract their
views, in proportion to the increasing cloud of
difficulties; but had a contrary effect upon the
mind of the Governor-general. To his eye, these
crude attempts to thwart his plans presented but
the means of establishing the settlement he de-
signed for India upon a broader and more solid
foundation; so just and so unbounded was his re-

liance on the machinery he had prepared for the accomplishment of his purpose.

Unlooked-for circumstances, however, combined to put his Lordship's fortitude to the test. Having by his advance to the Sindh enforced upon Sindheea the acceptance of the treaty of concert, he was, in the middle of November, moving leisurely with the centre division to take up such a position, as might be calculated to connect the object of keeping that chief in awe, with the interception of the Pindarees, should they attempt to penetrate by the north or east : when his army was afflicted with a pestilence as violent and destructive, as any recorded in the pages of history. The malady, from some similarity in its principal features to that previously known by medical men under the title of the *cholera morbus*, has usually been designated by this appellation. It was, however, decidedly epidemic, and, like all similar visitations of nature, its source is matter of pure conjecture, though its progress has been distinctly traced. It was first observed in the Delta of the Ganges, about the commencement of the rainy season of 1817 ; and, from the early part of September, its ravages were felt at Calcutta, where for a long time it destroyed upwards of two hundred persons daily. Spreading thence up the course of the Ganges and its tributary waters, it reached the camp of Brigadier-general Hardyman about the beginning of October; but as it was pitched in a healthy country, and his force consisted of but one European and one native battalion, with a regiment of cavalry, the destructive effects of the disease, though serious, were not particularly marked, in comparison with what had previously been felt in its progress thither. Continuing westward, however, it fell with extraordinary violence upon the army commanded by Lord Hastings in person, which it overtook very soon after the conclusion of the treaty with Sindheea. The year was one of scarcity, and grain had been collected for the troops and camp followers with extreme difficulty, and of course of very inferior quality. That part of Bundelkhund, where the division was encamped when the disease first showed itself, was, moreover, low and notoriously unhealthy; besides which, except when obtained from running streams, the water was generally indifferent. The time of the year too was precisely that, at which the heat of the day is most strongly contrasted with the cold of the night. All these circumstances, superadded to the crowded state of the camp of so large an army, gave to the epidemic, when it did break out, a degree of violence much exceeding what it had manifested in other parts of the country. For about ten days, that it raged with particular fury the whole camp was a hospital*; and the deaths in this short period amounted, according to the nearest estimate that could be made, to a tenth of the whole number collected. Europeans and natives, fighting men and camp followers, were alike affected ; but the latter, being generally worse clothed and fed, suffered in a greater proportion, Of the Europeans there were fewer cases of seizure ; but those which occurred were more frequently fatal, and usually so within a few hours. The camp continued for some days to move eastward, in the hope of finding a better climate, as soon as it should reach the Betwa ; but each day of march many dead and dying were abandoned on the route, and many more fell down on the road, for whom it was impossible to furnish the means of transport, though the utmost possible provision had been made by the previous distribution of carts and elephants for the accommodation of the sick. Such indeed was the general distress, that, so

* The narrator himself lost seven domestic servants and a *moonshee* in about four days, besides twelve others who were sick and unserviceable for a month, out of an establishment of fifty-three ; and others of the staff were equal sufferers. The fighting men filled the whole of the hospitals in the first two days ; and for servants and followers every man's tent was his only receptacle, and himself the only doctor.

long as the epidemic raged, even the healthy were
broken in spirit, and incapable of labour or fatigue ;
while the bazars and public establishments were
deserted, and the whole efficiency of this fine army
was, for the time, apparently destroyed.

The symptoms of the disease may be described
in a few words. Its approach was indicated by a
giddiness that came on suddenly and without
warning, attended with an immediate and total
prostration of strength; insomuch, that men fell
from their horses in the line of march, and were
unable afterwards to rise from the ground, though
perfectly well when they had started in the morning.   A nausea succeeded, with purging and
vomiting, so violent as tó defy the power of medicine.   Laudanum was generally given at this
stage in large quantities ; but the stomach would
retain nothing, throwing up a peculiar green
or whitish fluid.   After this, the patient was
seized with cramps and coldness from the extremities upwards, even to the parts about the heart.
In the midst of his agonies, he felt a burning thirst,
and called incessantly for cold water, but vomited
it the instant it was given.   This lasted from
twenty-four to forty-eight hours, and the person
affected, either died under its severity, or was
left in a state of such extreme debility, that the
utmost power of medicine availed nothing.   The
cure was very rare, when these spasmodic affec-

tions came on with any degree of violence. It was observed of this malady, that neither the voice, nor the power of swallowing, nor the intellect, were ever lost, while life remained ; also, that after death the bodies had a peculiar smell, which was immediately perceptible at some distance. Medical men have never yet discovered wherein the disease lay ; much less have they found any probable cure. Laudanum or opium to allay the irritation within, and calomel, the universal specific of India, with stimulants when the patient is about to sink from exhaustion, formed the general practice, on the first appearance of the disease : bleeding has since been tried with effect, when administered shortly after the first attack, but it is in vain to try this remedy after the cramps have commenced. The hot bath has also been occasionally adopted successfully in different stages of the disease, and so have other remedies of more capricious selection. The most experienced medical men are not quite agreed as to the precise course that is most efficacious.

Towards the end of November, the Governor-general had reached a healthy station at Erich on the Betwa, and the epidemic had visibly expended its virulence. The camp was, however, still crowded with convalescents, when the march of the Pindarees towards Gwalior threatened to call for the active exertions of the centre division, and the personal appearance of its noble commander upon the scene of operations.

It has before been mentioned, that one detachment had been sent from this division, under Major Cumming, to cover the civil station of Bundelkhund. This had subsequently been pushed forward as far south as Tehree; while a second detachment, chiefly of cavalry, under Colonel Philpot of His Majesty's 24th dragoons, was in the course of November stationed at Burwa-Sâgur, so as completely to connect the centre division at Erich, with that of General Marshall, then moving on Seronj. But, as soon as it was ascertained that the durras of Kureem, and of Wâsil Mohummed, had decamped to the northward, Lord Hastings ordered the detachment from Burwa-Sâgur to move through Dutteea, across the Sindh, to cut them off from Gwalior; and, at the same time, seeing reason to suspect the fidelity of his ally to his new engagements, he again marched upon the Sindh, from his station near Erich, calling in the detachment from Tehree. This movement had the double object of giving a support to Colonel Philpot, and more effectually overawing the counsels of the Gwalior durbar. His Lordship reached Soonaree, which is only thirty miles S. S. E. of Gwalior, on the 11th of December, where his unexpected appearance had the desired effect. Sindheea was alarmed, and the Pindarees halted in consternation in the junguls and broken ground about Shahabad, not knowing what course to pursue, or whither to direct their march. Despairing of aid from Gwalior, they could not retrace their steps; for General Marshall, though he had not been able to make all the progress expected, had nevertheless reached Nya Seraee on the 12th of December, while Colonel Adams was with his force at Googul Chupra on the Parbutee; both of which points were particularly well adapted to intercept the return of the marauders southward. To force the passes of Haraotee to the S. W., or those of the Chumbul towards Jypoor, seemed the only modes of escape now left to the fugitives: but the state of the river, and a variety of precautions, which had been taken to strengthen the principal passes in the latter quarter, by troops from Agra and from General Donkin's division, rendered the passage of the Chumbul, lower than Haraotee, wholly impracticable. Sir David Ochterlony had also arrived with the reserve in the neighbourhood of Jypoor, and was prepared to support this line of defence. Again, with respect to escaping by Haraotee, the country there was in the hands of the Raj-Rana Zalim Singh, manager for the Raja of Kota, who was now in strict alliance with us. Immediately upon the conclusion of the treaty with Sindheea, Captain Tod had been ordered from Gwalior, where he was acting assistant to the Resident, in order to cement a closer union with this chieftain ; and he had not only been successful in this object, having obtained from the Raj-Rana the blocking up of all the passes through his dominions, but had further induced him to place a contingent at the disposal of the British authorities, which had for some time been in the field. General Donkin also, with the right division, arrived at Boondee on the 10th of December ; and hearing from Captain Tod of the situation of the Pindarees about Shahabad, was now in full march eastward to cut them off, in case of any effort to escape in that direction.

On the 13th of December, General Marshall made a move towards Shahabad, where he was informed the united durras still remained encumbered with their baggage and families. At the same time Colonel Adams crossed the Parbutee, and took the same direction, to co-operate with the above movement. General Marshall arrived in the afternoon of the 14th at the Lodwana Ghât, one of those leading into Haraotee, which he found the Pindarees had lately forced, in consequence of the ill conduct of Zalim Singh's troops there posted. Here he was told, that the freebooters were still encamped at Bichee-Tal, a short distance only from the top of the Ghât. Accordingly, he lost no time in pushing forward his advanced guard with all the cavalry, in the hope of giving them a surprise. A party of about one thousand of the best mounted, immediately on perceiving the approach of the advance, presented themselves as if to oppose it ; but, instead of abiding a charge, led Colonel Newbery, who commanded the cavalry, into a long pursuit, away from the route by which the rest effected their escape. General Marshall, however, took much baggage that day, notwithstanding that no more than fifty or sixty of the enemy were killed. In the course of his advance next morning, he found the road strewed with loads of grain and other baggage, thrown away in the confusion of the flight. Kureem and Wâsil had moved off westward, intending to cross the Chumbul by the Loharee Ghât, in the hope of being joined by Muhtab Khan, one of Ameer Khan's principal officers, as soon as they should penetrate to Jypoor. That Ghât, however, was guarded by the wing of one of General Donkin's battalions, previously detached for the purpose ; and the General himself, after crossing the Chumbul on the 13th, was now in full march towards Burôd, which lay in the direct line of their retreat by this route. The Pindarees did not hear of General Donkin's approach, until he had surprised their advanced guard, in a night bivouac, about four miles north-east of Burôd, capturing the wife of Kureem Khan, and all his state elephants, kettle-drums, standards, and other insignia of command. The main body of the two durras was then, only six miles distant; but, on finding themselves intercepted, they instantly called a council of the leaders, when it was agreed, that, burning their tents and abandoning their baggage, all but the *elite* or fighting men should disperse, every one free to seek his own fortune. The two chiefs, with less than four thousand, all well mounted, went off in the utmost haste to the south; and passing to the left of Colonel Adams' division, while he was manœuvring on the right bank of the Parbutee, made good their passage through Zalim Singh's territory, although Colonel Adams, immediately on hearing of their flight that way, detached his cavalry under Major Clarke in pursuit. Of those left behind, many were cut up by the different divisions, some in attempting the Loharee Ghât, and the remainder by the villagers, who now regarded their destruction as certain, and no longer hesitated to retaliate on them the cruelties they had so often suffered at their hands. So complete was the despondency of these once formidable hordes, and so hopeless their present situation, that the appearance of the smallest party of our sepahees was enough to make a large body of them throw every thing away and disperse. Availing himself of this feeling, on the night of the 23d of December, an Havildar, with only thirty-four men of Captain Tod's escort, ventured to attack a very considerable body, as it lay encamped in a part of Zalim Singh's territories. The whole galloped off on the first volley, deserting their camels, and even many of their horses; but when the morning dawned soon after, and they saw the smallness of the party, they rallied, and showed a disposition to dispute the prize. The Havildar, however, manœuvring as if he was merely the advance guard of a larger force, put them a second time to flight : nor did they venture again to turn. Khooshal Koonwur a Sirdar of note, was the commander of the routed party. The Havildar secured a large booty, and gained great credit by the enterprise.

The object having been thus accomplished in this quarter, Major-general Marshall was ordered to return with the head-quarters of his division to Seronj, in order to be at hand to prevent any broken parties of the marauders from re-appearing in their previous haunts, as well as to hinder other powers from establishing their jurisdiction in the territory whence they had just been expelled, unless with the express authority of the

Governor-general or Sir Thomas Hislop. The scene of operations, as far as concerned the Pindarees, was now entirely confined to Mewur, in which direction Cheetoo had originally retired, and whither the remains of Kureem's and Wâsil's durras had directed their flight.

A new plan of operations was forthwith devised, in order to surround them similarly in this quarter. Colonel Adams moved down upon Gungrar to hem them in on the east; while General Donkin, recrossing the Chumbul, proceeded to take post at Shahpoora, westward of the Bunas, so as to inclose them on the north. The Marquess of Hastings also despatched Major-general Brown from the centre division at Sonaree, with a light force, composed of the 3d native cavalry, the dromedary corps, one troop of horse artillery, and some companies of light infantry; which, after being reinforced by a regiment of cavalry *, some irregular horse, and a battalion from Major-general Marshall's army, was directed to march by the line of Shahabad, and to the southward of Haraotee, so as to be available to the north of Colonel Adams, in case its services should be required in that direction. In the mean time, the divisions from the Dukhun, under Generals Sir Thomas Hislop and Sir John Malcolm, as well as

* Fourth native cavalry, and 2d battalion of 1st native infantry.

the army from Goozerât under Sir William Keir, had become available in the same quarter. But, before we follow up the operations against the Pindarees, it will be necessary to relate the other more important transactions, in which the two divisions from the Dukhun had just been involved with the army of Holkur.

CHAPTER XVI.

HOLKUR.—HINDOOSTAN.

1817–18. December, January, February.

Brigadier-general Malcolm pursues Cheetoo — Meets the army of Holkur—Falls back on Oojein—Overtures from that durbar—Effect of Pêshwa's defection—Army advances —Junction of the divisions of Malcolm and Hislop—Negotiation tried—Regent put to death—Hostilities—Battle of Mehudpoor—Junction of the Goozerât division—Terms offered—Treaty of Mundisôr—Affair of Rampoora —Effect on Sindheea—Juswunt Rao Bhâo—Affair of Jawud— Kumulnèr and other forts taken—Final settlement in that quarter—Pindarees expelled from Mewur—Surprised at Kotree—Further pursuit—Submission of Namdar Khan— Wâsil Mohummed—Kureem and his son—How disposed of—Cheetoo.

IT has been mentioned in the preceding chapters, that Sir John Malcolm, with the third division of the army of the Dukhun, arrived at Tullain on the 26th of November. Here being informed of Cheetoo's flight to the west, and that Kureem and Wâsil had taken the northward route, he resolved to move in pursuit of the former, and proceeded by Sarungpoor to Agur. But the motions of the army of Holkur having latterly been very suspicious, it was arranged between the Brigadier-general and Colonel Adams, that the latter should move westward also as far as Rajgurh-Patun, to afford his support in case of necessity. Sir John Malcolm arrived at Agur on the 4th of December, and from this point opened a communication with Captain Tod at Kota, whose information confirmed the reports of his own intelligencers, representing the intentions of Holkur, or at least those of his army, to be decidedly hostile. The reception of Cheetoo, whose camp was pitched close to that of Holkur, and who was himself admitted to an audience before he set off to deposit his family with Juswunt Rao Bhâo in Kumulnèr, was a sufficient proof of the sentiments of the ruling party at this durbar. Sir John Malcolm, therefore, having in the interim heard that Sir Thomas Hislop was on his return to Oojein, resolved to fall back upon that *appui*, and to let Colonel Adams advance to the north, in co-operation with the division of General Marshall, which was on the point of moving from Seronj. It will be necessary to give some explanation of the conduct of Holkur's administration at this juncture.

It will be recollected, that it formed part of Lord Hastings' general plan, to conclude with this durbar a treaty of concert similar to that

effected with Sindheea; with the difference, however, of detaching Ameer Khan from his depen-
dency upon the chief, and procuring the acknowledgment of his independent sovereignty over such
districts as might be in his actual possession. In
conformity with this plan, a letter had been addressed to the Regency of Holkur by the Resident at Dehlee, at the same time that negotiations
were opened with Sindheea and Ameer Khan,
inviting it to send a confidential agent to Dehlee
to treat, and intimating the terms on which it
was the Governor-general's wish to form a closer
connexion with the durbar. For a long time no
answer was returned to this communication; but
on the 15th of November, Mr. Metcalfe received
an overture from the Regent, Toolsee-Baee, offering to place herself and the young Mulhar Rao
under the protection of the British government.
This overture, though conveyed with much secrecy, came either from the ministers of the day,
Gunput Rao and Tanteea Jog, or at least with
their knowledge and concurrence. Accordingly,
on Captain Tod's being sent to Kota, he was instructed to open a communication through the
ministers; and as it was supposed to be the Baee's
principal object in making the offer, to rid herself
and her ward of the influence of Ameer Khan and
the rebellious commanders of infantry, General
Donkin was apprised beforehand of the probability

that the Baee might need the active aid of a British force; and this had been one of the objects of his advance up the left bank of the Chumbul.

Soon afterwards, however, the news of the Pêshwa's defection spread abroad, and the first impulse of the sirdars of Holkur was to march immediately to the south, in order to rally round the legitimate head of the Mahratta nation. The intention to move in that direction was soon publicly announced; but it was at first supposed to be a feint on the part of the Baee and her ministry, who, finding it impossible to control the soldiery, were thought to have taken this step with a view to deceive them by the appearance of a cordial unison of sentiment. But the sirdars were not to be so deceived; and suspecting that the ministry was intriguing underhand with the English, resolved upon its removal from office. On the 24th of November, Tanteea Jog was accused in open durbar of a conspiracy to betray the principality to the English; and he was accordingly stripped of his office and placed in close confinement. Gunput Rao was left nominally in the chief conduct of affairs; but the real power fell into the hands of the Putan sirdars, at the head of whom was Ghufoor Khan, the avowed agent of Ameer Khan, and Ramdeen, one of the most considerable of the infantry officers. The march from Rampoora was commenced very soon after-

wards; and it was resolved to move by Indrok on
Mehudpoor, and thence by Indore across, the
Nerbudda by the ford of Choolee-Muheshwur.
Every effort was made to collect the dispersed infantry of Holkur's establishment; and, before the
28th, fourteen additional battalions under Roshun-
Beg and Roshun Khan had joined on the line of
march.   Things were, in this state in the camp of
Mulhar Rao, when Cheetoo formed a junction
with it; and the near approach of Sir John Malcolm brought it more directly into contact with
the British armies.   The mutinous troops were
kept together by the promise of being paid their
arrears on arriving at Indore, and the hopes of
all were buoyed up by the expectation of a liberal
supply of money from the coffers of Bajee Rao, as
soon as they should have crossed the Nerbudda:
assurances to this effect had been received from
Poona but a few days before, so that it was no
time to expect any favourable disposition towards
ourselves, nor indeed was the soldiery inclined to
pay much attention to the remonstrances addressed to the sirdars by Sir John Malcolm, in consequence of their reception of Cheetoo; or to the
efforts of that officer to persuade them to relinquish the design of espousing the cause of the
Pêshwa.   The sirdars themselves, however, were
liberal of their professions, and answered the letters both of Sir John Malcolm and of the Resident

at Dehlee, with general protestations of their desire to maintain the existing relations of amity. The march to the south was nevertheless continued; all ranks, particularly the regent princess, expressing the most enthusiastic devotion to the cause of the Mahratta sovereign. Seeing, therefore, to what issue matters were fast verging, Sir John Malcolm, as above mentioned, fell back upon Oojein, in order to effect a junction with the division of Sir Thomas Hislop.

The two divisions met on the 12th of December; and, after a halt of two days at Oojein, advanced on the 14th towards the camp of Holkur, for the purpose of giving effect to the negotiation. A draft of treaty was prepared, similar in most of the terms to that concluded with Sindheea, and was proffered to the acceptance of the durbar. Its reception was at first outwardly favourable; and, to carry on the deception as long as possible, a confidential agent was sent to treat and discuss the several articles. Things continued in this uncertain state for some days, the two armies lying all the while within fourteen miles of each other; that of Holkur being at Mehudpoor, while Sir Thomas Hislop was at Punbehar, a little to the north of Oojein. On the 17th of December, the mutinous spirit of the Putan sirdars openly gained the preponderance; and, distrusting the designs of Gunput Rao and the Regent Baee, whom they still suspected of a secret design to throw themselves upon British protection, they seized and confined both, and broke off all further communication with Sir John Malcolm. It was the general feeling of the sirdars, that if the court were to accede to the terms proposed, they would themselves lose all personal consideration; and there was little difficulty in persuading the troops, that such a measure would necessarily deprive them for ever of their means of livelihood. In this feeling, it was unanimously resolved to offer battle to the English, in preference to accepting the terms; and, with a view to prevent any future intrigues from interfering with the resolution, the regent, Toolsee Baee, was carried down by night to the banks of the Soopra, and there put to death, by order of Ghufoor Khan and the Putans.

The ascendancy of the war faction was immediately apparent in the attacks made upon our foraging parties, from which cattle were daily carried off, not without some loss of lives. On the 20th of December, Sir Thomas Hislop, thinking thereby to curb this spirit of hostility, advanced to within seven miles of Holkur's camp; but that very day a picquet of Mysoor horse was attacked by a party of about two hundred of Holkur's Barabaee horse, under circumstances which showed that they were not actuated by any motive of plunder. It was accordingly resolved to enforce immediate submission to the terms proposed to the acceptance of the durbar, or to bring on a general action without further delay.

On the morning of the 21st of December, the British army again advanced; but its march was more openly opposed by bodies of Holkur's horse, which appeared on every side. A letter had been written over night to invite the durbar to submission; and another to the agent employed to negotiate, to know why communication had been so abruptly broken off. To both of these answers were received on the march: the reply to the former contained mere general assurances; but that of the negotiator explained more fully, that the sirdars were bent upon abiding the result of an action. Sir Thomas Hislop, therefore, no longer hesitated as to the course to be pursued.

On approaching Mehudpoor, the enemy were discovered drawn up in line on the opposite bank of the Soopra, as if they intended to dispute the passage of that river by the most practicable ford, which lay a little above their position, that is to say, to the south of the town. A reconnoisance was immediately made by Lieutenant-colonel Blacker, the quarter-master-general, who ascertained that there was ground on the opposite side of the river, and within its bed, for the troops to form upon after the passage, where they would be completely sheltered from the fire of the enemy's

artillery by the brow of the over-hanging bank.
He likewise observed, that on ascending the bank
the men would only have to advance three hundred yards before they reached the enemy's guns.
Upon this report, it was determined to attack in
front by the ford, notwithstanding the obvious
disadvantages of the ground, in preference to manœuvring so as to turn the position, which would
have required a long detour and much time, while
any appearance of hesitation could not fail to produce a very prejudicial effect. The enemy's right
was protected by a deep ravine, and his left by a
slight bend of the river, and a deserted village
called Sitawud, not far from its bank. The
ground on which the British army had to form
itself, after crossing the ford, was within the two
horns of this position ; the enemy's line retiring a
little in the centre to make the most advantage of
it. Sir Thomas Hislop placed the baggage in a
village on the right bank called Doolait, under
protection of the rear-guard and a few Mysoor
horse ; and then, while Sir John Malcolm with
the cavalry drove off the hovering parties of the
enemy's horse, a few light troops were pushed
across the ford, followed by fourteen guns of the
horse artillery and a troop of rocketers. The
passage was effected without much difficulty, although the enemy brought up some guns to bear
on the ford. The horse artillery immediately

opened a battery on the enemy's line, while the rest of the army crossed to the low ground under cover of the bank, in order there to form for the attack. The enemy were so superior in artillery, that in a short time the whole of our guns were disabled. Four guns of the foot artillery were, however, opened with good effect, from a position they had taken on the opposite side of the river, a little nearer Mehudpoor, whence they enfiladed the left of the enemy's line, which had been advanced between the village of Sitawud and the river, in order to open with more effect on the ford.

By the time the horse artillery were nearly silenced, the British army had passed the ford, and was formed for the attack. The first brigade, composed of the flank companies of his Majesty's Royal Scots and the Madras European regiment, with the second battalion of the Madras 14th N. I., the whole under Lieutenant-colonel R. Scott, was destined to the attack of the enemy's left. The light brigade, consisting of the rifle corps, with the Palam-cotta and Trichinopoly light infantry, the whole under Major Bowen, formed the centre : and the second brigade, composed of the 2d battalion of the 6th Madras N. I. and the Nizam's battalions under Captain Hare, formed the left of our infantry line. The cavalry were directed to operate against the enemy's right, where the ground was most favourable for this arm. The main attack, however, was entrusted to the first brigade, where the enemy was strongest in artillery, and the distance to be passed under his fire the longest. Sir John Malcolm solicited permission to lead this attack, which was granted; and in the same manner Lieutenant-colonel M'Gregor Murray, Deputy Adjutant-general to the king's forces, obtained leave to head the detachment of the Royal Scots, which had precedence in it. These dispositions were no sooner completed, than the attack was commenced. The enemy's artillery was extremely numerous and well served, so that our loss was very severe, particularly in the first and in the light brigade, which latter being in the centre, was exposed to the cross fire of the whole line. The troops, however, advanced with great steadiness, the Europeans *, in particular, reserving their fire and trusting to the bayonet alone. Holkur's artillerymen stood to

---

* Sir John Malcolm, observing a sepahee battalion stop and fire in its advance, turned round to the men and said, " My lads, there is little use in that; I think, we had better give them the cold iron." Whereupon he was answered with characteristic bluntness from the ranks ; " Yes, your Honour, I think we had ;" and the line advanced with shouldered arms in high glee, notwithstanding the destructive fire then playing upon it.

their guns till they were bayonetted ; but his
infantry battalions gave way as soon as the guns
were carried.

Meanwhile, the cavalry had turned the enemy's
right, and driving off the horse who opposed
them, made a dreadful slaughter of the broken
infantry. Holkur's camp was directly opposite
to Mehudpoor, a little to the north of the field
of battle. This, with all the artillery, was soon
in our hands ; but on the pursuit being continued, the fugitives attempted to rally, and got
together some guns to cover their retreat across
a ford about four miles lower down the river than
Mehudpoor. Upon this, Sir Thomas Hislop ordered his line to be again formed ; but the guns
were soon taken, and the feeble resistance offered
at this point overpowered by the rapid advance of
Sir John Malcolm with the cavalry and a light
detachment. Our camp was formed upon the
field of battle, while Sir John Malcolm continued
the pursuit across the river with the regular cavalry, and Captain Grant with the Mysoor horse
moved down the left bank. The enemy's flight
was supposed to be directed northwards towards
Rampoora. An immense booty fell into the
hands of the Mysoor horse. Eight elephants and
some hundred camels were brought in chiefly by
them. The camp itself was found deserted when
entered by the regular army : sixty-three guns

were, however, captured, and the total destruction of so many disorderly battalions was a yet more important consequence of the success of this day.

Our loss was severe, amounting to one hundred and seventy-four killed, and six hundred and four wounded ; among the former were three officers, Lieutenants M'Leod, Colman, and Glen ; amongst the latter, no less than thirty-five, whereof eight were of the rifle corps alone *.

Sir Thomas Hislop resolved to remain himself a week at Mehudpoor, and to establish a hospital and depôt there ; while Sir John Malcolm fol-

* Names of officers severely wounded :
        Quarter-master Griffin, horse artillery.
        Lieutenant Campbell, royals.
        Lieut. Hancome, European regiment (since dead).
        Captain Norton,
        Lieutenants Gwynne,
                Shanahan,
                Drake,   rifle corps.
                Calder,
                Eastment,
           Ensign Gem,
        Lieutenant Jones, Palamcotta light infantry.
        Major Bowen,
        Lieutenant Palmer, } Trichinopoly ditto.
        Lieutenant Gibbings, quarter-master-general's
           department.
        Lieutenant Lyon, brigade-major of cavalry.
Besides twenty other officers slightly wounded.

lowed up the victory with a light division from
his army. One of the principal reasons of this
delay was, to allow of the junction of the Bombay army from Goozerât, which arrived at Rutlam
on the 24th of December. This army had also
been directed to move on Oojein, and, according
to the original plan of operations, would have
been in time to have taken part in the battle of
Mehudpoor, had not its march been arrested by
an order of recall addressed to Major-general Sir
William Keir by the Bombay Government, immediately on hearing of the defection of the Bhoosla.
This event, it seems, was so totally unexpected at
that Presidency, that in the uncertainty how far
the appearance of fidelity kept up at Brodera
could be trusted, the Governor in council felt
alarmed at the idea of the Goozerât force being so
far removed from the territory of his government,
and wished to retain it for the protection of Su-
rat and the Gykwar state from the secret or
open attempts of Bajee Rao. The Marquess of
Hastings was by no means pleased at this diversion of the Goozerât army from the part assigned
to it in his original plan ; and no sooner heard of
it, than he called upon the Bombay government
to rectify the error without delay. In the interim, however, the strong representations addressed to Sir William Keir by Sir Thomas
Hislop, showing the necessity of his advance into

Hindoostan, had induced that officer to resume his forward march after a short retrograde, before he received the positive order to that effect, addressed to him by the Marquess of Hastings in person ; and he had from Rutlam furnished a light reinforcement to Sir John Malcolm, which joined at Kurdla on the 27th of December. On the 30th, the Goozerât army effected a junction with the head-quarters of the army of the Dukhun, and the united force then advanced upon Mundisôr in support of Sir John Malcolm, who had already reached that point.

There was, however, little further to be done in this quarter, except to receive the submission of Holkur, whose power had been completely broken by the defeat of the 21st, and who, finding retreat cut off by our divisions on every side, had no longer the means of resistance or evasion. The negotiation was opened by Ghufoor Khan, who sent the agent that had conducted the previous negotiations, to make inquiries about a son-in-law left wounded on the field of battle. This opportunity was taken to forward the most humble assurances of the present altered sentiments of the leading men of the durbar. Tanteea Jog had already been released from confinement and restored to office ; and Sir John Malcolm, in his reply to the above unofficial communication, caused it to be suggested, that the

durbar could adopt no fitter course than to de-
pute that minister immediately to the camp of
Sir Thomas Hislop, to tender the submissions of
the court, and conclude a treaty on the best
terms hé could obtain. In conformity with this
intimation, Tanteea Jog came into Sir John
Malcolm's camp at Mundisôr on the 1st of January.

By this time, the Brigadier-general had received the instructions framed by the Marquess of
Hastings in the contemplation of a rupture, and
prescribing the terms on which Holkur's submission was to be accepted and his authority
re-established. He accordingly entered at once
upon the negotiation. The terms proposed were,
that Mulhar Rao Holkur should place himself and
his dominions under British protection; that he
should confirm the engagement already concluded
with Ameer Khan, and renounce all sovereignty
over the lands guaranteed to that chieftain; the
four pergunnas of Puchpuhar, Deeg, Gungrar, and
Ahoor, which Zalim Singh of Kota had for some
years rented, to be ceded to the British in perpetuity, to enable them to recompense the useful
services of the Raj-Rana; also, all territories possessed by Holkur north of the Boondee hills or
south of the Sâtpoora range, including the fort of
Sindwa in the latter, with a glacis, to be ceded to
us, together with all claims for tribute on the

Rajpoot princes. The state to be placed on the footing of other powers connected with us in subsidiary alliances, and its contingent to be fixed at three thousand horse. The Governor-general's plan for settling the factious differences that for so many years had distracted this durbar, was to invest Ghufoor Khan, the avowed head of the Putan interest, with an hereditary jageer to be held of Holkur in perpetuity under our guarantee. It was thought that this measure would satisfy the expectations of that party, and probably tend to separate it for ever from the intrigues of the durbar; and it was hoped the lands known to be already in Ghufoor Khan's possession would prove an ample provision. It was not known to his Lordship, when these instructions were issued, that Ghufoor Khan was suspected of being the principal instigator of the murder of Toolsee Baee; else in all probability a different arrangement would have been devised. As it was, however, Sir John Malcolm executed his instructions to the letter, and effected all these objects after a short negotiation, in which Tanteea Jog insisted principally on three points: first, the extent of the cession for the benefit of Zalim Singh, which he wished to limit to two instead of four pergunnas; secondly, the arrears due on account of the past year's tribute from the Rajpoots, for which he solicited our guarantee; and thirdly, the retention

of the forts of Chandore and Umba, with some
villages in Kandês and the Dukhun. Sir John
Malcolm distinctly refused to give up either of the
above points, but promised to submit a request on
behalf of Mulhar Rao, that some hereditary civil
rights in several of the villages in the Dukhun
should be reserved to the family, after and although the sovereignty should be ceded to us.
The treaty was signed and executed on the 6th
of January, in conformity with the original draft.
The jageer secured to Ghufoor Khan, under its
stipulations, included the pergunnas of Sunjeet,
Mulhar-gurh, Tal Moondawur, Joura, and Burôd,
with the Peeplouda tribute : and the condition of
tenure was the military service of six hundred
select horse, the number to be liable to increase
on the eventual improvement of the jageer. The
ratification of the Governor-general was affixed on
the 17th of January 1818 ; and at the same time
Sir John Malcolm was authorised to make an advance of five lakh of rupees on the revenues of
Koonch, one of the pergunnas of Holkur not included amongst the cessions, but bordering on
our own territory of Bundelkhund. An arrangement had been made some years before with this
durbar, by which we had undertaken the collection of its revenues, and annually paid them from
the Dehlee treasury. The pergunna having been
assigned to a sister of Mulhar Rao, its cession was

not insisted upon ; and the sum advanced upon it was necessary to the peaceable settlement of his government in its new relations.

Immediately on the conclusion of the above treaty, Mulhar Rao came in, with Gunput Rao, Ghufoor Khan, and his principal Sirdars, and placed himself under the protection of the British army. Tanteea Jog was vested with the principal administration of the public affairs, the prince being a youth of about twelve years of age. Gunput Rao, who held the high office of hereditary dewan, was reduced to the exercise of a mere nominal authority.

An occasion very soon occurred to call forth the active exercise of our protective engagements. Roshun Beg and Roshun Khan, two principal officers of the infantry destroyed at Mehudpoor, had, with a few hundred men, the poor remnant of their fourteen battalions, fled to Rampoora ; where, hearing of the submission of their chief, they exhibited symptoms of discontent, and acted as if they meant to set up for themselves. Sir Thomas Hislop, sensible of the necessity of vigorously suppressing the first symptoms of such a disposition, was about to direct the force under Colonel Adams, still posted at Gungrar, to the punishment of these refractory leaders : but hearing, in the mean time, of the arrival of General Brown, with the detachment from Lord Hastings' camp, at Sonel, in the direct line of Rampoora, thought it most convenient to use its services for this object. General Brown, with his usual activity, hastened forthwith to the spot; and appearing before Rampoora on the 10th of January, immediately made his dispositions to carry the place by assault, notwithstanding that it was surrounded by fortifications of some strength, and well capable of defence. About four hundred of the infantry collected by the Roshuns were put to the sword in the town; and some horse, who fled in the opposite direction, were also cut up by the cavalry of our detachment, which had been sent round to intercept their escape. The two leaders themselves got clear off, but several other principal Sirdars were killed or taken prisoners. After this successful enterprise, the settlement of this territory proceeded with the utmost tranquillity under the superintendence of Sir John Malcolm and Major Agnew, which latter had been appointed by the Governor-general to act temporarily as Resident at that court.

Thus was peace re-established with the second of the three principal Mahratta powers, who had risen in arms to oppose the execution of his Lordship's plans. The immediate effect of so sudden an annihilation of the power of Holkur was apparent in the altered conduct of the Gwalior durbar, which from this time forward resigned itself to the most perfect acquiescence in every arrangement, indicated by the British Resident as the wish of the Governor-general. Juswunt Rao Bhâo, too, the most turbulent of Sindheea's Sirdars, became somewhat more tractable; and, dismissing Cheetoo with his durra, which had remained for some time in his neighbourhood, received Captain Caulfield, the officer appointed by Lord Hastings to act with his division, under the stipulations of the treaty of Gwalior, with every assurance of deference to his Lordship's commands. But these professions were soon found to be deceitful; for it was ascertained, that he was at the same time giving underhand the utmost protection in his power to the leaders and their banditti, by admitting them into his ranks, or concealing them in his different forts and villages. A body of five hundred Pindarees, under Fazil Khan, were declared by Juswunt Rao to be a part of his regular establishment; and he went so far as to request a protection for them, in case they should fall in with any of the divisions of our army. Captain Caulfield granted the desired protection provisionally, until he should have ascertained the wishes of the Governor-general in respect to this party; but, in the interim, Sir William Keir, who had been despatched by Sir Thomas Hislop in pursuit of Cheetoo, was led by his hurkaras to the village where Fazil Khan had been reported to be quartered, under information that a large party of Cheetoo's durra were there harboured. Upon the first appearance of the British troops, numbers of armed horsemen were seen to gallop forth from the opposite side of the village, which confirming the previous information, he ordered the cavalry to give chase to the fugitives, and immediately attacked the village. It was carried in a few minutes, and many Pindarees and others had been put to death, before the head man had time to produce Captain Caulfield's protection, upon sight of which instant orders were issued to stop the pillage. This was not effected without resorting to the extreme measure of hanging a sepahee caught in the fact; but the circumstances induced Sir William Keir to institute an inquiry upon the spot, when it was indisputably proved, both by the confessions of many of the prisoners and by other evidence, that the major part of the horsemen found in the village had but very recently parted from the durra of Cheetoo, there to seek an asylum. This was one of many instances of Juswunt Rao's unwarrantable conduct. He harboured Bheekoo Seyud of Kureem's durra, the very Sirdar who had led the expedition into Guntoor in 1815, in a yet more barefaced manner; suffering him to come within his camp, and pitch his tents within a short distance of that of Captain Caulfield: and, although the man was clearly identified, and Captain Caulfield made the most earnest demands for his arrest or expulsion, he could procure no redress.

The Marquess of Hastings, being apprised of this conduct, sent instructions on the 24th of January, authorising Juswunt Rao to be proceeded against as a public enemy, pursuant to the conditions of the Gwalior treaty, unless he should in the intermediate space have adopted a different course of conduct. The detachment of General Brown was directed to give effect to these instructions; but, before the arrival of the orders, matters had already been brought by this force to the issue of the sword with the refractory chieftain.

On General Brown's approach to Jawud, Capt. Caulfield renewed his remonstrances, but still without producing any change in the conduct of Juswunt Rao. Accordingly, on the 28th of January, after having in vain waited the expiration of the period prescribed for compliance with his demand of the surrender of the harboured Pindarees, Captain Caulfield retired from Juswunt Rao's camp to that of the General; and on the morning of the next day, having intelligence that arrangements were making secretly to remove the Pindarees to some place of safety, suggested the

sending round a squadron of our regular cavalry
to counteract this intention, by occupying the
road through which they must pass. In perform-
ing this duty, the squadron was fired at both from
the town and camp; whereupon the General ordered out his whole line, and determined on the
immediate assault of all Juswunt Rao's posts. The
third cavalry, under Captain Hodges, were ordered down with the horse artillery to the support
of Captain Swindell, who commanded the squadron
that had been fired upon. This force was immediately led by Colonel Newbery, the brigadier of
cavalry, to the attack of one of Juswunt Rao's
camps, which lay on the south of the town : it
was soon carried. General Brown determined to
follow up his success against the town itself: and
blowing open the gate with a twelve-pounder of
the horse artillery, while the rest of the guns were
employed in taking off the defences, the Major-
general caused the place to be stormed by the
first battalion of the first, under Major Bellingham,
and by the dromedary corps, which was dismount-
ed for the purpose, and led by Lieutenant Patton,
the only officer wounded in the whole affair.
Captain Ridge, with the fourth cavalry, and a
party of Rohilla horse, had in the mean time
been sent round the town, under the guidance of
Lieutenant Franklin of the quarter-master-gene-

ral's department, to attack another camp to the north-west, in which a large portion of Juswunt Rao's force was cantoned. There were in this encampment six guns and two battalions, besides horse. Captain Ridge came upon them in a quarter whence he was exposed to the fire from the town as well as that of the troops in the camp. Leaving the town to the general, whose attack had by this time commenced on the opposite gateway, he charged at once into the camp, dispersed and cut up the battalions, and captured all the six guns. The Rohilla horse were led on this occasion by Lieutenant Turner, and behaved with as much spirit and steadiness as the regular cavalry. The result was complete success in every quarter, without a single check. Juswunt Rao himself owed his escape to the fleetness of his horse, and got off with very few attendants.

As soon as information was received of matters having been brought to this issue, General Donkin, who was still at Shahpoora, was ordered down to occupy the possessions of Juswunt Rao Bhâo in Oodeepoor, and particularly the forts and districts of Kumulner, Rypoor, and Ramnugur, three recent usurpations from the Rana, who had a few days only before placed himself under our protection. The acquisition of these fortresses was effected by the middle of February, the garrisons agreeing to evacuate on receiving their arrears, which in no instance exceeded four thousand rupees. Kumulner is one of the strongest hill forts in India, and there it was that the Pindarees had been desirous of depositing their families and baggage during this campaign. It was now restored to the Rana of Oodeepoor, along with the other recent usurpations. Jawud and Neemuch, two of Sindheea's pergunnas assigned to Juswunt Rao, were likewise seized by us, and held for some time, but afterwards restored to Doulut Rao, in order to enable him to make a peaceable settlement with a man, who had otherwise sufficient influence to give trouble. It had been distinctly intimated to him, at the time of concluding the treaty of Gwalior, that in the event of any of his Sirdars requiring chastisement for infractions of the articles, the acquisitions made from them would be retained by us as a remuneration for the trouble of inflicting it. Wherefore this attack of Juswunt Rao and seizure of his territories gave little umbrage, and occasioned no discussions with the durbar.

It is now time to notice the further operations against the Pindarees, after the remnant of the durras of Kureem and Wâsil Mohummed had effected their escape through Haraotee to Mewur, where they had hoped to share the promised protection of Juswunt Rao Bhâo. Early in January, Colonel Adams had taken up a position at Gun-

grar, and General Donkin another to the north of
Mewur, while General Brown was advancing towards Rampoora.   Upon the conclusion of the
treaty with Holkur, Major-general Sir William
Keir was immediately despatched with his fresh
division in a north-westerly direction from Mundisôr, to operate against Cheetoo, or any other of
the Pindaree chiefs of whom he might receive intelligence.   The durra of the former was partially
cut up in the neighbourhood of Satoolla ; and several were taken in villages, where they had singly
or in small parties sought protection. Sir Thomas
Hislop remained in the mean time at Mundisôr, a
centrical point, well calculated for the general direction of affairs in this quarter.   Harassed by
the activity of Sir William Keir's pursuit, the
marauders resolved to endeavour to retrace their
steps to their haunts in Malwa, and in the valley
of the Nerbudda.   Cheetoo succeeded in baffling
every effort made to overtake him, and effected
his object, by penetrating through a most difficult
country to the south of Mewur.   He reappeared
near Dhar, where a very high range of hills sends
forth the streams which form the Mhye, a considerable river emptying itself into the Gulf of
Kambay.   In this march he was obliged to disencumber himself of his baggage, and lost many of
his horses ; while Sir William Keir, being unable
to follow by the same route, made a circuit by

the open plain beyond the sources of that river, and then moved southward up the Chumbul in the same direction.

The wreck of Kureem's durra, under Namdar-Khan,—for both Kureem and his son had been left behind in a jungul in the flight through Haraotee,—had rejoined Wâsil Mohummed; and both were driven, by the operations just described, to attempt, in common with Cheetoo, a return towards Malwa and the Nerbudda. After having rounded the camp of Sir Thomas Hislop at Mundisôr, they were proceeding easterly, with the confidence of no other British force being in their neighbourhood, when, after crossing the Chumbul, they bivouacked on the 12th of January, at a small village named Kotree, on the Kalee-Sindh. By good fortune, Colonel Adams was still lying at Gungrar, within a few miles of their bivouack. He detached the 5th Bengal cavalry to give them, if possible, a night surprise. Major Clarke, who commanded this regiment, fell in with their encampment about an hour before daylight of the 13th, and found them either in such security, or so worn down by continued fatigue, that they evidently had no intelligence whatever of his approach, when he was within sight of their fires. Perceiving that he was quite undiscovered, he resolved to wait until the first appearance of dawn, that their flight might not be aided by the cover of darkness. On the first blush of day, he divided his force, ordering three troops under Lieutenant Kennedy to attack in front, while with the other three he made a detour himself round the village, to come upon them in the direction their flight would obviously take on the first alarm of danger. The manœuvre was most masterly; and the loss of the durras in this affair was greater than they had sustained in any previous attack, not excepting that of the year before, when surprised by Major Lushington in the Dukhun. The whole body was completely dispersed, and many leaders of note left dead on the field.

Soon after this success, Colonel Adams having ascertained that the freebooters had entirely evacuated Mewur, with the intention of returning into Malwa, hastened after them without delay, and sent notice of this movement to General Marshall, who had for some time been in the neighbourhood of Bairsea and Seronj expecting this event. On their march, the Pindarees were severely handled by detachments from the divisions of Adams and Marshall, and in the end harassed to such a degree, as to be unable longer to keep their followers together.

It would be uninteresting to follow the track of these miserable fugitives with further minuteness. Such was the extremity of their distress, that Colonel Adams, judging them to be now ripe for

unqualified submission, caused an intimation to
be conveyed to them through the Nuwab of Bho-
pal, that, if they were willing to throw them-
felves entirely on the mercy of the British government, surrendering their arms and horses, the
Sirdars might expect a livelihood in some part of
our provinces remote from their old haunts, and
the lives of their followers would be spared.
Namdar Khan was the first to avail himself of
this intimation. He delivered himself up to
Colonel Adams on the 3d of February at Deoraj-
poor, in the Bhopâl territory, with all his yet remaining followers, which were no more than
eighty-seven. He required no other terms than
a bare assurance that he should not be sent to
Europe or Calcutta : on receiving which he surrendered without further stipulation. Others
came in daily by twos or threes ; and all reported
that Wâsil Mohummed was in equal distress, and
ready to avail himself of the same proffer of pardon. He had penetrated further to the east; but
soon after fled for refuge to Gwalior, where Sindheea, though from a point of honour he at first
refused to seize and deliver him up, when the
Resident discovered the place of his concealment,
and demanded his seizure and surrender, was ultimately obliged to do so, at the express requisition
of the Governor-general. The rest, for the most
part, followed the example of Namdar Khan.

Kureem, it appeared, was alone in concealment at
Jawud, when the place was stormed by General
Brown. He escaped with extreme difficulty on
foot, and lived for some time in the neighbouring junguls; but, after a variety of risks and
adventures, finding the restoration of his affairs
utterly hopeless, he surrendered himself to Sir
John Malcolm on the 15th of February. His
son, Shuhamut Khan, with Rutun Koonwur, a
noted leader of luhburs, and about two hundred
followers, were still lurking in the junguls and
mountains of Haraotee and Boondee, when Zalim
Singh of Kota conveyed to them the assurance of
life, and induced them to yield on the same terms
as had been granted to Namdar Khan. Kureem
Khan was settled with his family on an estate
purchased for him in the Gourukpoor district, of
the value of about one thousand rupees a month.
Wâsil Mohummed was on his seizure kept in strict
surveillance at Ghazeepoor; but continued evidently restless, and refused to send for his family,
or to take measures to settle himself in the manner desired by the British government. At the
close of the following rains he attempted an
escape, having by some means or other procured
relays of horses to be laid to carry him beyond our
frontier; but being detected in the act of getting
out of the house in which he resided, he destroyed
himself by taking poison.

Thus were the two durras of Kureem and Wâsil Mohummed annihilated. Cheetoo, though he had suffered much in detail, had hitherto avoided a rencounter with any of the British corps in the field. But, on the 25th of January, he was heard of at Kurnôd by Colonel Heath, who commanded the garrison and post of Hindia. A party was immediately sent out, which beat up his bivouack in the night, and utterly dispersed the remnant of his durra. The Bheels and Grasseas were encouraged to plunder and destroy the fugitives, a commission they zealously executed. After this, Cheetoo wandered about Malwa a short time, with about two hundred followers; and seeing his affairs to be nearly desperate, endeavoured, through the Nuwab of Bhopâl, to make terms for himself, in conjunction with his remaining adherents. For this purpose, he suddenly entered the Nuwab's camp; but when he learned that Nuzur Mohummed had nothing to offer, beyond a slender personal maintenance in some distant part of Hindoostan, while he demanded a jageer in Malwa, and the entertainment of himself with his men in the British service, he decamped as suddenly as he had come. While he staid, his horses were constantly saddled, and the men slept with the bridles in their hands, ready to fly instantly, in case of an attempt to seize them. Preparations were making for the purpose

the very night he went off; but he was too well
on his guard, and too much alive to suspicion, to
allow them to be completed. He was instantly
pursued by the Nuwab's people ; and General
Malcolm also sent out parties to take him, which
distressed him so much, that Rajun left him, and
made his submission. Yet he subsequently found
his way into Kandês and the Dukhun, and made
common cause with the Arabs and chiefs of the
Pêshwa's routed army, with whom he became
assimilated, receiving occasional protection from
the Kiladar of the fortress of Aseergurh. His
durra was completely destroyed, and his followers
almost entirely deserted him, but nothing could
subdue his spirit, or induce him to surrender.
His end was tragical and singular, and deserves
to be recorded. Having joined Apa Saheb, he
passed the rainy season of 1818, in the moun-
tainous heights of the Mohadeo range ; and upon
that chief's expulsion in February 1819, accompanied him to the Fort of Aseergurh. Being
refused admittance, he sought shelter in the
neighbouring jungul, and, on horseback and alone,
attempted to penetrate a thick cover known to be
infested with tigers. He was missed for some
days after, and no one knew what had become of
him. His horse was at last discovered grazing
near the margin of the forest, saddled and bridled,
and exactly in the state in which it was when

Cheetoo had last been seen upon it. Upon search, a bag of two hundred and fifty rupees was found in the saddle ; and several seal rings, with some letters of Apa Saheb, promising future reward, served more completely to fix the identity of the horse's late master. These circumstances, combined with the known resort of tigers to the spot, induced a search for the body, when, at no great distance, some clothes clotted with blood, and, further on, fragments of bones, and at last the Pindara's head entire, with the features in a state to be recognised, were successively discovered. The chief's mangled remains were given over to his son for interment, and the miserable fate of one, who so shortly before had ridden at the head of twenty thousand horse, gave an awful lesson of the uncertainty of fortune, and drew pity even from those who had been the victims of his barbarity when living.

The notice of this event has been introduced thus prematurely in order to show to what desperation the whole tribe was driven by the declared hostility and active pursuit of the British. The name of this chief will again recur when the operations against Apa Saheb come to be related at length.

CHAPTER XVII.

POONA.

1817-18, NOVEMBER TO APRIL.

Pêshwa's flight and pursuit—Is cut off from the north—Returns to the south—Affair at Koragâon—Resolute defence of Captain Staunton—Repulse of the enemy—Remarks—Flight of Bajee Rao continued—Brigadier-general Pritzler's pursuit—Bajee Rao turns north—Met by General Smith, and pursued up the Kishna—New distribution of British force—Sutara taken—Plans of Governor-general in respect to Pêshwa and Sutara Raja—Reasons and reflections—Instructions issued—Sutara Raja proclaimed—General Smith pursues Bajee Rao—Comes up with him at Ashtee—Gokla slain—Sutara family captured—Notice respecting Gokla—Pêshwa's distress—Capture of his forts—Desertion of his Jageerdars—Joined by Gunput Rao and Ram Deen—Flight to the northward.

IT is now time to revert to the transactions of the war with Bajee Rao in the Dukhun. For the purpose of preserving the continuity of the narrative of occurrences in other quarters, we have reserved these for separate notice, there having as yet been no such direct connexion be-

tween the operations on the two opposite sides of
India, as to require the relation to be interwoven.

After his defeat at Poona on the 16th of November, the Pèshwa fled southward towards his
strong holds in the vicinity of Sutara. It was
at first believed, that he intended to shut himself
up in some one of them, there to abide a siege.
It appeared, however, that he had no such design,
the recent fall of Hutras having shaken the confidence of all the native chieftains in their fortified
places. His march to the south had no other
object than to effect a junction with a party sent
before to carry off the family* of the Raja of Sutara from Wusota. Fearing to trust a race of so
much political importance to the safe keeping of
even the strongest of his forts, he resolved to
carry the principal members of the family along
with him, in order to prevent the possibility of
their falling into our hands, or being set up by us
in opposition to his own authority.

Towards the end of November, Brigadier-general Smith, having completed his arrangements
for the occupation and eventual defence of Poona,
set off in pursuit of the fugitive prince. On the
morning of the 29th, he forced the passage of
the Salpa-Ghât, leading to the high land in which
the Kishna takes its rise. Gokla, with a body of

* Vide Forbes' Oriental Memoirs.

five thousand of the Pêshwa's best horse, had, since the 22d, been continually hovering about the Brigadier-general's line of march, for the purpose of taking advantage of the least confusion. It would have been far too harassing a duty for the single regiment of cavalry, and few irregulars attached to the division, to have attempted to keep at a distance an enemy that never ventured to stand a charge. However, by occasionally masking a galloper gun, and employing Shrapnell shells, the General was enabled to make the service of Gokla's horse rather too perilous for a continuance. On the day of his forcing the Salpa-Ghât, the nature of the ground gave an opportunity of opening the battery of a whole troop of horse-artillery in this manner, and with such effect, that for some days afterwards, indeed, until the 6th of December, the hovering clouds of horsemen completely disappeared. Bajee Rao himself usually kept at the distance of two long marches in advance.

Nothing of interest occurred in this very long and arduous pursuit : it will be sufficient, therefore, to notice the line of the enemy's flight. Passing Sutara, he went as far south as Poosa Saolee (Possessolee.) From this point, either to avoid falling in with Brigadier-general Pritzler, who was advancing with the reserve from the ceded districts, or having no object in remaining

to the south of the capital after the junction of
the Sutara Raja's family, and naturally wishing
to be joined by the support he expected from
Hindoostan, he made a few long marches eastward, as far as Pundurpoor ; and thence getting
round Brigadier-general Smith, marched rapidly
in a north-westerly direction, and, passing half-
way between Poona and Seroor, moved northward as far as Wuttoor, on the direct road to
Nassik.   Here he was joined by Trimbukjee
Dainglia, who brought with him a considerable
reinforcement of horse and foot, raised in Kandês,
or invited down from Hindoostan into the service.
General Smith followed close at his rear, arriving
at Pundurpoor on the 8th of December, the second day only after Bajee Rao had left it.   As
soon as the Pêshwa had passed clear of Poona,
the Brigadier-general moved to the old cantonment of Seroor, and, after recruiting his cattle,
resumed the pursuit on the 22d of December.
Keeping now greatly to the east of the enemy's
route, he entered the valley of the Godavuree, by
the Nimba-Deora Ghât, in the hope thus to intercept his retreat northward : for the Pêshwa,
finding himself less pressed, had loitered some
days at Wuttoor, and in the neighbourhood of
the strong fort at Jooneer.   He was still in the
vicinity of that place on the 26th of December,
when his pursuer had already advanced to Hun-

wuntgâon, yet further northward than himself. He then attempted to continue his march towards Nassik ; but General Smith was gaining fast upon him from the east, and he had scarcely descended the Ghât to the valley of the Peeree, on the 27th, when he heard that the Brigadier-general had already passed Sungumner, and was in full march to intercept his flight. Finding it now impossible to prosecute his march to the north without taking a more westerly route, he moved first to Kootool ; but then fearing to be entangled with his cavalry in the difficult country in the immediate neighbourhood of the western ghâts, he determined to give up the intention of continuing his flight in that direction, and, re-ascending the table-land he had quitted only the day before, returned to Wuttoor, on the 28th of December, and thence hastened his flight in a southerly course on the direct road to Poona. This gave occasion to one of the most memorable actions that has ever been fought in India.

Colonel Burr, the officer left in command at Poona, hearing of the Pêshwa's advance by the direct road to that city, and not being sufficiently aware of the manœuvres that had forced him into this line of retreat, and the closeness of the pursuers in his rear, thought an attack upon the capital was meditated. He accordingly solicited the reinforcement of a battalion from Seroor, the better to be prepared for defence. The following is an accurate account of what befel the re-inforcement forwarded at his request.

The detachment consisted of a detail of Madras artillery, with two 6-pounders, the 2d battalion of the 1st Bombay N. I., about five hundred strong, and three hundred auxiliary horse, the whole under Captain Staunton of the Bombay establishment, who commanded the battalion. It began its march from Seroor for Poona, at eight P. M. on the 31st of December, and at ten next morning reached the heights overlooking Koragâon, about half way to the city; when the whole of the Pêshwa's army, estimated at twenty thousand horse, and several thousand infantry, were discovered on the plain to the south of the Bheema. Captain Staunton found his march to Poona intercepted, and himself in great danger of being cut off. In order to avoid the exposure of the plain, which would have given an immense advantage to the Mahratta cavalry, he advanced hastily to seize the village of Koragâon, before it should be occupied by the enemy's infantry. On perceiving his intention, they made for the same point, and Captain Staunton succeeded in part only; for half the village, and several of the strongest positions, remained in the hands of the enemy, who manned the whole of their portion with Arabs, whom he found it impossible to dislodge, notwithstanding several attempts for the purpose. A most desperate struggle now commenced between this mere handful of men and the whole of the Mahratta army, which fought under the stimulus of the presence of the prince himself, who personally witnessed the action from an adjoining height.

The enemy also had but two guns; but his infantry outnumbered ours in the proportion of more than ten to one, and the majority were Arabs *, a race whose determined courage, or rather desperation of boldness, had frequently been experienced in former wars, and was, perhaps, never more conspicuous than at Nagpoor, and in this affair. The Arab infantry had also the support of immense clouds of cavalry, before whom the few horse that accompanied the battalion dared not show themselves; indeed, Captain Swanston, who commanded those auxiliaries, was wounded early in the day.

The contest continued until after sunset, and

---

* It may be proper to mention, as a proof of the estimation in which the Arabs are held as soldiers by the native powers, the rate of pay they received in the Peshwa's army, in comparison with natives of other countries.

Arabs, natives of Arabia - - 15 rupees a month.
Their descendants born in the country 10 ditto.
Hindoostanees, (the same as our sepoys) 8 ditto.
Mahrattas and Dukhunees - - 6 ditto.

was a series of obstinate attacks and defences of such posts, as the situation of the houses and circumjacent buildings afforded. In actions of this nature, the advantage of having fresh troops to bring up is every thing, and this the enemy possessed and availed himself of to the utmost degree ; while Captain Staunton had scarcely sufficient for the defence of the ground he occupied, much less any men to spare for reserve, or for the occasional relief of his different posts. The attack commenced a little before noon, and was not discontinued till nine in the evening, during the whole of which time our men remained without refreshment ; and, what was of more consequence, no water was to be had in that part of the village in their possession. In the evening their situation was peculiarly critical. Lieutenant Chisholm, the officer of artillery, with most of his men, had been killed at a post near a pagoda in the village, against which the Arabs principally directed their efforts. At the same time, the exertions that the European officers had been called upon to make, in heading repeated charges, had so reduced their number, that, of the whole, three only remained undisabled, Captain Staunton himself, Lieutenant Jones, and Assistant-surgeon Wylie, the two latter nearly exhausted. The Arabs at this time charged and obtained possession of the gun at the pagoda, round which

many of our wounded were lying; among the rest,
Assistant-surgeon Wingate of the 2d bat. 1st N. I.
Captain Swanston, and Lieutenant Connellan,
were there, all in a helpless state. The Arabs
immediately commenced a massacre of the wounded, and the mutilation of the bodies of the deceased. Dr. Wingate was the first victim to
their cruelty ; he was literally hacked to pieces,
as was the body of the deceased artillery officer.
But they did not long enjoy the triumph ; for the
three remaining officers, immediately upon the
loss of the gun, although themselves almost exhausted, and their men fainting from want of
water, exerted themselves to bring them on to a
final charge. On this occasion Lieutenant Pat-
terson, who had been wounded and lodged in a
place of safety, appeared again at the head of his
men, and continued to exert the little strength he
had left, until he received a second wound, which
utterly disabled him, and in the end proved
mortal. The charge fortunately was successful,
and was executed with such judicious celerity
and spirit, that it saved the lives of Captain
Swanston and Lieutenant Connellan, both of
whom were in the Arabs' hands, and having just
witnessed the massacre and mutilation of their
comrades, were expecting a like fate to themselves. Every man of the Arabs, who had penetrated to the pagoda, was bayoneted without

mercy, and from this time the enemy relaxed much in the vigour of his attacks. As it grew dark, the men were enabled to procure a supply of water, which was the only refreshment they received for the whole day and night. By nine P. M. the enemy was driven out of the positions he had till then held in the village, and the rest of the night was passed by the detachment without molestation, but under the alarming anticipation of a renewed attack, with fresh troops, on the ensuing morning, and the certainty of their ammunition failing in that case after a few rounds. At daybreak it was found, that although the Mahratta army still hovered about the village, it was not disposed to renew the attack. The day was, however, passed under arms, and without any opportunity of procuring a supply of provisions. On the night of the 2d of January, Captain Staunton, despairing of being able to effect his march on Poona, prepared to move back to Seroor. Wherefore, sacrificing much of his baggage in order to provide the means of transporting his numerous wounded, he commenced his march in the dark, and reached Seroor by nine next morning, bringing back not only his guns, but likewise all his wounded.

Brigadier-general Smith arrived at Koragâon with all his division in the course of the 3d of January. But Bajee Rao had previously de-

camped, and continuing his flight to the southward, had on the same day ascended the Boor-
Ghat beyond Poona, passing a second time
within twenty miles of the capital. The approach
of General Smith had obliged him to allow the
battalion to march back to Seroor without further
molestation.

The extraordinary obstinacy of Captain Staunton's defence against such overwhelming numbers,
and his ultimate success in driving off the enemy,
are amongst the most surprising exploits that our
Indian army has ever achieved. There were but
six officers and two assistant-surgeons * with the
detachment; but the latter felt themselves called
upon for exertions altogether out of their profession, and frequently lent the influence of their example, in leading the sepoys to the charge of the
bayonet, and inspiring them with that confidence
of success, which the ascendancy of the European
character never fails to produce. Our loss in the

---

* Names of the officers:

    Captain Staunton, commanding.
    Lieutenant-adjutant Patterson, died of his wounds.
    Lieutenant Connellan, wounded.
    Lieutenant Jones, doing duty.
    Assistant-surgeon Wingate, killed.
    Lieutenant Chisholm, artillery, killed.
    Assistant-surgeon Wylie, artillery.
    Lieutenant Swanston, auxiliary horse, wounded.

affair was three officers killed and two wounded, out of the eight engaged. In the artillery the loss of men was most severe, twelve being killed and eight wounded, out of a detail for two six-pounders only. Of the battalion, fifty killed and one hundred and five wounded. It may be worth while to compare the loss suffered on this occasion with that of other hard-contested actions, in order to enable us to form a just estimate of the degree of credit to which the troops were entitled for their exertion and endurance in this memorable defence. At the battle of Mehudpoor, the rifle corps suffered undoubtedly a more severe loss in officers; and of the men, there were no less than one hundred and thirty killed and wounded, which, as the corps was weak, is nearly an equal proportion : but this was one regiment of an army; and had it been cut off to a man, the victory might still have been gained by the rest of the troops : no analogy can be drawn between the behaviour of a battalion executing part of a combined movement, even though it should bear a disproportionate share of the brunt of the action, and the conduct of one that has to fight by itself without support or hope, except from its own exertions. The Nagpoor affair, where the whole of the troops were actively engaged, and nearly in an equal degree, is probably that which, in its circumstances, was most similar to the affair of Koragâon. The duration and obstinacy of the attack in both cases; the description of troops engaged; the partial success and ultimate discomfiture of the Arabs, are all so many points of resemblance between the two; and many more might be pointed out. At Nagpoor, however, the general loss was nearly equal to that of the Bombay battalion, while that of the first battalion of the twenty-fourth* alone amounted to one hundred and forty-nine killed and wounded, which is only six short of the loss of Captain Staunton, although the proportionate number of combatants was rather in favour of the latter. On the whole, therefore, the contest may be considered to have been nearly as severe in one case as in the other, and in each the alternative of victory or ignominious death was presented to the combatants, which may account for the perseverance and resolute valour evinced on both occasions. But the discouraging circumstances under which the Bombay battalion fought, having to take up its ground hastily after a long and fatiguing march, and being forced to fight without food or refreshment, and without water, give to its efforts a character of

---

* This distinguished battalion was originally the first battalion of the first; but in consequence of its concern in the mutiny of Vellore, it had been degraded from the highest to the lowest place in the numerical scale of the native corps. Its behaviour at Nagpoor, and general good conduct, has since obtained the restoration of its former rank and number.

desperate and deliberate gallantry, much beyond what the most distinguished corps on any other occasion of the war had displayed, as indeed was universally acknowledged. To testify the sense entertained by the Supreme Government of the conduct of Captain Staunton, in this affair, the Marquess of Hastings nominated him an honorary aid-de-camp, and subsequently conferred on him the command of the fortress of Ahmednugur, when formed into a regular garrison. The government further ordered the erection of a public monument at Koragâon to the memory of those who fell.

After this repulse, Bajee Rao a second time ascended the table land, whence the Kishna takes its rise, and continued his flight south-eastward through Poosa-Saolee to Merich. In the mean time, Brigadier-general Pritzler, who, on the first rise of Bajee Rao in arms, had been summoned to take part in the operations against him, had advanced with part of the reserve by the route by Bejapoor, and was between Peergâon and Pundurpoor on the Bheema, when he heard of the Mahratta army being in full march to the south. He immediately moved westward, with a view to intercept them ; but finding the enemy had already ascended the Ghâts, followed in the same direction, and passed the Salpa-Ghât on the 6th of January. On the next day he fell in with Bajee Rao's rear-guard, and pressed it with his cavalry under Major Doveton, by which means about sixty or seventy of the Mahrattas were killed. The Brigadier-general continued the pursuit, following them close at the heels to Poosa-Saolee and Merich, and thence crossing the Kishna after them by the ford of Erroor a little lower down the river. It was given out in the Pêshwa's army and through the country it traversed, that he meditated the invasion of Mysoor and our own ceded districts. With this view he went as far south as Gokâk on the Gutpurba, and endeavoured to open a correspondence with the Raja of Mysoor : failing in this, however, and hearing that the country on the other side of the Gutpurba had been armed against him by the exertions and popularity of Brigadier-general Munro: and, moreover, finding that the same indefatigable officer had collected the scattered and inconsiderable force of regular troops at his disposal, and was already prepared to oppose his further progress to the south, he resolved, on the 15th of January, to retrace his steps, and from Gokâk turned eastward, and recrossing the Kishna at Gulgula, diverged thence to the west, and marched by Hutanee on Merich, thus circumventing General Pritzler's division, in the same manner as he had done that of General Smith in his flight to the south. But in this he did not succeed without being hard pressed by his pursuers, and particularly in the turn he made to the east. On the 17th of January, Brigadier-general Pritzler's cavalry had a smart brush with a part of the Mahratta army, and occasioned it very considerable loss. General Pritzler was stronger in this arm than General Smith had been, having two squadrons of the twenty-second dragoons, besides the seventh native cavalry: but the enemy could never be brought to stand a charge, and it was only by means of galloper guns, or by breaking our line in pursuit, that they could be materially injured: and the latter could rarely be hazarded in the face of such disproportionate numbers.

While General Pritzler was tracking the Pêshwa's flight in the manner above mentioned, General Smith, having again recruited his division at Seroor, prepared to move likewise to the south with the major part of his force lightly equipped, in order to act against the enemy as circumstances might enable him. He started from Seroor on the 8th of January with this intention, leaving a part of his force, under Lieutenant-colonel Boles, to follow with the stores and heavy guns. On the 12th of January he was near Fultun, and thence directed his march on Malwullee, pursuing a southerly course. On the 21st of January he heard of the enemy having wheeled round General Pritzler's division, and of his being in full march on Merich from Hutanee. General Smith was at the time

not far from Hingungâon, whence he immediately
moved on Merich to take up the pursuit. On
the 22d he arrived at Oogar on the Kishna, a
little above the town, where he learnt that the
fugitive Pêshwa had encamped only the day before.
From this point Bajee Rao, crossing the Kishna,
made a feint of descending into the Konkan by
the Amba-Ghât, but soon giving up that design,
continued his flight up the right bank, while General Smith followed on the opposite side, hoping
by this means to prevent any escape to the east.
The pursuit was very close; yet the enemy was
enabled, by a rapid march from Sutara, on the
28th of January, to cross the river and clear the
Salpa-Ghât with the loss of only part of his rear-
guard, which was intercepted in the defiles. On
moving forward, however, towards the Boor-Ghât,
he was met and cannonaded by the detachment
under Colonel Boles, and in the end fled eastward
through Fultun to Pundurpoor, and afterwards to
Solapoor, where he hoped to gain possession of the
treasures of his old minister Suda-Sheeo-Bhâo-
Mankèshur, who had died but a few months before.

Here he halted, and was left for some days
unmolested; while General Smith, finding himself
in the neighbourhood, resolved to call up his
heavy guns and employ them in reducing Sutara,
still the nominal capital of the Mahratta empire.

Besides the *éclat* and political importance that would necessarily result from the capture of this celebrated fortress, the Brigadier-general had other motives for undertaking the enterprise. He was desirous of effecting a junction with General Pritzler, who was still considerably in his rear, and of then making a new disposition of the troops composing the two divisions, by forming all the cavalry and light troops of both into an active corps for the pursuit of Bajee Rao; while the heavy artillery and a sufficient force for sieges and similar operations were left to reduce the many strong places in the country south of the capital. This most politic and judicious plan was adopted at the suggestion of Mr. Elphinstone, and it would have been earlier put in practice, had not the hope of coming up with the Pêshwa's army carried off General Pritzler in another direction, and prevented his having the necessary communication with General Smith. The mere pursuit of the fugitive prince from place to place, without wresting from him the occupancy of the country, had proved to be productive of little benefit hitherto, and seemed moreover likely to be spun out to an indefinite length, unless prosecuted on a very different plan. Whereas, on the contrary, by employing the troops according to the new and improved military arrangement, it was not improbable, that rather than submit quietly to the loss of his fortified places, the enemy would risk a general action, which was exactly what we most desired. Resolving to act upon this principle, General Smith waited the junction of the reserve division, which was coming up with a convoy, an encumbrance it had not been able to rid itself of during the whole line of pursuit, and himself employed the interval in laying siege to Sutara. The place surrendered the same day that the Brigadier-general appeared before it, the garrison offering to evacuate, the moment the mortar battery was brought to play with effect. It was taken possession of next morning, the 11th of February; but instead of hoisting the British flag on the walls, the standard of Sevagee was again made to float over the ramparts of this his ancient seat, while Mr. Elphinstone took the occasion of publishing a manifesto to the Mahratta nation, declaring it to be the intention of the British government to restore the Sutara family to an independent sovereignty, and to punish the long-continued treachery and ultimate defection of Bajee Rao, by the perpetual exclusion of his dynasty from all authority or concern in the affairs of the Mahratta empire, and by the assumption to itself of all his territorial possessions.

This course of policy was taken under orders from the Governor-general, which were not issued without very mature consideration of the question.

On the first occurrence of the rupture, the Resident at Poona had addressed to the Marquess of Hastings a solicitation for special instructions, respecting the conduct to be observed in the event of Bajee Rao's capture or submission, and generally upon the question, whether the present prince was to be reinstated upon any terms in any portion of the dominions of his family. In case of its being resolved to restore him to some share of nominal authority, Mr. Elphinstone submitted a plan for imposing such complete restraint upon all his actions, as he hoped would afford a sufficient safeguard against any future ill effects from his ambition and rooted fondness for intrigue. He proposed, however, at all events, to curtail his means effectually, as well by requiring compensation for the charges of the war, as by the demand of the arrears of the pension paid to Umrit Rao, his father's adopted son, under the agreement made with that chief by the Duke of Wellington on his first advance to Poona; besides insisting on the cession of a territory, to be conferred on that prince in lieu of the pension for the future. The policy of setting up Umrit Rao himself, as well as that of placing Chimnajee, the brother of Bajee Rao, on the Guddee, were at the same time brought under consideration, in case the deposition of the present Pêshwa should be determined on. In submitting these points, the

Resident did not express any preference of one plan above another, conceiving the choice to lie peculiarly in the judgment of the Governor-general; and the Marquess of Hastings, whose closest attention had already been turned to the subject, decided in favour of the total expulsion of Bajee Rao from the Dukhun, the perpetual exclusion of his family from any share of influence or dominion, and the annihilation of the Pêshwa's name and authority for ever.

These were certainly strong measures, and may at first sight carry the appearance of harshness. But he considered them to be warranted by the uniform conduct of our insidious ally for the four preceding years; and both the manner in which he had placed himself at the head of the confederation against the British power, and the critical time he had chosen to set the example of defection, demanded that his treatment should be a warning example to the sovereigns of India, and an awful lesson on the consequences of incurring the full measure of our just indignation. The mere removal of the individual from the seat of imperial sway, for the purpose of elevating either Chimnajee, or Umrit Rao, or any other member of the same family, would have had the effect of impressing the minds of other princes with the idea, that the personal chastisement of the delinquent was to be the extreme consequence of the most implaca-

ble and persevering hostility ; while the dignities
and advantages of sovereignty, nominal at least,
if not real, would still, under any circumstances
of provocation, be left to descend in the uninterrupted line of hereditary succession. But how
many men are there, that would set wealth, rank,
and even life at hazard, in a desperate grasp at personal or political advancement, howsoever preca-
rious or remote, who yet would hesitate to set on
the same cast the fortunes of an entire family, and
the extinction in perpetuity of an ancient and
illustrious house ? There can be no doubt that
Bajee Rao and his advisers never acted under the
belief that they were putting so much at stake :
they had misconceived the motives by which the
British government had all along been actuated.
Construing its signal moderation as a mark of politic prudence and fear, and arguing from the aid
we had afforded in establishing the authority of
the Pêshwa, as well as from the uniform desire we
had testified to keep on good terms with his government, that its maintenance in the existing
form was indispensable to the stability and duration of our system, they were led into the presumptuous hope of succeeding, by menace and
opposition, in exacting an equivalent for this ima-
ginary benefit : hence · too, they reckoned with
confidence upon being always able to save themselves by a timely accommodation, however justly

or deeply they might incur our resentment by the display of a rancorous animosity. The Prince himself had, since his defection, made several overtures for this purpose, and was not a little surprised to find them uniformly rejected, or answered by a declaration, that nothing short of unconditional submission could be listened to, or more than life be guaranteed. It was observed, that the recollection of the negotiations and disasters which attended our first connexion with the Pêshwas, when the Bombay government espoused the desperate cause of the father of Bajee Rao, had far too much influence on the counsels of this durbar, and had from the first infused a most ambitious and arrogant spirit. The Marquess of Hastings had hoped, that the humiliations imposed by the treaty of Poona, concluded in the preceding June, would have subdued or abated this spirit; but a contrary effect had followed; and there seemed now to be no choice left to the British government, but for ever to annihilate the state of things that had first generated it, and to show that it could itself occupy the guddee of Poona, and direct its control over the chiefs of the Mahratta nation to the maintenance of public tranquillity, with yet more efficiency than it possessed when the first Bajee Rao and Balajee united the race for the devastation of the rest of India.

These were the principal motives, that fixed

the Marquess of Hastings in the resolution to annihilate the authority and name of Pêshwa; and, with the reservation above noticed for the Sutara family, to assume the whole authority and dominion into the hands of the British nation. In December, he issued his instructions to this effect, constituting Mr. Elphinstone commissioner, with full powers for the execution of his plan. The Jageerdars, who had heretofore held of the Pêshwa, were to be admitted to hold on the same terms of the British government, unless they should engage in active hostility against us, or delay their submission for too long a period. The lands of Gokla were directed to be immediately resumed; and it was to be a part of any arrangement that might be made, that his person, together with that of such other chiefs as were equally active in the same cause, should be lodged in safe custody. It was likewise to be an article, that the parties concerned in the hanging of the two Vaughans should be given up for execution. The Raja of Sutara was to be established in a territorial possession, to be held either as a dependent Jageer, or as a distinct sovereignty, under stipulations securing the supremacy of the British government. The declared object of this part of the plan was, to conciliate the Mahrattas to the new order of things, and establish a counterpoise to the remaining influence of the Pêshwa's Brahminical administration. The mode, and form, and amount of the provision, were left to Mr. Elphinstone's discretion, so that the object might be most securely attained. The above, with a territorial reservation for the settlement of a Jageer upon Chimna Apa, formed the outline of the plan devised by the Marquess of Hastings : in prosecution of which, immediately upon the capture of Sutara, the Mahratta flag was again hoisted on its walls, in the manner above mentioned, and a proclamation issued, inviting the Mahrattas to rally round their rightful hereditary sovereign, for whom it was declared, that Sutara and the adjacent territories would be reserved as an independent dominion under British protection. In this form Mr. Elphinstone thought the establishment of the Sutara Raja would be effected with most advantage under existing circumstances ; and the early submission of several jageerdars, who were eager to establish a prior claim to the honours and advantages of the restored dynasty, attested the policy of the measure. Events occurred within a very few days after the fall of Sutara that materially forwarded the completion of these arrangements.

After the capture of that fortress, Brigadier-general Smith, in concert with Brigadier-general Pritzler, formed a light division in the manner proposed, with which, on the 13th of February, he moved to the eastward on the route to Pundurpoor. Arriving at Yellapoor, on the 19th, he heard that Bajee Rao had left Solapoor, where he had remained during the operations against Sutara, and was on his march due west. Hoping, therefore, to fall in with him about Pundurpoor, the Brigadier-general made a night march on that point, but heard in the morning that he had gone off to the northward, and was at Kurkumbh, totally unconscious of the vicinity of a British force. Upon this intelligence he crossed the Bheema at Keroulee, and pushed on with all his cavalry and horse-artillery, in the hope of coming up with the enemy. At half-past eight in the morning he had the gratification of hearing the state kettledrums of the Pêshwa beat in preparation for a march, which had been hastily resolved upon in consequence of information of General Smith's approach having just got the start of him. The British troops were concealed by the brow of a hill from the enemy's view, until the cavalry appeared on the ridge drawn up in battle array. Gokla, now seeing that it would be impossible for the Pêshwa's army to escape without sacrificing nearly all its baggage, took the resolution to risk an action, in the hope of saving it. General Smith had with him the 2d and 7th regiments of Madras light cavalry, and two squadrons of his Majesty's 22d dragoons. He had also a troop of horse-artillery; but the ground was too rugged to expect much benefit from this arm. Some of the guns were, however, brought up by the exertions and zeal of Captain Pierce, so as to have opened with effect; but the Brigadier-general, observing the enemy disposed to stand a cavalry charge, resolved to bring the matter to this issue in preference. He accordingly advanced in three columns, the dragoons forming the centre. The enemy was formed on the other side of a difficult ravine at the foot of the hill, which our troops had to pass before they could reach him. On forming line, the 7th cavalry, which was on the right wing, came soonest upon the ravine, and, getting in some degree entangled in it, Gokla took the opportunity of pushing a body of horse beyond its right flank, and even into its rear, which, coupled with a demonstration of simultaneous attack in front, created some confusion in the 7th regiment. But Major Davies, who commanded the detachment of the 22d dragoons, immediately ordered a troop to fall back and scour the rear; and the commandant of the 2d regiment also adopted the same precaution. By this means, the body that had succeeded in getting to the rear were completely dispersed. A *gole*, led by Gokla, was charged by the troop of dragoons in the most

gallant manner, on which occasion that distinguished chief was himself slain. He died bravely,
having wounded several of our men with his own
hand before he fell, and amongst the rest Lieutenant Warrand, of the 22d dragoons, the first who
attacked him. The death of Gokla left the
enemy without a head : for Bajee Rao had
already gone off with his personal guard and attendants, deserting his palanquin, and mounting
a horse for the purpose as soon as the battle commenced. From this moment there was no longer
any appearance of order in the resistance opposed.
Our cavalry, particularly the dragoons, charged
successively several masses of the enemy's horse,
until the dragoons penetrated to their camp and
baggage, the whole of which, after a slight resistance, fell into their hands. The person and
family of the Sutara Raja were found there and
secured, and were by no means the least important prize obtained on this occasion. The family
consisted of the Raja, Noor Nerayun, a young
man about twenty years of age, his two brothers,
and mother. There were also twelve elephants
and fifty-seven camels taken. Our loss was very
trifling, being only one officer, Lieutenant Warrand, and nineteen men, wounded. The Brigadier-general was himself surrounded, and received a slight wound on the head, at the time
when Gokla and his party had penetrated to the

rear; but this accident did not prevent his continuing to direct in person the operations of the day. Besides Gokla, the enemy lost another sirdar, Moro Punt Aptee; but the death of the former in particular, and the capture of the Sutara family, gave peculiar importance to the battle fought at Ashtee, on the 20th of February. Bapoo Gokla was reputed a good officer; he was one of the sirdars who accompanied the Duke of Wellington throughout his campaigns in the Dukhun, during the Mahratta war, and was then well esteemed for his services and general character, insomuch as to be particularly recommended to the favour of the Pêshwa's government on the close of that war, besides deriving other substantial advantages from the General's good opinion. He had subsequently been yet more deeply indebted to the favour of the British government, which more than once interfered to secure his possessions from his master's rapacity, at a time when the latter was stimulated by private pique*,

---

* The Pêshwa's animosity was long irreconcileable, in con - sequence of Gokla's refusing to suffer his wife to visit at the palace, where she could not have gone without dishonour; such was the sensuality that prevailed there. Gokla yielded the point, when the prospect of guiding the counsels of the state was opened to him; and " was generally known to have owed his former disgrace and subsequent favour to his tardy acquiescence in the dishonour of his family."—*Elphinstone's Despatches.*

as well as by avarice, to aim at his ruin. These benefits were of course forgotten, as soon as ambition and the desire of restoring the Mahratta empire to its ancient splendour became the ruling passions of his soul. Since 1814, he had uniformly been the adviser of the most decided hostility, and the avowed head of the war faction. When Bajee Rao conceived the project of rising against the British power, he found it convenient to court Gokla, and subsequently, at different times, added largely to his military fiefs, besides giving him a command in his immediate and personal troops. His post, since the rupture, had been always in the rear guard, or wherever else there was most danger ; and his master's confidence was unbounded and well-merited. After his death, the Pêshwa himself directed the movements and operations of the Mahratta army, there being no other chief on whom he could place equal reliance.

The routed host fled northwards, towards Kopergâon and Kandês ; their numbers now thinned daily by desertion. The capture of Sutara and of its Raja, added to the distress and precipitation of the flight, made even the most sanguine of the Mahrattas themselves regard the cause of their chief as altogether desperate. The daily fall of some one or other of his southern forts before Brigadier-general Pritzler confirmed this impression.

On the 20th of February, that officer appeared before Singurh, which capitulated on the 2d of March. He thence proceeded to the attack of the two contiguous forts of Viziergurh and Poorundur, which were also taken after two days' cannonade and bombardment. This occurred on the 15th of March. The garrisons amounted to one thousand one hundred and thirty-six, while in Singurh there were upwards of one thousand three hundred, whereof three hundred were Arabs. After the fall of these two of the Pêshwa's strongest holds, Wundun-Chundun, Nundgaree, Wussuntgurh, Kurnalgurh, Pandoogurh, and Kalinja, surrendered as soon as the army appeared before them ; the two last-mentioned only having waited for the batteries to open. After these successes, Brigadier-general Pritzler prepared himself, on the 31st of March, to proceed against Wusota, reckoned the strongest of all the forts in these parts ; and in the repair and improvement of which large sums had recently been lavished. Châkun, a place on the north-west of Poona, had previously been reduced by Colonel Deacon, who was bringing up a reinforcement from Berar. Colonel Prother, who had been despatched with an armament from the Bombay Presidency into the southern Konkan, was equally successful. In the course of January and the commencement of February, Kurnala, Bopâlgurh, Kotillagurh, Oochitgurh, and Sungurh, surrendered successively to this officer. The fort of Pâlee, which commanded the Ghât of that name, was also reduced after a short resistance. The seaport of Sevandroog had been taken some time before, by a force equipped for the purpose, from Fort Victoria, or Bankoot. In addition to the above captures, General Munro, having completely occupied the country to the south as far as the Malpurba, and driven out the officers placed there by Bajee Rao or Gokla, had proceeded against Badamee, a place famous for its long resistance to Nana Furnavees, who had attacked it with all his means. It soon yielded to General Munro; and Bhagulkôt, in the same neighbourhood, fell very shortly after. All these forts were no doubt ill defended; but their garrisons felt themselves wholly without hope of support, and, therefore, were impressed with an early conviction that the cause was hopeless, and could be but little advanced by their best exertions. They were also strangers to the effect of shells thrown with precision; and there being no protection against this artillery within the forts, the defenders were soon disheartened by its destructive effect, and our divisions, aware of the nature of the service, were well provided with this arm.

This uninterrupted chain of success induced many of the principal jageerdars of the Mahratta empire to make their terms with Mr. Elphinstone. The Putwurdhuns were the first to desert the standard of Bajee Rao. The Prithee-Nidhee and Punt-Suchem, the two chief officers of the Sutara family, sent to offer their submission immediately on the publication of the manifesto; others followed every day; insomuch, that in the southern portion of his dominions the influence and hold of the country, possessed by the Pêshwa, were fast passing away. He was, however, reinforced in his flight to the north by the junction of Ramdeen, with part of Holkur's broken infantry. Gunput Rao, with the remnant of the army of Apa Saheb, had previously joined, at the time Bajee Rao was loitering between Pundurpoor and Solapoor. The troops he brought were chiefly horse, who, after their defeat by General Doveton, were successfully conducted through the Nizam's dominions by that leader, notwithstanding the various attempts to intercept their march made by different detachments of our troops, as well as of those of the Nizam.

The flight of Bajee Rao northward towards Hindoostan brought him into contact with divisions of our army, different from those with which he had been hitherto engaged; and his operations also became thenceforward connected with the transactions of the other durbars. With a view, therefore, to perspicuity of arrangement, it will be proper to bring up the relation of events in Hindoostan and at Nagpoor to the same period.

CHAPTER XVIII.

HINDOOSTAN—KANDÉS.

1818. FEBRUARY, MARCH.

Holkur—Ameer Khan—His crafty conduct—Guns obtained —Troops disbanded—Takes refuge in Kota—Putans taken . into British service—Policy of the measure—Proceedings of Sir David Ochterlony—Troops in the field in February —Exchanges with Sindheea proposed—Lord Hastings quits the field with the centre division—Sâgur—Its reduction ordered—Reasons—Terms offered to Bunaeek Rao—and accepted—Dhamonee reduced—Mundela stormed—New distribution of the forces—Sir Thomas Hislop's return—Soandwara reduced—Sindwa occupied—Resistance at Talnêr—and storm—Loss of officers—Garrison put to the sword—Kiladar hanged—Sir Thomas Hislop in communication with Brigadier-general Doveton.

To return to Hindoostan; we have seen already, that, before the close of the month of January, the bond of union, that kept together the turbulent bands attached to the standard of the Holkur family, had been completely dissolved. Their collective strength had been irretrievably broken at Mehudpoor; while the example of Rampoora and of Jawud had seriously impressed on the sirdars individually the necessity of conforming to the new order of things, which it was the design of the Marquess of Hastings to introduce. Ameer Khan had all along been sensible of this necessity; but his subordinate sirdars were by no means satisfied with the terms he had procured, the advantages of which were entirely personal to himself. It appeared, indeed, that the Putan chief had not scrupled to deceive his associates in arms, causing the agent he employed at Dehlee to forward accounts of the negotiation in progress there, much more favourable to their interests than the truth warranted. This deceit was continued, even at the conference held by appointment between himself and Sir David Ochterlony, on the 18th of December, for the express purpose of exchanging the mutual ratification. A number of additional stipulations were then brought forward, as having been agreed to by Mr. Metcalfe at Dehlee; amongst others, the promise of a jageer to his son Wuzeer Mohummed, and of similar grants to other sirdars. In proof of these having been agreed to, the above letters were produced, bearing the seal of Nerunjun Lal, his Dehlee agent, who was himself called into Sir David's presence to make an oral declaration to the same effect. Fortunately, the Major-general was well acquainted with the Putan character;

and, having been furnished with correct information of all that had passed at Dehlee by Mr. Metcalfe himself, at once declared his disbelief of the
whole, stating that he had come to receive the
ratification of the engagement actually signed;
and, as he knew nothing of any further concessions, must insist on an explicit answer, whether
the chief was prepared to ratify that engagement
or not. This peremptory demand had the effect
of procuring the delivery next day of the ratified
engagement, by the terms of which there can be
little doubt that Ameer Khan was from the first
prepared to abide, though the total insubordina-
tion of his army, and the independence of the
sirdars possessed of influence or command in it,
had obliged him to practise the above deceit, in
order to amuse and feed them with delusive
hopes, while he was making separate terms for
himself.

After the ratification, Ameer Khan came into
Sir David Ochterlony's camp, and took up his
quarters there for some time, until he should succeed in persuading his mutinous officers to disband
and deliver up their guns. It is to be observed,
that each brigade of infantry, with its equipments,
was considered as the especial property of some
one sirdar, who derived his profit from the sale
or hire of its services, or the share of its plunder
and exactions. The motive that led so many of

them to rally round the standard of Ameer Khan was, the want of regular employment elsewhere, and the idea that his talents for command promised to afford, in the spoils he would put them in the way of sharing, a better livelihood than could be elsewhere obtained. Many of the brigades were undoubtedly of Ameer Khan's own raising, but more than half had been raised by others; and he had bound himself to disband the whole, and deliver up their artillery, with only five lakh of rupees in hand to effect the business. It may easily be imagined, that, in order to satisfy the greedy wants of an army so composed as his, which had been living as it were from hand to mouth for several years past, and was now called upon to surrender the very means of subsistence, and to abandon for ever the inveterate habits of military licence, no distribution of those very limited means at Ameer Khan's command could make them suffice. The sirdars and troops consequently remained for some time sullen and dissatisfied, and the brigades would not give up their artillery, notwithstanding the most earnest endeavours on the part of the chief to obtain their compliance. But the Marquess of Hastings had never expected to wring from them these implements of trade, by any other motive than the strong and immediate influence of fear. The destruction of Holkur's infantry at Mehudpoor, whose case they felt to be exactly their own, and the judicious advance of Sir David Ochterlony with the reserve, to a position * directly between the two principal divisions of the Putan army, those of Muhtab Khan and of Raja Buhadur, had at last the desired effect; and the artillery of both were procured in the course of January. Other sirdars continued refractory for some time longer ; particularly Jumsheed Khan, whose guns were not obtained until the end of March, and were then yielded on compulsion only, and in consequence of the threat of immediate attack by a detachment sent for the purpose.

It was a yet more difficult task to procure the quiet dispersion of the Putan soldiery, than to obtain the surrender of their guns. Ameer Khan exerted himself with zeal to effect this, as indeed every other part of his agreement, but for a long time with little success. His soldiers had before them the prospect of absolute starvation, if they abandoned their present livelihood and habits ; while the money at the chief's disposal, however fairly distributed, afforded no compensation to the individuals for so great a sacrifice. The well

* The Major-general was already in the neighbourhood ; and he made this movement on the pretence of greater convenience of forage : nor were the Putan sirdars aware of the commanding nature of the position, until it was actually taken up.

known address of Sir David Ochterlony, brought in aid of Ameer Khan's exertions, was scarcely equal to the task of inducing so many armed men to return quietly to their respective homes, notwithstanding the awe inspired by his position, and by the efficiency of the army under his command. Ameer Khan was so beset by the discontented rabble thus turned adrift, who depicted to him in glowing colours the hardships and disgrace of their present situation, that, after trying every means in his power to allay the ferment, and practising in vain all manner of deceit, in order to ged rid of their importunities, he found it necessary at last to retire with precipitation to Sheergurh, a fort in Zalim Singh's territory, until this feeling of irritation should in some degree have subsided. His son had already arrived at Dehlee as a hostage; and the sincerity of the chief's individual efforts and intentions was never doubted for a moment, notwithstanding the suddenness of this flight and his notorious want of integrity*.

The difficulty of completing this part of the Governor-general's plan for the final settlement of

---

* Amongst other modes of avoiding the present importunity of his troops, he gave many of the sirdars drafts on the Resident at Dehlee, which he must have known would not be honoured, as he had already overdrawn the amount stipulated. He drew in this way for nine lakh beyond his credit.

Rajpootana had been distinctly foreseen ; and Major-General Sir David Ochterlony, to whom the
execution was entrusted, had been empowered, in
case it should be found indispensable to adopt such
a means of allaying that discontent, which would,
unavoidably be excited, as a temporary expedient
to entertain a portion of the most efficient of
Ameer Khan's troops in British pay, under such
regulations, as would best adapt them to our
system of discipline and organization.   Acting
upon this authority, the Major-general, in the
course of February, made the tender of British
service to eight of the best Putan battalions and
to about three thousand horse.   The former, after
pensioning off the native officers above the rank of
soobadar, and thinning the ranks by the strictest
scrutiny into the character, age, and general qua-
lifications of the men, were formed into four battalions for provincial duties, of which two were
sent to the Dehlee territory, and the other two retained for similar service in Rajpootana, under the
conduct of British officers appointed to command
them.   These battalions were found extremely
serviceable ; and, in the existing demand for
troops in every quarter, the arrangement was attended with essential benefit.   The horse were
formed into bodies called *rusalas*, of five hundred
each ; and, as the very best only were taken, they
also rendered good service ; while, the arrange-

ment being merely temporary, and recruiting disallowed, the expense was continually decreasing.

It was a most important point of the original plan, not hastily to drive to despair the whole swarm of military adventurers, by depriving them suddenly and entirely of their habitual means of subsistence; but to destroy those only, whose habits or ambition prevented their conforming to our system of rule, and so to hold the balance between the hopes and fears of the rest, as to render them instrumental to the establishment of order, and content with the offer of a moderate and regular provision. It was partly with this view that the stipulation for an auxiliary force had been introduced into the treaty of Gwalior, to open a field of employment to many of the unsettled characters, who must else have been turned loose upon society, and allure them with the assurance of fixed and regular pay under British guarantee. The same policy had dictated the large extension of irregular levies on our own establishment, and the formation of the auxiliary contingent at Poona before the commencement of operations.

No fitter agent could have been chosen, for the practical application of these principles to the settlement of affairs with the army of the Putan chief, than Sir David Ochterlony himself. By his consummate address and judicious arrangements, the whole affair was completely settled before the end of Feb-

ruary, by which time all the sirdars had submitted, with the exception of Jumsheed Khan and
one or two subordinate officers, who vainly hoped,
by holding out to the last, to advance instead of
impairing their interests. Notwithstanding the
natural turbulence of the Putan character, all the
divisions, not even excepting those who last submitted, were restrained from any kind of violence
in the interim; so that, in fact, the destruction of this predatory association, which seemed
more likely than those of the Pindarees to require a great display of our military strength, was
brought about wholly by negotiation, aided by
the awe that our attitude of preparation was calculated to inspire. The merit of this early and
entire success is due principally to Sir David
Ochterlony's personal skill and judgment, which
met with the Governor-general's uniform approba-
tion, and to the imposing force of the division
placed under his command, which consisted of two
very strong brigades of regular infantry, with a
regiment of cavalry, and two corps (one thousand
each) of native horse, raised and embodied by
Colonel Skinner. Besides these, the contingents
of the military chiefs, to whom lands had been assigned on our western frontier, on the settlement
of 1805-6, were for the most part attached to the
reserve division, when called out to take a part in

the present operations; by which means its numerical strength was more than doubled.

The concentration and advance of the reserve had been connected with the further object of carrying into effect the arrangements intended to be made with the Rajpoot chiefs. The greater part of these were in train long before the close of the month of January; but the mention of them has been purposely omitted, that the narrative of the events and military transactions might not be interrupted by the constant recurrence to measures of a purely political nature. As these all formed part of a general system of permanent pacification, it has been thought more convenient to reserve them for separate mention, when the result of the whole operations and the nature of the final settlement of our Indian empire come to be explained. It will be sufficient, therefore, to mention in this place, that, with the exception of Jypoor, the counsels of which evinced their usual indecision and imbecility, all the Rajpoot states entered readily into the terms and propositions offered for their acceptance: nor was there one that did not show the utmost eagerness in the promotion of the Governor-general's views, for the restoration of order in that part of India, occupied by their dominions.

The Marquess of Hastings, seeing every thing

to be in a train of easy adjustment with the Rajpoot princes, and feeling equally confident respecting the settlement with Ameer Khan and the Putans, the detail of which had been left to Sir David Ochterlony, thought himself at liberty, by the beginning of February, to relax a little the military attitude he had assumed on the side of Hindoostan. He accordingly resolved upon a new distribution of the force there collected, in order, if possible, before the close of the season, to secure every remaining object. The predatory power of the Pindarees had by this time been completely destroyed. Of the routed bands of Holkur, some had rallied again round that chief, whose government having fallen into the hands of ¡Tanteea Jog, and being aided by the advice and exertions of Sir John Malcolm and the British representative at the durbar, was fast assuming a regular shape. Many more had been destroyed piecemeal at Rampoora and elsewhere; while all, who still remained in arms, had fled into the Dukhun, and were gathering round the banners of Bajee Rao, who alone still kept the field, and maintained the cause of opposition and disorder. On the 1st of February, the British force actually in the field to the north of the Nerbudda was thus disposed. The reserve division, under Sir David Ochterlony, in the neighbourhood of Jypoor; the centre division, under Lord Hastings' personal command, still

SINDHEEA. 199

posted on the banks of the Sindh; the right division, that of Major-general Donkin, was proceeding to take possession of Kumulner and the usurpations of Juswunt Rao in Mewur; of the left
division, part was with General Marshall about
Seronj and Bairsea, and of the remainder, a quota
had been furnished to the force with Major-general Brown, who was still in the vicinity of Jawud,
and two battalions had joined his Lordship's head-
quarters, under Brigadier-general Watson.

Of the army of the Dukhun, the divisions of Sir
Thomas Hislop and Sir John Malcolm were still
near Mundisor, while Lieutenant-colonel Adams
was in the Bhopâl territory, employed in receiving
the submission of the Pindaree chiefs. The Goozerat army, after a long pursuit of Cheetoo's durra,
was now halted in the neighbourhood of Indôr,
to receive its further destination according to circumstances. Besides the above, a corps of observation was still posted on the southern frontier of
Buhar, under Brigadier-general Toone; and Brigadier-general Hardyman with his corps occupied
Jubulpoor.

The present humility of Sindheea, as evinced
by the readiness with which, since the destruction
of Holkur's army, he had forwarded the levy and
equipment of the auxiliary horse stipulated in the
treaty of Gwalior, and more recently by the indifference he had manifested at the attack on

Juswunt Rao Bhâo, satisfied the Marquess of
Hastings, that it was no longer necessary for the
army under his personal command to occupy the
forward position it had assumed to awe the
counsels of this durbar. It was accordingly resolved to break up the centre division of the
grand army, and march the greater part of it
back to its cantonments within the Company's
provinces, whereby an important saving of expense would be effected. However, before this
measure was carried into execution, it was
thought right to open to that durbar the ulterior
views of the British government, and to sound its
disposition in respect to them. The principal remaining points, which it was the wish of the
Governor-general to obtain, were—the cession of
Ajmeer to ourselves, in order perpetually to exclude the Mahratta influence from that part of
Rajpootana; the transfer of Islamnugur to Bhopâl, with a view to a similar exclusion from that
quarter; and, lastly, the cession in perpetuity of
all the Maha-Raja's claims on the Boondee principality, as well as of lands obtained from time to
time in lieu of such claims. As an equivalent for
these sacrifices, the Marquess of Hastings was
prepared to offer the lands of the Vinshorkur
(except the portion already given to Bhopâl), together with those of other late tributaries of the
Pêshwa similarly circumstanced, and the tributes

and personal rights of that prince in Hindoostan, which had been assigned to us by the recent treaty of Poona. The Vinshorkur's lands had become justly forfeit, in consequence of his continued adherence to Bajee Rao, since his defection. The value of the equivalent about to be offered considerably exceeded that of the cessions intended to be demanded ; besides which, Sindheea relied upon our bounty for the restitution of Jawud, and the territory lately resumed from Juswunt Rao Bhâo ; so that there was little reason to expect any serious opposition on his part to the arrangement. Yet it was impossible to estimate beforehand, with any degree of certainty, what sensation the demand of a permanent cession would make on a Mahratta court. His Lordship accordingly resolved to ascertain this beyond a doubt, before he should relinquish the attitude which had given him such advantage in the past negotiations. For this purpose, before finally quitting the banks of the Sindh, the Marquess of Hastings caused a proposal for the above exchanges to be submitted to the Gwalior durbar.

Finding it to be well received, his Lordship did not think it necessary to wait the complete execution of the arrangement ; but on the 13th of February commenced his homeward march to our own provinces, having for some days previously

moved gradually along the right bank of the
Sindh from Sonaree and Oochar down to Beer-
cha, which lies but a few miles above Seonda,
the point on which he had first moved in the
November preceding, to enforce the signature of
the treaty. Of the troops composing the centre
division, the Europeans for the most part returned to the cantonment of Cawnpoor ; while
the native infantry were so disposed along the
Bundelkhund and Etâwa frontier, as to be capable of immediate reunion, in case any appearances
in the court or army of Dowlut Rao Sindheea
should require their second advance. A brigade
of three strong battalions, however, with the 7th
native cavalry, and the heavy train, which had
purposely been attached to this division, were
sent, under the command of Brigadier-general
Watson, to reinforce the troops under Major-
general Marshall, which it was determined to
employ in the reduction of the territory of Sâgur,
with a view to its permanent annexation to the
British dominions.

The right of paramount sovereignty over this
territory formed part of our acquisitions, by virtue
of the late treaty of Poona ; and it will be recollected, that, in assertion of that right, Bunaeek
Rao, the occupant, had been called upon in the
September preceding, either to fulfil the terms, on
which the fief was held of the Poona state, by

furnishing the quota of six hundred and sixty-six horse, and paying the tribute of one lakh of rupees to the British government, or to agree to an advantageous money commutation, offered to be taken in lieu of that contingent. The letter containing the offer of commutation was answered evasively; the more positive demand of the fulfilment of the original terms, which was accompanied by a notice that General Marshall was already advancing against the Pindarees, and a requisition, that the quota of six hundred and sixty-six horse should join his division, and cooperate on the service, was equally disregarded: besides which, instead of receiving assistance in the procurement of its supplies, the left division experienced every sort of impediment, and was uniformly treated as an enemy in the Sâgur territory. As a further proof of Bunaeek Rao's infatuation, no effort had subsequently been made to calm our just resentment, notwithstanding the favourable turn of affairs in every quarter. Neither had he offered a rupee of the tribute due, or the service of a single horseman. Under these circumstances, the Marquess of Hastings resolved to regard the occupant of Sâgur as a feudatory, who had incurred the forfeiture of his fief; more especially as there was evidence forthcoming of his correspondence with the Pindarees since the commencement of operations against them, and of his attachment to the cause of the Pêshwa. Wherefore, no sooner did the state of affairs in Hindoostan permit the allotment of a sufficient force to this object, than the reduction of this province was resolved upon. Accordingly, in the middle of February, Major-general Marshall was ordered to proceed against the capital of the principality, so soon as he should be joined by the battering-train and reinforcement sent to him for this purpose from the centre division.

The following were the modified terms, to which submission within three days was now to be peremptorily demanded. The present government to be displaced, and the territory transferred to the administration of British agents ; the revenue actually realised to be allotted as follows :—

	Sicca rupees,
Tribute to the British Government	100,000
Commutation for military service, with 666 horse	159,840
Total payment to the British government	259,840

This, together with 10 per cent. on the gross assets, for the expense of administering the affairs of the province, to be the primary charge on the total receipts *. After defraying which, the revenues to be next charged with a stipend of two

---

* This ratio was assumed, on an estimate of the past revenues of Sâgur and its dependencies, at 698,000 rupees.

lakh and a half, as a provision for the maintenance of Bunaeek Rao, and Rukhma Baee, the widow of the former possessor, in whose name Bunaeek administered the country ; any excess of the revenues beyond this, to be allotted to the hereditary proprietor of the territory, that is to say, to Nana Govind Rao, the holder of Jaloun, who had already made his separate terms for the portion of the family dominions in his own possession. It was, however, to be distinctly explained, that if any improvement should be effected in the revenues of Sâgur proper, in consequence of our management, beyond the estimate of their former product, taken at six lakh and ninety-eight thousand rupees, the same was to be the exclusive profit of the Company. The extreme limit of the stipend to the Nana of Jaloun was therefore one lakh and eighteen thousand three hundred and sixty rupees, being the total surplus above the forementioned charges, in case the whole of that estimate and no more should be realized.

In obedience to these instructions, Major-general Marshall, reinforced by Brigadier-general Watson, appeared before Sâgur, on the 8th of March. Bunaeek Rao was now convinced of his danger, and resolved upon submission. The capital of Sâgur was accordingly surrendered on the 11th of March ; and the other forts and territories were quietly taken possession of in the course of the month. General Marshall's force then proceeded against Dhamonee, a fortified town belonging to the Raja of Nagpoor, situated to the north of the Nerbudda, and thus comprised within the late cessions of Apa Saheb, though the Kiladar and garrison had refused to comply with the order for its evacuation. The general appeared before the place on the 17th of March, and tendered the payment to the garrison of their arrears, as far as ten thousand rupees, on the condition of immediate evacuation. The garrison demanded the full arrears of two years and a half, declaring that, for the whole of that period, they had received no pay whatever. As this amount greatly exceeded what the Major-general thought himself authorized to offer, the town was immediately invested, and batteries having been raised within breaching distance, the garrison surrendered as prisoners of war, on the 24th of March; when the Kiladar and principal officers were in the first instance dealt with as rebels, and sentenced to confinement in different forts, but subsequently pardoned and released.

The division was now directed to effect the reduction of Mundela, on the Nerbudda, which had in like manner resisted Apa Saheb's public order for its surrender. The main difficulty here was to bring up the heavy artillery through the roads and passes that led to the town. This being at last effected, two batteries were raised, and opened their fire on the 26th of April. The fire was so accurate, that the besieged were driven entirely from the angle of the wall attacked, which being observed by Captain Tickell the engineer, and by Lieutenant Pickersgill, of the Quarter-master-general's department, they approached the spot in the afternoon, and ascertained by close inspection, both that the breach was practicable, and the wall abandoned. On receipt of their report in the trenches, a storm was immediately resolved on. It was led by Brigadier-general Watson himself; and, after some fighting in the streets, the town was carried. Of the garrison, part escaped into the fort, but the rest were either cut up in the streets, or, in attempting to escape by an opposite gate, were attacked and cut to pieces by the cavalry, previously posted to complete the investiture on that side. The fort surrendered at discretion next morning, the Kiladar having been taken during the night, while endeavouring to cross the river in a boat. The Marquess of Hastings had ordered him to be dealt with severely, not only for his rebellion in resisting the order of evacuation, but likewise and specially, because he had attempted to circumvent and cut off Major O'Brien, the officer who had been despatched with a mere escort to present it. He was accordingly tried for his life by a drum-head court martial; but acquitted, on exhibiting proof that he had the private orders of Apa Saheb not to deliver up the place. Another active partisan, of the name of Nathoo Ram, was similarly tried and acquitted. Although this did not occur until the end of April, it is here introduced by anticipation, in order to complete the notice of General Marshall's operations for the season.

Before proceeding further, it will be necessary to explain the part assigned, under the new distribution of February, to the other divisions of the British armies then in activity on the side of Hindoostan. Major-general Donkin's, or the right division of the grand army, was ordered to be broken up as soon as it should have succeeded in occupying Juswunt Rao's possessions in Mewur. The European portion of the troops composing it, (8th dragoons, his Majesty's 14th foot, and the artillery), were ordered back to the cantonment of Meeruth : from the native troops, a reinforcement was to be furnished to Sir David Ochterlony. The detachment, which had been sent in advance from Lord Hastings', the centre division, under the command of Major-general Brown, was, immediately after the affair of Jawud, likewise made available for the purpose of strengthening the force to be left in Rajpootana, which it was determined to put in a most efficient state, for the completion of the settlement of that quarter. This reinforcement afforded the means of forming an additional brigade of infantry, which, together with a regiment of cavalry, and a complement of the other arms, it was intended to station at Holkur's capital, for the defence and protection of that chief's remaining dominions. Lieutenant-colonel Ludlow was appointed to the subordinate command of this corps, which, after the execution of the service, was to be annexed to the division of Sir David Ochterlony. Such was the new distribution of the troops, that had been brought into the field on the side of Hindoostan. The whole arrangement was ordered and carried into execution by the Marquess of Hastings, by the middle of February; and, at the same time, the two corps of observation to the east were recalled from their advanced positions. Of the native troops composing the latter, a competent force for the occupation of Jubulpoor was detached by Brigadier-general Hardyman, and left under the command of Major O'Brien; while the troops requisite for the military occupation and settlement of the Jungul tract to the south of Buhar, lately ceded by the Bhoosla Raja, were furnished from the corps of Brigadier-general Toone. Major Roughsedge commanded the detachment employed on this latter duty, and by his means Sirgooja, Jushpoor, Sohagpoor, and Sumbhulpoor, were quietly annexed to our dominions ; though the wildness of the country, and of the native tribes that inhabit it, rendered its peaceable settlement a work of time and attention.

Of the three divisions of the army of the Dukhun, still in the field to the north of the Nerbudda, that under the personal command of Sir Thomas Hislop, and the 5th, commanded by Lieutenant-colonel Adams, were directed to return forthwith to aid in the early restoration of the affairs of the Dukhun. Colonel Adams was ordered to proceed, in the first instance, upon Chouragurh, a fort in the northern extremity of the Mohadeo hills, which, like Dhamonee and Mundela, had refused to obey the orders of surrender forwarded for the purpose from Nagpoor. We shall come presently to the detail of the operations of this force. Sir Thomas Hislop was ordered to conduct back his division by the route of the Sindwa Ghât and Kandês, so as to admit of their immediate employment in the reduction of Bajee Rao's possessions in that province, and in the occupation of the recent cessions of Holkur within it. The country was remarkably strong by nature, and was besides full of fortresses and Arab colonies, that promised no inconsiderable trouble and impediment in the way of its quiet settlement. It had at first been resolved to employ the head-quarter division of the Madras army, in co-operation with that of Brigadier-general Doveton, in the reduction of Aseergurh; but the evident importance of early reducing the strong-holds of Kandês, and of making further means available against Bajee Rao, who still kept the field in formidable force, prevailed with his Lordship to give the above plan the preference, leaving Aseergurh until such time as our armies might be less extensively employed in other directions.

It was further suggested to Sir Thomas Hislop, that, as the objects, with a view to which the several subsidiary forces had been formed into divisions of the same army, and placed under his own personal command as general in chief, had now been entirely accomplished, by the dispersion of the Pindarees and the destruction of the military power of Holkur's predatory adherents, there was no longer any occasion for continuing the same organization of the troops under the general control of a commander-in-chief: and, as the subsidiary forces of the Nizam and Bhoosla might conveniently be replaced on their former footing, under the direction of the Residents at the respective durbars, who had special and immediate instructions from Lord Hastings, there was little necessity for the Lieutenant-general's further presence in the field. The Poona subsidiary force, which temporarily formed the third division of the army of the Dukhun, had previously been separated from that army, and placed again at Mr. Elphinstone's disposal, in the same manner as before Sir Thomas Hislop took the field in person; and, as the services in other quarters would now become equally insulated, the motives which had suggested the measure in one case, were obviously applicable to the other forces of the same description. The army of the Dukhun was accordingly ordered to be broken up without delay. The Marquess's present plan was, to direct Brigadier-general Doveton to prosecute the operations in Kandês, the settlement of which province, as well as of the rest of Bajee Rao's dominions in the Dukhun, was subjected to Mr. Elphinstone's general control and superintendence; and to distribute the troops composing the division of Sir Thomas Hislop in the reinforcement, as well of the corps to be so employed, as of the other corps at present acting against Bajee Rao, the regulation and disposition of which had equally devolved on Mr. Elphinstone as commissioner. By this means, an overwhelming force would be collected to ensure the subjugation of the country still adhering to the cause of Bajee Rao by the close of the passing season.

The above orders and instructions were issued by the Marquess of Hastings on the 2d of February. By the middle of the month, the head-quarter division of the army of the Dukhun commenced its southward march, by the route of Indôr, and Muheshwur. Brigadier-general Malcolm retained the Madras troops attached to his division; the corps of Bengal troops allotted for the protection of Holkur's dominions not having yet been organized. He was also desirous of employing a military force for the reduction of Soandwara*, a province lying west of Malwa; the natural difficulties of which encouraged its inhabitants to persevere in the predatory habits they had been bred to, notwithstanding the change of system proclaimed on the establishment of our influence in those parts. The early repression of the smallest indication of a marauding spirit was of course an essential object; and in this view the enterprise was promptly undertaken. In addition to the troops of his own division, Sir John Malcolm also retained for this service a strong brigade of infantry, and a battering-train from the Goozerat army, which, under the recent military arrangements, the Marquess of Hastings had ordered back to the Gykwar's dominions. Of these elements, a field force was soon formed, which, after the junction of the troops of Zalim Singh of Kota,

---

* A tract extending from Agur to the Chumbul east and west, and from near Bhanpoora to Oojein north and south. In this tract, the freebooters mustered near two thousand horse. Lalgurh was their principal hold.

and those of Holkur's present government, penetrated into the country. The capture of a few
strong-holds, which were carried with great spirit,
completely effected the business before the end of
March. The troops of Holkur and of Zalim
Singh* co-operated with the utmost alacrity, and
did good service on all occasions. Indeed, it was
by no means the least gratifying circumstance in
the accomplishment of the object contemplated in
this expedition, to observe the promptitude and
good will with which our new allies came forward
with their contingents to aid the enterprise. The
spirit they displayed afforded the most satisfactory
test of the policy whereon the new system was
founded, and the best security for the solidity and
permanence of the arrangements either made or in
progress.

Pending the settlement of Soandwara, Sir
Thomas Hislop was on his way to the Dukhun, as
above mentioned. Having crossed the Nerbudda
at Mundisôr, a little above Muheshwur, he moved
direct to the Sindwa Ghât, where he arrived on
the 22d of February, The fort was surrendered
on the 23d, agreeably to the orders to that pur-

---

* Muhrab Khan, his general, particularly distinguished
himself in the attack of the village and fortress of Narela,
which he stormed, though the breach was hardly practicable,
and took, with the loss of two hundred of his troops, and
several officers of rank.

port, brought from Holkur's court. A battalion was left to garrison it, and overawe the country between the Sâtpoora range and the Nerbudda; and Sir Thomas Hislop continued his march to the south. On the 27th of February, he reached the post of Talnêr, commanding the ford over the Taptee, and one of the places ceded by Holkur under the late treaty of Mundisôr, the orders for the surrender of which were in Sir Thomas Hislop's possession. It had been reported that the Kiladar intended to refuse compliance; and, on the approach of a party of our troops, a fire was opened upon them. The Kiladar was warned, that, if he continued to resist the order of his master, he would be dealt with as a rebel; but this produced no abatement of the fire from the walls. The Petta, or open town, was accordingly occupied; and the artillery of the division, consisting of ten six-pounders, with two five-and-a-half inch howitzers, was opened from a position it afforded about three hundred yards distant from the fort. The fire was directed chiefly at the defences, and was briskly answered by matchlocks from the wall. In the evening, it was resolved to attempt to force the gate of the place; for which purpose, two six-pounders were carried up to the outer gate by the flank companies of the Royal Scots and the European regiment, the whole led by Major Gordon, accompanied by Lieutenant-

colonel M'Gregor Murray, Lieutenant-colonel
Conway, and other officers of the staff. On reaching the first gate, it was discovered that the fire
during the day had so injured the wall beside it
that the men got through without finding it necessary to blow it open. Wherefore, leaving the
guns on the outside, the storming party pushed
on to the second gate, which was found open.
At the third gate they were met by the Kiladar,
who came out by the wicket, along with some
buneeas, native merchants, and proffered his surrender to Colonel Conway. The third and
fourth gates were then opened, and the party
advanced to the fifth, which led into the body of
the place. This was found closed, and the
garrison from within demanded terms, and expressed their dissatisfaction. After a very short
parley, in which they were distinctly summoned to surrender at discretion, the wicket-gate
was opened from within, and Lieutenant-colonel
Murray and Major Gordon, with three other
officers, entered, followed by about ten or twelve
grenadiers.

In the mean time, the Arabs of the garrison
understood little of what was proposed to them,
for, unfortunately, none of the officers in advance
could speak their language : hence, distrusting
the intention of the British towards themselves, and seeing every thing on the point of

being lost, they worked themselves up to a frenzy of desperation ; and either resolving to sell their lives as dearly as possible, or hoping yet to be able to save the place, made a sudden attack with swords, spears and knives on the few who had already entered the wicket. Major Gordon and Captain M'Gregor were presently killed. Lieutenant-colonel Murray received several wounds, and was at last cut down and disabled, as were the other two officers who had accompanied him, Lieutenants Chauvel and M'Gregor : most of the foremost grenadiers were also killed or wounded. However, as those who entered first had maintained their ground, others crowded through the wicket to their support; and, in the end, the Arabs were driven to seek shelter in the circumjacent houses. The guns were also brought up after blowing open the outer gate, upon which the place was soon carried, and the garrison, in number about three hundred, were put to the sword. The Kiladar was executed next morning, on the twofold charge of original resistance to the order of his sovereign and supposed implication in the treachery of the garrison. The example was probably useful,* and no doubt influenced the subse-

* I wish not to be understood as the apologist of this act of severity. The motive which induced the Marquess of Hastings to take upon himself the responsibility of its approval may easily be appreciated, but to have ordered such

quent surrender of the much stronger forts of Gâlna, Chandôr, and other places, immediately on the presentation of the orders by the several detachments sent to occupy them. The total loss on the part of the British was seven officers and eighteen men killed and wounded. The death of Major Gordon was the subject of universal regret, as he deservedly enjoyed the highest estimation of his brother soldiers, as well as of the government he served.

Leaving a garrison to occupy Talnêr, the Lieutenant-general crossed the Taptee, and advanced by Umulnêr to Pahrola, where he came into communication with Brigadier-general Doveton, then posted at Outrân. This officer, having already completed the settlement of affairs at Nagpoor, had returned westward by Ellichpoor in the course of January, expecting orders to proceed against Aseergurh; but, on the abandonment of the intention of reducing that fortress in the current season, he had been ordered to direct his march upon the point of

a thing would have been quite foreign to his nature. The manner also, even with the explanations given afterwards by the Staff Officers present or concerned, was extremely exceptionable, and very much in contrast with the course adopted under his Lordship's orders for the trial and eventual punishment of the Kiladar of Mundela, who was suspected of similar treachery, but who, when put on his defence before a tribunal not ordinarily addicted to leniency, viz. a drum-head Court-martial, was acquitted.

Ootrân, on the Gyrna. Sir Thomas Hislop now ordered him to move up the Gyrna to Bal, following himself the course of the Boaree, and sending a detachment to receive the surrender of Gâlna. No resistance was attempted ; and this, with several other of Holkur's possessions in the neighbourhood, was quietly occupied by the troops of the two divisions.

While these divisions were thus employed in Kandês, Sir Thomas Hislop received intelligence that Bajee Rao had penetrated the Ghâts separating that province from the valley of the Godavuree: whereupon he immediately hastened to the south, ordering Brigadier-general Doveton to move on a parallel line in the same direction, in the hope of being able to intercept him before he should be apprized of their approach. It will be convenient, however, to relate the intermediate occurrences at the court of Nagpoor, before we return to trace the motions of the fugitive Pêshwa, and the further operations against him.

CHAPTER XIX.

NAGPOOR.—DUKHUN.

1818, FEBRUARY TO MAY.

Nagpoor—ministry of restored Raja—his fresh intrigues and early treachery—Resident's suspicions and measures—Governor-general's first instructions—Detection of the plots—arrest of Raja and his ministers—Bajee Rao applied to by Bhoosla for aid—consequent proceedings—marches eastward—eludes Sir Thomas Hislop's division—Army of the Dukhun broken up—progress of Bajee Rao—Brigadier-general Smith co-operates with Brigadier-general Doveton—Lieutenant-colonel Adams—repulse of Gunput Rao—Lieutenant-colonel Adams at Hingunghât—waits for other divisions, and advances—rout of Soonee—pursuit by Brigadier-general Doveton—dispersion of Mahratta army—detention and submission of sirdars—Wusota invested and captured—new distribution of the forces—capture of other forts—affair of Solapoor—Chanda invested—its surrender.

THE affairs of Nagpoor have been passed over in silence, since Apa Saheb's return to the palace of the Bhooslas, under an arrangement confirmed by the Marquess of Hastings, as mentioned in the fifteenth Chapter. This occurred in the course of January, the date of the Raja's return being the 9th of that month.

It will be recollected, that, when Apa Saheb made his submission, the principal channel of communication between him and the Resident was Nurayun Pundit, one of the negotiators of the original subsidiary alliance. This man was rewarded for the share he had in that transaction, and for his former tried fidelity to the British government, by being immediately invested with the second place in the administration, under the name of Pêshkar. Nagoo Punt, however, the other negotiator of the alliance, a man more deep in Apa Saheb's confidence, was retained as dewan; and Ramchundur Wâgh, who had also submitted, together with his master, on the 16th of December, was not displaced, though known to have been an active instigator of the late hostilities. This man had been included in the indemnity for the past, by an express stipulation with Nurayun, before Apa Saheb could be induced to come in; and Mr. Jenkins, willing to regard the fact of his surrender along with his master, as a sufficient indication of his altered sentiments, not only showed towards him no displeasure at the part he had lately taken, but allowed him to retain his offices and influence in the court.

The European reader will scarcely believe it possible, that, after submitting to be reinstated on the Guddee of Nagpoor by the mediation of the

British Resident, at the sacrifice of his army and
political independence, Apa Saheb should again
have entered into treasonable plots against the
power which had thus restored him.   It would
seem, however, that no sooner was the personal
danger gone by, than he began to be ashamed of
the weakness that had urged him to throw up a
cause by no means desperate ; and, sensible that he
had acted more from fear than judgment, he could
scarcely divest himself of the idea of his having been betrayed into the step, by what he now
deemed to be Nurayun's interested exaggerations
of the danger.   Ashamed and mortified at the
folly and cowardice of the course he had taken,
he thought only of repairing the error, as soon as
he should recover the means ; and by way of
ensuring success, not only agreed with apparent
readiness to the terms proposed, but proffered
more than was asked, in the hope of regaining
our confidence, and thereby masking his future
conduct and designs.

So rapid was this change of sentiment in the
Raja, that, even while yet in our power, and
living at the Residency, nay, at the very moment
of subscribing to the terms which were to be the
price of his restoration, was he practising the deception, by which he hoped to retrieve his affairs
and renew our embarrassments.   In the interval
between the attack on the Residency and the ar-

rival of Brigadier-general Doveton, secret orders
had been issued to the several Goand and other
jungul and mountain Rajas, to call out their followers, and offer every annoyance in their power
to the British authorities, especially to cut off detachments in charge of convoys, and prevent the
country from furnishing supplies to the different
armies in the field.   Apa Saheb and his ministers,
while negotiating the terms of the treaty, perceiving, from the omission of any stipulation for
the recall of these orders, that Mr. Jenkins had
then no notice or suspicion of them, resolved to
allow them to take effect, though perfectly aware,
as they afterwards acknowledged, that the consequence of not recalling them would be, to raise
the whole country in arms, not only against us,
but against any government that might act under
our sanction.   This deception was continued in
the measures taken to prevent the due execution
of the treaty after its signature.   It was ascertained, that the Kiladars of Mundela and Chouragurh had from the first received private instructions not to surrender to the public orders
which should be presented.   The commander at
Dhamonee * also pleaded the receipt of similar in-

---

* The private orders to Dhamonee were in these words :
" Jysa Dekho, wysakuro ;" As you see, so do.   Meaning, as
the Kiladar naturally interpreted them, " Resist, if you think
_ yourself able."

structions, and the order, in this instance, to be effectual, must have preceded the signing of the treaty, or at least have followed so closely, as to be sure of anticipating the public summons ; which shows the early commencement of the plot. In prosecution of the same designs, orders were issued on the 18th of January, nine days only after the Raja returned to his palace, for the Kiladar of Chanda to recruit, and particularly to enlist Arabs. It was, moreover, subsequently ascertained, that, along with Gunput Rao, who carried off with him the remnant of the army defeated by Brigadier-general Doveton, an agent of the name of Sukha-Ram had been sent directly from Apa Saheb, carrying with him one of the seals of state in token of his mission, to convey the Raja's earnest request for immediate assistance towards throwing off the British yoke. The issue of this part of the intrigue will presently be mentioned, when we come to relate what was passing in the camp of Bajee Rao.

The first suspicion entertained by Mr. Jenkins of the existence of these designs was excited by the obstinate refusal of the Kiladars and garrisons to evacuate Mundela and Chouragurh, notwithstanding the liberal offer of all arrears ; for the rejection of which it was impossible to assign an adequate motive, without supposing them to have other resources or the assurance of other support in the back ground. Indeed, the Ki-ladar of Chouragurh asserted the receipt of private orders of a contrary purport, in reply to the summons sent to him by Lieutenant-colonel M'Morine. Coupling this obstinacy of the Kiladars and the reasons so publicly assigned for it with some appearances of a similar nature in the behaviour of the Prince himself since his restoration, Mr. Jenkins thought it necessary to take measures for ascertaining the truth or falsehood of the reports in circulation, and for watching the agents of the several parties, and endeavouring to intercept some of their confidential despatches. It was particularly an object to discover, whether the intrigues were confined to the ministry and inferior departments, or originated with the Raja himself. There was certainly ample ground to suspect Apa Saheb; for it had been observed, that, although he had since his return to the palace shut himself up in his own apartments, professing to be indifferent to all state concerns, still he was evidently discontented, and never saw Nurayun Pundit without reproaching him as the cause of his present degradation. At the same time it was known, that he had frequent private conferences with Nagoo Punt and Ramchundur, the purport of which was studiously concealed from their colleagues in administration, and from the Resident. His participation in whatever in-

trigues were on foot was also inferable from his
general character and conduct; besides which,
on more than one occasion, suspicion was excited
by Nagoo Punt's mode of conducting the internal
branch of the administration, particularly by
some measures he took to favour the interests of
those proscribed in consequence of their continued
disobedience. When Mr. Jenkins preferred a
complaint against him to Apa Saheb, the Raja
pledged himself for the Dewan's fidelity, and
would listen to no argument tending to impeach
it; thus evidently identifying himself with the
measures of the favourite. But the circumstance
which threw the strongest personal suspicion
upon Apa Saheb, was, the discovery that, instead
of bringing his treasures back to Nagpoor, along
with the women of his family, he had issued
secret orders to have the greater part conveyed
back to Chanda and other forts, and even what
was brought into the town was not openly depo-
sited in the palace, but given out in trust with
great secrecy and care.

Influenced by these suspicions, Mr. Jenkins
first set a watch upon a man named Govind
Pundit, whom he knew to be the agent at court
on behalf of Nathoo-Ram, an officer who had
been commissioned to expedite the surrender of
Mundela. On the 4th of March, having intelligence that a letter was on its way from him to
Nathoo-Ram, in the hands of a confidential mes-

senger, he caused the bearer of it to be seized, and thus obtained possession of it. The letter gave circumstantial details of what had passed at some conferences with Nagoo Punt, and Ramchundur, to which Govind had been admitted, and afforded abundant evidence of those ministers having instigated the refusal to surrender Mundela. Upon this, Mr. Jenkins caused Govind Punt to be arrested and examined; and being apprehensive of an attempt on the part of Apa Saheb to depart secretly, redoubled his vigilance, and, under the pretence of an improved police regulation, ordered every possible precaution to be taken to prevent any one from quitting the town by night. Though the suspicions were strong, nothing further had yet attached to Apa Saheb himself; when a private letter of date the 6th of March, was addressed by Mr. Jenkins to the Governor-general, pressing for early instructions for his guidance; he was answered in the same form by Mr. Adam, the Governor-general's secretary, that, without direct proof against the Raja, he was only to act against the ministers; but that he would be justified in taking the most vigorous measures to obtain the removal of such dangerous counsellors as Nagoo Punt and Ramchundur had now proved themselves to be, and the exclusion from the durbar of others of the same stamp. In the mean time, however, reports poured in from every quarter, of applications by Apa Saheb to

Bajee Rao for assistance, and of the hostile advance of Gunput Rao with succours. Mr. Jenkins, therefore, redoubled his efforts to penetrate the mystery. Having ascertained that two agents were about to be despatched by Ramchundur to Bajee Rao, one a confidential *chitnavees* (secretary) of Ramchundur himself, the other a *bareedar* (private servant) of the Raja, he caused them to be seized when just on the point of setting off. Before this strong measure, he had contrived to procure from the chitnavees an acknowledgment of the nature of his errand, which was made in a place where he could be overheard, and to a supposed friend, who was in reality a spy set to win his confidence. Atma-Ram, (so was the secretary named) destroyed a paper he had about him as soon as he found himself betrayed ; but it was discovered that this paper contained a few words in the Prince's own hand-writing, which were to give the assurance of his being a true messenger. Next morning, when Apa Saheb was informed of the arrest of the courier, he expressed the utmost anxiety to know if any paper had been found upon him, and seemed much relieved at learning that none was actually forthcoming. This occurred on the 14th of March ; and at the same time arrived the positive intelligence of Gunput Rao being in full march to Nagpoor, while it was confidently re-

ported, that the Pêshwa was himself following
with his whole army, and had already passed the
frontier of the Nizam's dominions in his way.
Previous accounts had reported him to have
moved in an easterly direction after evading the
pursuit of Sir Thomas Hislop, so as to render
such an intention extremely probable. It was
rumoured also, that the Raja was on the eve of
flying to Chanda to meet him.

The Pêshwa's detachment of Gunput Rao with
reinforcements, and movement with his main
army in a direction to support that chief, was so
strong a confirmation of the truth of the designs
said to be in agitation at Nagpoor, as, even without positive proof and on mere suspicion, would
have justified the most vigorous precautionary
measures. More decisive evidence had, however,
been obtained by the seizure of Atma-Ram and
his companion, evidence going directly to implicate
the Raja himself. Feeling, therefore, that, should
the Bhoosla prince escape and join Bajee Rao,
all that had been done to establish order in the
Nagpoor dominions would be undone again in a
moment, and being now armed with more con-
vincing testimony, the Resident resolved to wait
no longer for instructions, but to act upon his
own responsibility, and take the only step, which
could effectually secure the British interests intrusted to his charge against the impending dan-

ger. Up to this time he had confined himself to
measures of precaution and inquiry; but the
knowledge of these, and of the arrest of the
couriers, was calculated to precipitate the crisis
with the Raja, and to urge him to immediate
flight, as the only means of avoiding the consequences of detection. Thus, it was impossible to
delay for another moment the necessary measures
of prevention, however anxious the Resident might
have been to receive the instructions of the higher
powers, before he took so decided a step.

Accordingly, having determined immediately
to place the Raja under close arrest, he sent notice of this intention over night to Buka Baee,
whom the reader will remember to have been
before mentioned, as the favourite wife of the
deceased Raghoojee, and at all times attached to
the party opposed to the reigning Raja. In the
morning of the 15th of March, he despatched a
note to Apa Saheb, informing him that doubts
had arisen, which made it absolutely necessary
that he should come and remain at the Residency
till they were cleared up, representing strongly
the utter impossibility of resistance, and the prudence of immediate compliance, without rendering it necessary to resort to forcible measures.
Buka Baee in vain exerted her influence to induce
the Raja to attend to this very peremptory summons: whereupon, Mr. Jenkins being determined

to enforce it, sent a party of Sepahees unarmed, under the conduct of Captain Browne, 22d Bengal N. I., and Dr. Gordon, the Resident's assistant, who succeeded in effecting the arrest, and fortunately without the necessity of entering the apartments reserved for the women. Nagoo Punt and Ramchundur Wâgh were in like manner seized, and all three brought to the Residency, and placed under separate guards. They in some measure confessed their participation in the plot, particularly Nagoo Punt, who accused his master of being the cause of his ruin by his incurable love of intrigue, and made it his principal request, that, if doomed to imprisonment, he might be separately confined.

The confessions of the Raja and of his ministers were quite unnecessary to convince the world of their criminality. Proofs multiplied from every quarter immediately after their apprehension ; while the daily advance of Bajee Rao, and the gradual development of the intrigues that had been passing between him and the Bhoosla, satisfied every one of the necessity of the Resident's precautionary measures. Amongst other articles of accusation that transpired in the course of the inquiries instituted on this occasion, the circumstances of the murder of Pursajee first came to light on the day before the arrest. Indeed, one of Mr. Jenkins' motives for holding the Raja in close confinement was, the idea that Lord Hastings might perhaps desire so heavy an accusation to be brought to trial, in order to visit the crime with the merited punishment, in the event of the charge being clearly established.

In this posture affairs remained at Nagpoor, while the Resident awaited the Governor-general's instructions as to the steps to be next adopted. And here we will for the present leave them, turning aside to notice the circumstances of Bajee Rao's advance into this territory, and the events to which it led.

We have already followed Gunput Rao to the time of his junction with Bajee Rao, at the head of the broken horse of the Nagpoor army. The junction took place in the neighbourhood of Tamboornee, before Bajee Rao's retreat on Solapoor, whither Gunput Rao accompanied him, and was afterwards present at the battle of Ashtee. Naroo Sukha-Ram, the agent before mentioned, had followed in the train of this Sirdar, and delivered the errand from his master, soliciting aid: and the course to be adopted in consequence was under consideration, when Bajee Rao's army was surprised on the 20th of February. In the flight, Bajee Rao had scarcely got as far north as Purinda, when two *hoojras* (confidential messengers) arrived also from Nagpoor, pressing for the early adoption of some plan for the Raja's relief. On

their heels followed two other similar messengers,
who repeated Apa Saheb's earnest entreaty for
assistance, bringing a letter in his own hand-
writing to confirm the veracity of their verbal
statement. The despatch was brief and simple :
" Sumana Meer to Gungana Dobeeya—Assist me
in any way you can." The names are those of
two holy men, famous in Mahratta legends for
the assistance they mutually rendered each other
in extremity. These messengers Bajee Rao carried along with him, and continued his flight
northward to Newasa, whence he endeavoured
without success to expel a garrison of Sebundees
left by Colonel Deacon in his way to the south-
west. From Newasa he directed his flight north-
west to Kopergâon, crossing the Godavuree at
Phool-tamba. Finding the heat of the pursuit
somewhat abated, he took the opportunity of visit-
ing Nassik, and then proceeded to Warner near
Chandôr, where he effected the before-mentioned
junction with Ramdeen, who had brought with
him some Pindaree horse, and a portion of the
routed infantry of Holkur. Hence the Nagpoor
messengers were at length despatched with a
written answer to the Bhoosla, the contents of
which never transpired ; but there can be no
doubt it conveyed an assurance of immediate help.
This was on the 2d of March ; and Gunput Rao
and Sukha-Ram at the same time solicited an ad-

vance of money, and leave to depart for Nagpoor,
stating that preparations for war had been making at Chanda, that a force under Chundojee
Bhoosla was at Bhundaree, and that they had
certain information of the hill people having risen
in arms, as well as of Mundela and Chouragurh
having been put into a condition to stand a siege.
With a small advance of money and troops, they
engaged to raise a general insurrection, as soon
as they should reach the Bhoosla territory ; and
strongly recommended the Pêshwa to proceed
himself in the same direction by the route of
Kandês and Boorhanpoor. Bajee Rao, though
he seemed to listen favourably to this advice,
could not be brought to give a distinct or immediate answer, but desired Gunput Rao to wait a
few days for his determination. He then skirted
the Ghâts into Kandês, collecting information as
he went, as to the practicability of the plan, and
the disposition of the several British divisions.
At Unkye he first learnt Sir Thomas Hislop's arrival in Kandês, and near approach in a direction
to intercept completely the route by Boorhanpoor;
whereupon he fled with the utmost precipitation
across the Godavuree at Kopergâon, and as far
south as Assee on the Peeree. Thence again,
fearing to fall in with the division of Brigadier-
general Smith in its advance from the south, he
turned off due east, and continued his march in

that direction. The suggestion of Gunput Rao was now openly adopted, and this chief sent forward by a parallel, but different route from that pursued by the main body, which passed the Nizam's frontier, and crossed the Godavuree at Rakhusbun to the south of Jâlna, with the evident and avowed intention of entering the dominions of the Bhoosla state.

On the 11th of March, Sir Thomas Hislop ascended from Kandês to the plain of the Godavuree, and made one or two ineffectual efforts to come up with the enemy; but, finding that he had escaped by the superior rapidity of his marches, first to the south and then to the east, the Lieutenant-general resolved, without further delay, to carry into effect the orders he had received from Lord Hastings. The several corps forming the head-quarter division were accordingly distributed amongst the other forces in the field; and, on the 31st of March, the final orders were issued from Lassoor for breaking up the army of the Dukhun. Sir Thomas Hislop himself, with the whole general staff of the army, prepared for his return to the Madras presidency with a slight escort of cavalry and infantry; and subsequently, in order to avoid the inconvenience of diverting so large a force as would be necessary to form an efficient escort, from the more important object of contributing to the settlement of the country, he resolved to proceed from **Poona** to Bombay, and thence round by sea to Madras, leaving all his escort at Mr. Elphinstone's disposal, along with the other troops in the field.

In the meantime, Bajee Rao was hastening his flight from his own dominions in the direction of Chanda. His march was marked with cruelties and excesses of the most wanton kind, which, indeed, were mostly attributed to the professional plunderers brought down by Ram - Deen from Hindoostan; for the Poona Mahrattas had hitherto shown much moderation and forbearance in their passage through the country. During the retreat, great pains were taken to mislead the pursuers. The Pêshwa himself always gave out the line of march for the day, withholding every morning from all his officers the next place of halting, until his standard and treasure elephants had actually moved forward. Brigadier-general Smith had not urged the northward pursuit of Bajee Rao after the action at Ashtee on the 20th of February; thinking it necessary first to escort the Raja of Sutara, to receive his formal investiture by Mr. Elphinstone. This occasioned a few days respite; after which the light division, under the Brigadier-general, again proceeded to the north, and having halted to refresh at Seroor, left that place to prosecute the pursuit on the 10th of March. Hearing at this point of Bajee Rao's march eastward, the Brigadier-general moved to-

wards Jâlna, in order to concert a combined plan
of pursuit with the division of Brigadier-general
Doveton. The latter, who was the senior officer,
resolved to march himself upon Basum, and thence
along the Ghâts into Berar, as far as Kurinja, in
the hope of, by that means, effectually cutting off
the Mahratta army from the north; and suggested
to Brigadier-general Smith the advantage of his
moving along the line of the Godavuree, at such a
distance‚ from the river, as should prevent the
enemy from turning his right without crossing,
which the difficulty of the fords gave him little
chance of effecting, or of getting off to the southward again, without laying himself open to attack.

The van of the Mahratta army, after having
traversed the Nizam's dominions from west to east
without resistance, appeared on the banks of the
Wurda‚ on the first or second of April, at a point
near Woonee, a little above the confluence of this
river with the Payn Gunga. In this quarter, however, Bajee Rao found his plans wholly disconcerted by the preparations made for his reception.
It will be recollected, that, after receiving the
submission of Namdar Khan and other Pindaree
leaders, the division of Lieutenant-colonel Adams
had been ordered to return from Hindoostan to
its original station in the valley of the Nerbudda,
there to prepare for the reduction of the fort of
Chouragurh, the Kiladar of which had been re-
peatedly summoned by Lieutenant-colonel M'Mo-

rine without effect. The beginning of March was passed by Colonel Adams in making ready for the attack of this place, and in procuring from General Marshall a reinforcement of heavy guns for the purpose, the two in the depôt at Hoshungabad having suffered a little in their carriages. While yet engaged in these preparations, the events above detailed were passing at Nagpoor; and Mr. Jenkins, having reason to believe that Chanda was to be the destined rallying point of resistance, even before it was certain that the Pêshwa was on his way thither, directed Lieutenant-colonel Adams' particular attention to the importance of summoning, and eventually reducing it before the close of the season, and therefore recommended his leaving Chouragurh for the present, in order to make Chanda his first object, in case there should not be time for the reduction of both before the setting in of the rains. It was further suggested that General Marshall's force might be advantageously employed against Chouragurh as well as Mundela, immediately after the taking of Dhamonee, on which service it was then employed; and this arrangement was afterwards ordered by the Marquess of Hastings to be carried into execution, as we have before incidentally noticed in the preceding chapter.

These discussions respecting the importance of reducing Chanda had prepared Lieutenant-colonel Adams for an early summons to the southward,

before the receipt of positive intelligence, that
Bajee Rao was on his way towards the same
point.   Wherefore, on the first advice of the probability of this event, he began to move by forced
marches upon Nagpoor, carrying with him the
5th Bengal cavalry, his horse artillery, and a brigade of infantry, and leaving Major Popham with
a detachment to bring up by easy stages the two
eighteen-pounders, forming the whole heavy train
at his command.   Mr. Jenkins had previously
summoned a detachment of the 8th Bengal cavalry from Jubulpoor to strengthen his force in
that arm ; and further, on learning that Chanda
was the point for which the troops from the westward were making, Lieutenant-colonel Scott had
been despatched with the greater part of the force
then at Nagpoor, in the hope of his being able to
cut off the enemy from any communication with
that strong fortress, and hold him in check until
the arrival of Colonel Adams with the main
body.   Colonel Scott reached Wuroda, or Wu-
roona, about fifteen miles from Chanda, on the
3d of April.   Here he fell in with the van of
the Mahrattas, under Gunput Rao, and drove
it back across the Wurda, though with the trifling
loss of ten or twelve only ; for the rencounter
was quite unexpected by the enemy, who fled
with precipitation on the first appearance of the
British force.   Thus stopped short in his advance, and at the same time apprized of the arrest

of Apa Saheb, and the little hope of support within the Bhoosla territory, Bajee Rao continued for some days irresolute, shifting his ground between the Wurda and the Payn-Gunga, but not daring to cross the former river. After the affair at Wuroda, Lieutenant-colonel Scott proceeded to Chanda, hoping to succeed in investing the place, or at least to cut off all communication from without; but he found the fortifications so extensive, that with his small force, consisting of only one weak brigade of infantry and the 6th Bengal cavalry, it was impossible for him to cover it entirely. Lieutenant-colonel Adams in the mean time, having made arrangements for the defence of Nagpoor, hastened his march to Hingun-Ghât, which he selected as the most appropriate point, both to cover the Bhoosla capital and to support Lieutenant-colonel Scott in case of emergency. He reached Hingun-Ghât on the 6th of April, and found, that Bajee Rao was still on the other side of the Wurda, undetermined what course now to pursue. Lieutenant-colonel Scott had left Nagpoor in such haste, that he had come away with insufficient supplies; and, as the country about Chanda was found to be wholly destitute of the means of support, he felt himself under the necessity of soliciting from Lieutenant-colonel Adams a part of his stores, which was instantly forwarded; but Colonel Adams thought it advisable in consequence to wait the arrival of a fresh supply

from Nagpoor, before he embarked any further in
a service, that promised to draw him into a long
pursuit through an impoverished country, and
away from his own resources. By good fortune,
the delay was every way advantageous, as it
would leave the enemy unmolested, and induce
his continuance in his present situation until Brigadier-general Doveton should reach the desired
position to the north-west of him, while Brigadier-
general Smith approached to cut him off from the
southward. With the three divisions thus closing
in upon him from opposite sides, it seemed utterly impossible he should escape. Halting therefore at Hingun-Ghât, the Lieutenant-colonel exerted himself to procure intelligence of every
motion of the enemy; and, ascertaining that he
still loitered about Pundur-Koura and Woonee
without attempting any thing, forbore for the present to disquiet him or beat up his quarters. On
the 11th of April, Lieutenant-colonel Scott was
called in from Chanda, in contemplation of an
eventual attack; and, on the information that
Bajee Rao had on the 13th ventured across the
Wurda, at a place called Poona, a little way up
the river, Colonel Adams on the 14th made a
westward movement on Alumda, which had the
effect of immediately driving him back. Brigadier-general Doveton had on the same day reached
Doodgâon on the Arun, fifty miles only to the

north-west of Pundur-Koura, whence he had
written to Lieutenant-colonel Adams, that he
should march by long stages directly on Pundur-Koura, so as to reach the latter place on
the 17th; and it was reckoned, that, by that
time, Brigadier-general Smith would be sufficiently advanced along the line of the Godavuree to intercept any retreat to the south. In
the course of the 16th, Colonel Adams received
the letter conveying this intelligence ; and learning from his own scouts that Bajee Rao was within
a forced march to the south of his position at
Alumda, resolved to march the same evening,
in the hope of either falling upon his encampment,
or driving him back upon the division of Brigadier-
general Doveton, on its advance to Pundur-Koura.
At eight in the evening, the Lieutenant-colonel
began his march ; and, on the morning of the
17th of April, arrived at Peepul-Kôt, where the
Pêshwa had been encamped the preceding day.
It was here found, that he had gone off to Soonee,
a village said to be six coss further to the south-
west. Upon this, not yet despairing to overtake
the fugitives, he called up the cavalry and horse-
artillery, together with a light infantry battalion,
and resolved to push forward with this force to
Soonee, leaving the rest of the troops to follow
more at leisure. Colonel Adams had with him
the entire 5th and 6th, and a squadron of the 8th

Bengal cavalry, a brigade of the Madras European horse artillery, and a troop of the native
corps of the same arm from the Bengal establishment. The light battalion was composed of the
light companies of the several corps originally
attached to the 5th division of the army of the
Dukhun, on its formation in the preceding October. With this force he hastened his march upon
Soonee. On approaching the village, he found
that Bajee Rao, whom his own advance had driven to the south-west, had just discovered himself
to be in full march on Brigadier-general Doveton's
line, which on the same day was marching to
Pundur-Koura, only twelve miles south of Soonee.
In the anxiety to avoid this new danger, he had
again taken a northerly route, and was making
off with all despatch along the very road by which
Colonel Adams was approaching. The advance
guard of the two armies met suddenly about five
miles from Soonee, the Lieutenant-colonel himself being the first who encountered the enemy as
he was marching at the head of the light battalion. He was indeed obliged to retire upon the
battalion, and throw it into square, to wait the
coming up of the cavalry, which was a little in
the rear; guessing, however, from the number of
elephants and standards he saw, that Bajee Rao
was present in person, immediately on its arrival,
he put the head of the column, consisting of the

5th native cavalry and horse artillery, into a gallop, and drove the enemy back in confusion for some miles. The course of the road led to the brow of a rising ground, whence, in the valley beneath, and on the opposite declivity, the main body of the Mahratta army was discovered in great confusion. The horse-artillery opened their fire with admirable effect upon them in this disorganised state, while the cavalry formed, and charging into the valley, in a short time completely cleared it. The Lieutenant-colonel, who led the charge himself, had by this time left the rest of his troops considerably in the rear: undismayed, however, by the numbers of the enemy, he determined to follow up his success with the single regiment and horse artillery he had with him. With this view, detaching one squadron to scour the rising ground on his right, he continued a hot pursuit with the two others, tracking the fugitives up the valley, which took a turn to the left of the road, until he reached another elevation overlooking a second valley watered by the same stream that runs by Soonee. The Mahrattas were here seen collected in greater numbers than before: the horse artillery again opened upon them with great effect, while Colonel Adams formed the two squadrons with him into line, and, charging a second time, drove every thing before him. At the further end of this second valley, two large bodies of the enemy's horse were drawn up, as if prepared to stand their ground. The first of these, however, dispersed quickly, on receiving the fire of the horse artillery, and on finding its flank threatened by the squadron that had been sent to scour the elevated ground on our right. The other body, which was posted on our left, was then driven off by a change of front and advance in that direction. The enemy was thenceforth seen only in broken detachments, flying through the surrounding jungul in complete rout. Five guns, the only ones he had with him, were captured in this action : three elephants and two hundred camels also fell into our hands. The elephants were of those which always preceded Bajee Rao's line of march, and on which his treasure was usually laden ; but no more than eleven thousand rupees in cash was found upon them, the rest having been made away with in the confusion. The Prince himself escaped with difficulty, by mounting a horse and galloping away on the first appearance of the British troops. One of his palanquins was taken, and proved to have been perforated by a round shot ; from its appearance, it was conjectured to have been the same in which he had just been riding. The British loss was only two wounded, the enemy never having stood a charge; whereas, in the pursuit, and particularly by the fire of the horse artillery, upwards of one thousand of the enemy were left dead on the field. Particular credit was due to the officers and men of both corps of horse artillery. Captain Rodber, of the Bengal native corps, had joined Colonel Adams at Alumda but eight hours before the march was commenced on the evening of the 16th; yet he was up with the foremost of the cavalry, notwithstanding the length of the march and pursuit, as was likewise Lieutenant Hunter, a very distinguished officer of the Madras artillery. Indeed, it was mainly in reliance upon his strength in this arm, that Colonel Adams ventured so far in advance of his main body, with only a single regiment of cavalry (5th), being determined to make the affair as decisive as possible, though at some risk, and aware that every moment afforded for escape would detract from the importance of the result. The rest of the cavalry, owing to some misapprehension on the part of Colonel Gahan, its commander, did not join until after the enemy had entirely disappeared. The troops were then encamped on the field of battle, after a continued march of upwards of thirty miles, and waited the coming up of their supplies, before the pursuit could be further prosecuted.

Brigadier-general Doveton arrived at Pundur-

Koura, on the morning of the very day on which this action was fought ; and, being only twelve miles distant, was not long in hearing of the success of the other division. The concurring reports of all his scouts having represented the line of the Pêshwa's flight to be to the southward of west, the Brigadier-general resolved to push forward and give chase in that direction. Consequently he divided his force into two bodies ; one of which he led himself, and of the other he gave the command to Captain Grant, of the Mysoor horse, with whom, besides his own corps, he detached for the purpose two squadrons of regular cavalry, two gallopers, and two light companies of infantry. In this manner the Mahratta army was followed at the heels for five successive days, during all which time it suffered the extreme of distress from famine and fatigue, the British officers making only occasional halts for the indispensable refreshment of their men and horses.

The routed Pêshwa was found to have taken a direction south-westerly, as far as Oomur-Kher, and thence due westward, by Kullumpoor to Boree. At this place, or in the way to it, disheartened at their uniform ill-success, and broken down by long privations, nearly two-thirds of his remaining adherents left his standard, with the intention of returning quietly to their homes.

Brigadier-general Doveton pursued without halting, as far as Oomur-Kher, where he waited three
days for his rear-guard, and in order to procure
supplies. Thence he continued the pursuit as
far west as Peepree beyond Jâlna, which he
reached on the 3d of May. Here, however, he
had the mortification to discover that he was
following a detached party led by chiefs of inferior note, while the Pêshwa himself had turned
off from Boree northwards, with the design of
crossing the Taptee, and penetrating if possible
into Hindoostan.

Of the countless host that had followed his
fortunes to the Wurda, there now remained with
him no more than eight or ten thousand at the
utmost. All the sirdars deserted after the affair
of Soonee, except Trimbukjee, Ram-deen, the
Vinshorkur, (Balooba), and the widow, with
some of the troops, of Gokla. This dispersion of
the several sirdars with their followers in so many
different directions, rendered it very difficult to
determine with precision the exact line of the
prince's flight. The party that Brigadier-general
Doveton pursued so far to the westward, proved
to be led by Madhoo Rasteea and Apa Dhun-
deree, Bajee Rao's father-in-law. The Brigadier-
general no sooner discovered his error, than he left
them to continue their route unmolested. Both
aiterwards made good their way to Kandês, and

sent their submissions thence to Mr. Elphinstone. In the same manner Apa Desaee, with Chimnajee Nurayun, Bajee Rao's own brother, separated themselves entirely from his standard at Boree, and fled directly to the south-west, crossing the Godavuree at Nander. Eesajee Punt, a Gokla nearly connected with the chief slain at Ashtee, and Wittojee Naeek, the same man who had delivered the declaration of war to the Resident at Poona, fled also in a south-west direction with another remnant of the fugitives. The pursuit of these parties was taken up by Brigadier-general Smith, who was at Neermul when the affair of Soonee took place, and, hearing of the total dispersion of the Mahratta army, started in pursuit on the 22d of April. Apa Desaee and Chimnajee surrendered to a detachment sent out by the Brigadier-general, under Captain Davies, of the Nizam's reformed horse, and were by that officer conducted to Ahmednugur, where they consented to abide the orders of Mr. Elphinstone. The other party was pursued by another detachment from the same division, under Major Cunningham, as far as Pundurpoor, whence their chiefs also sent in their submission.

In the interim, Brigadier-general Pritzler, whom we left preparing for the attack of Wusota, appeared before that place and closely invested it, on the 31st of March. Such, however, were the

natural difficulties of the ground, that the heavy
guns could not be brought into battery until the
5th of April. The fort itself, though nature and
art had done their utmost to strengthen it in
other respects, was commanded by a neighbouring hill, called Old Wusota, which was accordingly chosen as the position for the breaching
batteries. Such was the effect with which they
opened, that the Kiladar stood out but one day's
fire, and surrendered the place on the 6th of
April. The remainder of the Raja of Sutara's
family was found here, and the Kiladar declared
that he had received orders from his master to
put the whole of them to death, sooner than
allow them to fall into the hands of the British.
These orders he found an obvious interest in
neglecting, in the present depressed condition of
Bajee Rao's fortunes. Lieutenants Morrieson
and Hunter, whose capture at the commencement
of the war was before noticed, were also found
immured in the dungeons of this fort. Valuables
belonging to the Sutara family, estimated to
amount to near three lakh of rupees, were likewise captured : for these, however, the troops
were allowed a compensation, in order to admit
of their restoration to the Raja. On the reduction of Wusota, the force under Brigadier-
general Pritzler was broken up ; the corps of it
drawn from the reserve, after being reinforced by

a Bombay battalion, were sent to meet Brigadier-general Munro *, who was advancing from the south to attack the infantry and guns that Bajee Rao had left behind at Solapoor. The remainder proceeded against the strong holds to the north of Poona. Brigadier-general Pritzler in person led back the troops of the reserve, and received on his route the submission of all the forts along the line of the Kishna, none of which offered the slightest resistance. Major Eldridge, of the Bombay European regiment, commanding the troops detached to the north, obtained possession, in the course of April, of Sheeoneer, or Jooneer, which had been evacuated, and of all the other forts south of the range that separates the sources of the Bheema from those of the Godavuree. Lieutenant-colonel M'Dowell, in the mean time, with a detachment from Brigadier-general Doveton's division, reduced the important forts of Unkye, Rajdeho, Dhoorup, and Trimbuk, which

* Brigadier-general Munro was not strong enough without this reinforcement, and though repeated requests had been addressed to the Madras government, not a single company was allowed to join him from within our provinces in that quarter : indeed, the march of a reinforcement, which the commanding officer took upon himself to furnish, was specially countermanded from the Presidency, on the plea of its being required to guard our own frontier; as if the destruction of the enemy were not its best possible defence.

gave to us the entire command of the valley of
the Godavuree, and a ready entrance into Kandês.
Captain Briggs, who had been placed in the political charge of the British interests in this quarter, in subordination to Mr. Elphinstone, the
supreme commissioner, now resolved to employ
the force of Lieutenant-colonel M'Dowell, though
consisting of only eleven hundred firelocks, in the
reduction of the Pêshwa's remaining possessions
in Kandês, from which object the pursuit of Bajee
Rao had necessarily diverted the Brigadier-general. The influence already possessed there,
from the occupation of all Holkur's late cessions,
gave us advantages that led Captain Briggs to
hope for success, notwithstanding his very inadequate means ; and the event justified the correctness of his calculations, although a temporary
check was experienced at Maleegâon, as will presently be mentioned.

Meanwhile, Brigadier-general Munro, having
advanced with the available portion of the reserve
under his command, and effected a junction with
Brigadier-general Pritzler, cleared the south country of several detached marauding parties, driving
them before him till he reached Solapoor, on the
9th of May. He there found the main body of
Bajee Rao's infantry, with eleven guns of his field
train, encamped under the walls, and the fort and
town strongly garrisoned with Arabs. On the

morning of the 10th, the Brigadier-general marched with all his brigades of infantry but one to the
north side of the place; and forming them into
two columns with a reserve, advanced for the purpose of carrying the *petta* by escalade. Besides
the fort, there was an inner and an outer petta; the
latter of these was soon in our possession, and a
lodgment was also effected in the wall of the inner
petta close to the fort. However, while this operation was going on within, Gunput Rao Panre,
the commandant of the infantry of the garrison,
brought a party round to the east of the fort, and
unexpectedly opened five guns on the troops left
in reserve with the artillery, consisting of six flank
companies. The fire was answered, though not
silenced, by ours; but, after carrying the petta,
Lieutenant-colonel Dalrymple, the commanding
officer of artillery, and the only field officer with
the reserve, perceiving the enemy to be in the act
of retiring his guns, led the companies of the reserve to the charge. In his advance he was
reinforced by Lieutenant-colonel Newal from the
petta, and succeeded in capturing three of the
guns, and driving the enemy back with considerable loss of men. Partial firing continued in
the petta; nor did the action cease till four P. M.,
at which time Brigadier-general Munro, observing
the infantry to be moving off in small parties
from the camp adjoining to the fort, ordered Bri-

gadier-general Pritzler in pursuit, with the cavalry attached to his force, consisting of not more than three troops of the 22d dragoons, and about four hundred irregulars. At the head of this small force, Brigadier-general Pritzler came up with the enemy a few miles from the town, and found him marching in pretty close column. The gallopers were opened, and one troop detached to the right, and another to the left, with orders to charge. The column was completely penetrated and broken, the dragoon officers judiciously restraining their men from using their pistols, until this first object had been fully accomplished. The infantry was then cut up in detail by the dragoons and irregulars, a duty in which the latter troops are in general particularly alert. The greater part of the fugitives threw away their arms and escaped; but considerable havoc was made amongst the Arabs, who disdained to secure their flight by such means. Gunput Rao had already been wounded in the attack on the reserve, and Veetul Punt, the second in command, killed on the same occasion. But Major de Pinto, a Portuguese officer, who had raised some battalions for Gokla, and had been actively engaged at Kirkee, was slain in this pursuit, together with more than eight hundred of the fugitives. The fort of Solapoor surrendered on the 15th of May, after one day's bombardment; and

with it all Bajee Rao's remaining artillery fell
into our hands, while the previous destruction of
his infantry left his cause entirely destitute of
adherents within his late dominions, except in the
garrisons of a few remaining forts in Kandês.
Of brigadier-general Munro's division, ninety-
seven were killed and wounded in the course of
these operations. The capture of thirty-seven
guns on the surrender of the place, most of them
in very serviceable condition, affords a fair cri-
terion of the importance of the success, and the
credit due to those who conducted the enterprise.

While Bajee Rao was thus hunted down, and
his country reduced by the several British divisions and detachments in the field, Lieutenant-
colonel Adams, having ascertained that the direction of the flight from Soonee was due west,
and that Brigadier-generals Doveton and Smith
were both hotly engaged in the pursuit, resolved
to lose no time in moving the force under his
command towards Chanda, in order to summon
that important fortress. He accordingly called
up the two 18-pounders, which had been directed
to follow him from Hôshungabad: and, having
obtained another of the Nizam's from Major Pitman at Umraotee, proceeded with this weak
train, and set himself down before Chanda on the
9th of May. The poisoning of the wells on his

approach indicated the Kiladar's determination
to hold out to the last extremity; nevertheless,
the Lieutenant-colonel forwarded a letter, containing the most moderate proposals, offering to
the garrison permission to march out with all
their private property and arms, and only requiring them to account for the treasure and
public property, which he was instructed to hold
in deposit for the successor of Apa Saheb. The
Kiladar not only sent no reply, but detained the
bearer of Colonel Adams' letter, and blew him
from the mouth of a gun in defiance, having the
utmost confidence of his ability to resist. The
place was so extensive, that the whole of the 10th
and 11th was occupied in reconnoitring * and
fixing upon the point of attack. Good ground
for the breaching battery was, however, found in
a *nala* about two hundred and fifty yards to the
south-east of the place. On the 13th, therefore,
the British camp was moved from the north-west
angle to the south of the fort, and a battery of
light guns made to play upon this face, in order
to divert the enemy's attention from the main
attack. This object was completely attained;

---

* A random shot from the last gun that was fired at the
reconnoitring party unfortunately killed Surgeon Anderson,
a valuable and much esteemed officer of the Bengal medical
establishment.

and the place having been invested at the same time to the north and west, the garrison, though it amounted to upwards of three thousand men, was kept in a state of constant alarm and uncertainty, and obliged to spread itself over the whole extent of the defences, instead of being concentrated on the single point of importance. The breaching battery opened on the morning of the 19th of April, from the ground originally selected for it. Before evening the breach was perfectly practicable; but the great extent of the works, and number of the garrison, made the Lieutenant-colonel averse to a night assault. Major Goreham, who commanded the artillery, undertook to prevent the garrison from throwing up any intrenchment or other defence behind the breach during the night; and the morning of next day, the 20th, was fixed for the storm. Lieutenant-colonel Scott, of the 1st battalion of the 1st Madras N. I., late the 1st of the 24th, the next in command to Colonel Adams, volunteered to lead the attack, and the utmost ardour and confidence were shown by the troops. Two squadrons of the 5th N. C. consented to dismount, and act with the light infantry battalion as a reserve. The place was carried in the course of the day, with the loss of eleven killed and fifty-one wounded on our part, while, of the enemy, Gungadeen the Kiladar was killed*, with at least five hundred of the garrison. No British officer was amongst the slain ; but Major Gore-ham, a most valuable officer of the Madras artillery, who had directed the operations of this arm during the siege, died of fatigue in the course of the day, and Captains Charlesworth and Watson, of the 1st battalion of the 1st Madras N. I., were wounded severely ; as were also Lieutenant Fell, of the Bengal Pioneers, and Lieutenant Casement, of the 1st battalion of the 19th Bengal N. I. Two other officers were also wounded, but very slightly. The storm of Chanda closed the campaign in the Bhoosla territory. Chouragurh had already been evacuated on the approach of Brigadier-general Watson, who was detached against it by Major-general Marshall, immediately after the capture of Mundela.

The division of Lieutenant-colonel Adams had now completed the object of its destination to the southward. As it was quietly returning to the cantonment at Hôshungabad, it was, however, attacked by the same fatal disorder, which, in the preceding November, had thinned the ranks of the centre division of the Bengal army. In a few days the casualties far exceeded what the troops

---

* He was wounded in a gateway near the breach, but knowing that he had no mercy to expect after what had passed, took poison immediately, and thus destroyed himself.

had suffered in the whole course of those military operations, in which they had borne so active a part. The symptoms and effects of the disease were precisely similar to those already described, when we had occasion before to mention it, and there is no need again to dwell upon them. Major-general Marshall's division also had experienced the destructive ravages of the pestilence in the course of the operations against Mundela; and no part of India, from the hills of Nipâl to Cape Comorin, escaped this dreadful visitation.

CHAPTER XX.

NAGPOOR—PÊSHWA, &c.

1818, MAY, JUNE, JULY.

Apa Saheb's exile — and escape — consequent measures—
Bajee Rao's designs—frustrated—He sends an agent to
Sir John Malcolm—is surrounded — negotiates—terms
offered—intentions of Governor-general — approach of
Brigadier-general Doveton—arrested—Bajee Rao submits
—terms—objections — Reflections — Dispersion of Bajee
Rao's army—Trimbukjee seized—Arabs refractory—General submission of the country—Review of Mr. Elphinstone's proceedings—their effect on the several classes of
the population—cultivating — religious — military—commercial—Arabs of Kandês—their expulsion resolved—
Siege of Maleegâon—vigorous sally—repulsed—Assault
fails—Reinforcements—bombardment—explosion of magazine—surrender of the place—mistake in the terms—Close
of the campaign.

PENDING the operations that terminated in the
rout of Soonee, Apa Saheb was held in close confinement at the Nagpoor Residency, along with
his two confidential ministers, Nagoo Punt and
Ramchundur Wâgh. The military defence of
the capital, in the expected event of the Pêshwa's
approach, was the object which at this time engrossed all the attention of the Resident. No

sooner was he relieved from apprehension for the
capital by the successful issue of this affair, and
the consequent dispersion of the Mahratta army,
than he selected from the troops at Nagpoor a
strong escort, for the conveyance of his prisoners to
a place of greater security within our own immediate provinces. A communication of the Governor-General's wishes in this respect had reached
the Resident, accompanied by an intimation, that
an old palace of the Moghul's, within the fort of
Allahabad, was every way the place best fitted
for the ex-Raja's accommodation and safe custody.
Accordingly, on the 3d of May, Apa Saheb, with
his two ministers, was conveyed from Nagpoor,
under charge of a wing of the 22d Bengal native
infantry, and three troops of the 8th native
cavalry, the whole under the conduct of Captain
Browne of the 22d, the same officer whose judgment had been conspicuous in the previous arrest
of the Raja in his palace. Arrangements had
been made to provide a fresh escort to take charge
of the prisoners from Jubulpoor onwards; and,
on the 12th of May, Captain Browne's detachment arrived at Rychoor, one march only from
that place. In the interim, however, the captive
Prince had not been idle. It is conjectured, that,
by the agency of a Brahmin, who accompanied
the party from Nagpoor for the first few marches,
then left them, on some pretext or other, to

make his arrangements, and afterwards rejoined on the 12th, a few of the Sepahees of the 22d Bengal native infantry were seduced from their duty; and that, partly by representation of the merit and glory of the act of assisting a Hindoo of the race of Sevagee in his distress, but chiefly by the profuse distribution of bribes, a conspiracy was formed amongst them to aid in effecting the ex-Raja's escape. Accordingly, about two o'clock in the morning of the 13th, a Sepahee's dress was introduced into the tent: Apa Saheb, thus accoutred, joined the guard; and, under semblance of a relief, marched without interruption completely out of the camp. Every precaution was taken to prevent an early discovery, so that he succeeded in getting clear off. Six Sepahees of the regiment deserted along with the prisoner, carrying with them their arms and accoutrements; and a few others followed the example in the course of the succeeding week. Indeed, it appeared, from circumstances which came out before the court-martial appointed for the trial of Captain Browne for neglect in suffering this escape, that several other men of the corps were deeply implicated in the conspiracy; and there was reason to suspect even a Soobadar to have been corrupted. Besides the Sepahees, Apa Saheb took with him only two of his personal attendants. He had left Nagpoor with upwards of a hundred in different capacities, most of whom were allowed unlimited access at all hours ; and, as it was a part of Captain Browne's instructions, to treat his prisoners with the utmost consideration that was consistent with their safe custody, he had not thought it necessary to restrict this intercourse, or to have an European officer on guard night and day over the deposed Raja: though, considering the character and importance of the prisoner, he ought perhaps to have taken that precaution.

Every thing in the tent was left in its usual place, insomuch, that the two servants, whose duty it was to handrub (*shampoe*) Apa Saheb as he slept, continued to perform the same office to the cushions of his bed ; and, when the guard was changed at four in the morning, the native officer, who, according to Captain Browne's standing orders, looked into the tent to ascertain the presence of the Raja, seeing them so engaged, was satisfied, and entertained not the least suspicion of his evasion. However, as soon as the escape was discovered, Captain Browne sent off parties of cavalry in every direction, and despatched expresses to Brigadier-general Watson and Lieutenant-colonel M'Morine, then engaged in the act of taking possession of Chouragurh, which was evacuated on the very same day. Information was also sent to Major O'Brien, the commandant at Jubulpoor, and to all the civil authorities. But

it was found impossible to trace the flight of Apa
Saheb in time to seize him, notwithstanding the
utmost exertion of despatch and vigilance in every
quarter.

Ere long it was ascertained that he had fled in
the first instance to Hurye, a place about forty
miles south-west of Rychoor, and thence to the
Mohadeo hills, where he was harboured and concealed by the Goands, and particularly by one
Chyn-Shah, a Raja of considerable influence
among them. By the close of the rains, he was
enabled to collect round his standard a few followers from the wreck of Bajee Rao's army, and
from among the fugitive Arabs driven out of
Kandês. With this band he gave considerable
trouble in the ensuing season : nor was the consequent disturbance of that part of the country
remedied, nor the rising in his favour entirely
subdued, until the capture of Aseergurh on the 9th
April 1819, gave the finishing stroke to the war.
But of this more hereafter.

The government of Nagpoor, immediately on
hearing of the escape, authorised the offer of a
reward of a lakh of rupees in cash, and a jageer of
10,000 rupees a year in land, for the re-apprehen-
sion of the fugitive. The reward in ready money
was afterwards doubled ; and it was for some
time hoped, that the notoriously venal disposition
of the Goands would have induced them to violate

the rights of hospitality; but in the end these hopes proved in this instance fallacious, and the whole force of Lieutenant-colonel Adams was consequently obliged to take the field. Neither Nagoo Punt nor Ramchundur Wâgh were parties to the escape; but both were safely conveyed to Jubulpoor, and thence forwarded to Allahabad, the place of their original destination. The escape of Apa Saheb at this juncture was particularly unfortunate, as it gave a new head to the turbulent and factious, whose minds might else have been reconciled to submission, if not by the example of their neighbours, at least by the total want of organization and of union that must have followed the loss of every leader of note and personal influence.

Bajee Rao had himself been reduced to extremity by the battle of Soonee, and was on the eve of throwing up the game. We have mentioned, that from Boree he turned northwards, directing his flight towards Hindoostan, in despair of being able to gain any thing by returning towards his late dominions. The faint reed on which he now leant his hopes, was the idea, that, in the event of his reaching the territory of Doulut Rao Sindheea, he might, either through that chief's mediation secure advantageous terms of reconciliation with the British, or, by drawing him into his measures, obtain the necessary accession of strength, without which all further struggle was utterly hopeless. The reputation of Sindheea's military power had always stood pre-eminent among the Mahratta states ; and, as he alone had survived the general crash of the late events, it was not unnatural for the fugitive head of the nation to look to it as a resource in his present desperate condition. Submission, however, was at this moment the primary object of his desire ; and, in token of his humiliation, he despatched agents both to Mr. Jenkins at Nagpoor and to the commissioner at Poona, to intimate his readiness to tender his personal surrender. Meanwhile, having crossed the Taptee on the 5th of May, just below its confluence with the Poorna, he proceeded down the valley as far as Chupara, with a view to penetrate into Hindoostan by the Sindwa Ghât and Indôr. At Chupara he discovered that this route was altogether closed against him by our possession of Sindwa, as well as by the judicious precautions already taken by Sir John Malcolm for defence of the line of the Nerbudda from Hindia downwards to Muheshwur. Equally baffled in this attempt, as he had been in his former design of reaching the Bhoosla dominions, he sent forward an agent to Sir John Malcolm, retiring himself eastward towards Boorhanpoor, in order to wait the result of his mission. It appeared as if he intended, in case of failure, to shut himself up in Aseergurh as his place of final refuge, or explore a more easterly route to Hindoostan, should any one seem to be practicable.

Every exertion had been made to provide against the possibility and danger of his penetrating to the north, and to overwhelm the adherents that still clung to his fortunes. There was fortunately at Hindia, besides the usual guard of that important post, a strong detachment of infantry, having under its escort the guns taken at Mehudpoor, and the hospital establishment and convalescents left there by Sir Thomas Hislop, and now on their way to the Dukhun. The presence of these troops afforded the means of forming a force of sufficient strength to advance upon Bajee Rao from the north-east, and either attack him on that side, or at least effectually shut up the Ghâts of the Sâtpoora range. Brigadier-general Malcolm also prepared to advance in person, with what troops he could collect, from the neighbourhood of Indôr to the north-west, while Brigadier-general Doveton was known to be approaching from the southward. Hence it seemed more than probable that the enemy would be again hemmed in, and give the opportunity of another affair as important as that of Soonee. Eastward of Hindia, the defence of the Nerbudda was confided to Brigadier-general Watson, who, after occupying Chouragurh, and affording Lieutenant-colonel

M'Morine a reinforcement to assist in the pursuit of Apa Saheb, had retired to Sâgur with the greater part of his force, in conformity with orders received direct from the Marquess of Hastings for his occupation of that post. In anticipation of the possibility of Bajee Rao's success in getting to the northward, before the above precautions should be in a sufficient state of forwardness to cut him off entirely from this line of retreat, the Marquess of Hastings, on the first alarm, instructed Sir David Ochterlony to be in readiness to throw his force between the enemy and Gwalior, and in that case to take upon himself the personal and supreme direction of all the operations. Such were the accumulated means, with which, if necessary, it was determined to crush the expiring efforts of the fugitive Pêshwa. That Prince, however, distracted at the operations that he saw about to close upon him on every side, remained irresolutely hovering about Aseergurh, where he was visited by Sindheea's Kiladar, Juswunt Rao Lar, who, during the whole of his stay in the neighbourhood, participated in all his counsels, and rendered every assistance in his power. Indeed, the reliance upon this resource and upon the shelter of the fortress in case of need, appears to have been a principal motive of his delay at Dhoolkôt, in that vicinity.

While Bajee Rao was thus wasting his time in

indecision, and allowing the British forces to draw a net completely round him, Anund Rao Juswunt, the agent who had been sent to Sir John Malcolm, reached the camp of that officer at Mow, a few miles from Indôr, late in the night of the 16th of May. The letter he brought from his master contained an appeal to the generosity of the British Government, and a spice of adulation to the general himself, whom, in a strain of Asiatic compliment, he protested he had been looking out for on every side, as one of his oldest and best friends, in order to solicit him to become the instrument of peace and reconciliation with the British. Particular allusion was made to the liberality with which conquests heretofore made from Holkur and Sindheea had been restored without equivalent or reason ; with an evident insinuation, that a similar degree of generosity in his own instance was expected or hoped to result from his choice of this channel of reconciliation.

Sir John Malcolm resolved at once to convert this communication, which really differed little in substance from what Mr. Elphinstone had been in the habit of receiving from the outset of the campaign, into a negotiation for surrender upon terms. The vakeel accordingly, finding the General in this mind, pressed him earnestly to advance to a personal conference with his master, for the purpose of discussing the terms and receiving his submission. This, however, was refused; but Sir John's first and second political assistants, Lieutenants Low and M'Dowell, were despatched along with Anund Rao, bearing the General's reply; and Lieutenant Low was instructed, if possible, to open a negotiation on the following basis: first, Bajee Rao to renounce all sovereignty in the Dukhun for himself and family for ever; secondly, not to return thither on any terms; thirdly, the surrender of Trimbukjee and all persons concerned in the hanging of the two Vaughans at Tulligâon on the first breaking out of the war. In the event of the Pêshwa's agreeing to these preliminaries, Lieutenant Low was to insist upon his immediately separating himself from Ram-Deen and other proscribed rebels or Pindarees that might be with his army, and advancing to meet the Brigadier-general, who, in such case, engaged to be the medium of an adjustment with the British Government, on the basis of personal security to the prince himself, and a liberal maintenance at such holy city, as he might select for his future residence. Protection from the attack of Brigadier-general Doveton, or any of the other divisions that threatened him, was not to be granted, except on compliance with the requisition to advance in the direction prescribed.

Sir John Malcolm had, in due course, been furnished with a copy of the Governor-general's instructions to Mr. Elphinstone, which had put him in possession of the outline of his Lordship's intentions with regard to the personal treatment of Bajee Rao, in case of his being reduced to surrender himself unconditionally ; and the terms which Lieutenant Low was directed to offer, were framed upon those instructions. Conceiving himself to be acting according to their spirit, the General did not think it necessary to wait the result of a reference for special orders in the present instance : nor indeed would the distance from his Lordship's quarters have allowed of such a reference. The Marquess of Hastings, however, immediately on hearing of the step taken by Sir John Malcolm, could not avoid expressing his apprehension, that the deputation of an officer for the avowed purpose of negotiation would have the effect of cramping the military operations of the several divisions, which it was particularly desirable to leave as free as possible to the last. It was evident that Bajee Rao could have but one motive of desire to submit, viz. the desperate posture of his affairs. Another rencontre with any of our divisions must necessarily complete his ruin ; consequently, any thing that embarrassed the military movements, besides impeding the grand object of annihilating the military power of the Mahratta sovereign, promised to give him a further advantage in the negotiation also, as it

must create an impression, that the basis of treaty
was not that of an individual resorting to us for
personal safety upon any terms that he could get,
but a bargain, founded upon views of a mutuality
of interest ; in other words, a compromise, in
which he was to receive value for his forbearance
to exert his remaining means of mischief and annoyance. His Lordship particularly deprecated
this construction being put upon the measure by
other powers : nor did he feel less anxiety, lest
the government should be committed in respect
to the place of the captive's future residence, wishing to have this left to his own selection, as well
as the fixation of the amount of the stipend for
the chief's permanent establishment, which he
declared his intention of limiting to two lakh of
rupees per annum. Instructions to this effect
were issued from Gourukpoor, whither the Governor-general had retired on the breaking up of the
centre division of the grand army. As had been
apprehended, the letter containing them did not
reach Sir John Malcolm until every thing was concluded ; but the event of Lieutenant Low's deputation proved the correctness of his Lordship's
anticipation of its effect upon the military
operations ; while the deviation from his wishes,
in respect to the other points, showed that his
anxiety was not without sufficient grounds.

The Lieutenant proceeded on the 18th of May,

in company with Anund Rao Juswunt, and reached Mundlisôr on the Nerbudda next day. He was here overtaken by fresh orders from the Brigadier-general (who had on the night of the 18th received advice of the escape of Apa Saheb), in obedience to which the Lieutenant stopped short himself, and sent forwards a Soobadar of the Madras cavalry, by name Seyud Husein Ulee, whom Sir John Malcolm had selected for his native aid-de-camp, and another native, together with the vakeels. The latter were made acquainted with the conditions on which their master was expected to advance and meet Sir John Malcolm ; and the Lieutenant himself followed by easy stages, expecting that, by the time he arrived in the neighbourhood, the mind of the prince would be prepared by their representations for submission. Bajee Rao had all this while remained at Dhoolkôt, five miles north of Aseergurh, where every day his alarm increased at the approach of Brigadier-general Doveton from the south. On the 25th of May, this officer arrived at Boorhanpoor, and was on the point of equipping a light force for the immediate attack of the enemy, when he received a letter from Lieutenant Low, dated the 23d of May, giving him the first intimation of the mission and of its result being still in suspense. Although the letter contained no positive request to suspend his further operations, yet Brigadier-general Doveton could not but see the desire of the negotiator, that time should be allowed to Bajee Rao : indeed it was mentioned, that Colonel Smith intended to halt at Bheekungâon to the north-west, until apprized of the result. The Brigadier-general accordingly deemed it right to remain at Boorhanpoor for the same purpose. In the mean time, Bajee Rao, though still undecided as to the acceptance of the conditions, was most earnest in the expression of his anxiety for the arrest of Brigadier-general Doveton's advance. This Seyud Husein Ulee reported to Lieutenant Low, who, upon his arrival at Bheekungâon on the 25th, inclosed to the Soobadar an absolute requisition on the Brigadier-general to delay his advance conditionally, in case Bajee Rao should have made. a movement, howsoever short, in the direction indicated. The Soobadar was not himself in Bajee Rao's camp when he received this despatch, but forwarded the letter with two troopers, to whom he gave similar directions. The Brigadier-general having previously upon his own judgment resolved to wait the result, the receipt of any absolute requisition became a matter of no importance ; but it might have been otherwise.

Up to the 30th of May, Bajee Rao continued in his position at Dhoolkôt, still equally irresolute. In the interim, however, Sir John Malcolm had brought down the force he had collected at Indôr, as far as Bheekungâon, where he found Lieutenant Low, together with the Pêshwa's vakeels, who had come the day before to press him to proceed to their master's camp, which he accordingly did by the order of the Brigadier-general. The troops from Hindia also had advanced to Peeplouda, while Brigadier-general Doveton still occupied Boorhanpoor. Being now, therefore, completely surrounded, Bajee Rao, on the 31st of May, sent Balooba, dewan of the Vinshorkur Jageerdar, to Sir John Malcolm, and agreed to a personal conference on the following day, at Kiree, a village on the plain about half a mile from the Ghât of that name in the Sâtpoora range. The meeting took place according to this appointment, at five p. m. of the 1st of June, Bajee Rao having come to Kiree for the purpose with all his family, and an escort of about two thousand five hundred horse and foot. In the conference that ensued, Sir John Malcolm recapitulated the terms that had before been communicated, and pressed the immediate surrender of Trimbukjee: but this was asserted to be impossible, as that chief had a separate camp of his own, and was in too great strength. Sir John then declared his intention to attack him forthwith, whereupon Bajee Rao replied he was welcome for his part, using the expression, " *Mobâ-ruk*," " Success attend you." He subsequently,

T 2

however, solicited time to recall some of his own
people from Trimbukjee's camp, a favour that
was perhaps incautiously granted, and thus most
probably the opportunity was taken of warning
Trimbukjee of his danger : for the attempt, when
subsequently made, proved abortive. The conference lasted till ten p. m. when the Pêshwa re-
ascended the Ghât, where he had some guns
placed to protect his retreat ; all the neighbouring
passes were lined with his Arab infantry. Sir
John Malcolm retired to his tent, and the same
night prepared a written note of the conditions,
and forwarded it the next morning to Bajee Rao.
They differed little from those before tendered by
Lieutenant Low, except in the omission of the
article for the surrender of Trimbukjee. It was
insisted, however, that his Highness should proceed to Hindoostan without the delay of a day,
and come to the British camp for the purpose
within twenty-four hours. At the same time, Sir
John Malcolm took upon himself to guarantee,
that the annual allowance to be assigned for the
future maintenance of his Highness should not
fall short of eight lakh of rupees per annum ; and
the written paper further declared, that if his
Highness, by prompt and full performance of the
terms, should evince his entire confidence in the
British government, his requests in favour of
jageerdars and adherents, who had been ruined

by their fidelity to his cause, should meet with liberal consideration; also, that his representations in favour of Brahmins and religious establishments founded or supported by his family, should be treated with attention. This article was subsequently explained, in respect to the jageerdars, to mean, that they should be received upon the same terms as had been accorded by Mr. Elphinstone to those who had tendered their submission after the rout of Soonee; viz. to retain any lands which belonged to their families in absolute property; but lose those they held by *surunjamee*, tenure of military service. In order to enforce compliance, or, in case of refusal, to proceed to attack the enemy's position, Brigadier-general Doveton was requested by letter to interpose, if possible, between his camp and Aseergurh, whither the Pèshwa had before conveyed a great part of his remaining valuables. Lieutenant-colonel Russel was also ordered to advance from his position at Bhoorgâon, and combine with that officer in an attack upon Trimbukjee.

At length, upon these conditions, after a fruitless attempt at further procrastination, Bajee Rao joined the camp of Sir John Malcolm on the 3d of June, at 11 a. m. The engagement, although not exactly according with his Lordship's views, was nevertheless confirmed and ratified by the Marquess of Hastings; and Bithoor, a place of

Hindoo pilgrimage, distant a few miles only from the large cantonment of Cawnpoor, was subsesequently fixed upon for the residence of the deposed and exiled prince.

The principal objection to this arrangement was, the extent of the personal allowance promised to his Highness, amounting to no less than 100,000*l*. a year for life. This was far beyond the probable amount of his personal expenditure in retirement, and it was feared might leave a surplus applicable to purposes of intrigue and mischief. Sir John Malcolm had been guided in the fixation of the stipend, by a recollection of the amount enjoyed by Umrit Rao, under the arrangement made with that chief, by the now Duke of Wellington. He thought there would be some insult, both to the prince and to the feelings of the Mahratta nation, in offering less to one, who had so long sat upon the guddee as his birthright, than was enjoyed, as the price of abdication, by a claimant by mere adoption. The cases, however, seemed to admit of little analogy; for Umrit Rao was a chief of powerful influence and numerous adherents, bought over in critical times, and at the outset of a war of doubtful issue. And, even in his case, the extent of the stipend had enabled the chief to entertain a large retinue, and create an influence of most pernicious tendency, necessary as the purchase may have been to the success of the operations of that period. Experience, therefore, was against entrusting similar means to the discretion of chiefs so circumstanced; and the ex-Pêshwa's proneness to intrigue was too notorious to admit of the hope, that, if possessed of the means, he would forbear to employ them.

On the other hand, there were circumstances which, in Sir John Malcolm's opinion, rendered the early surrender of Bajee Rao an object well worth the purchase. His troops were considerably refreshed after their halt, and had been succoured from the fort of Aseergurh so as to be able to renew their flight; and, although the principal roads were guarded by British divisions, it was, nevertheless, possible for him to elude their vigilance. Even, however, if this resource failed, another seemed open to the ex-Pêshwa; for the Kiladar of Aseergurh had already afforded shelter to the baggage and valuables; and his conduct, in furnishing guns and other stores, had shown his readiness to receive his fugitive prince within the cover of his walls, in case of extremity. The near approach of the rainy season, and the absence of the small battering train attached to Brigadier-general Doveton's division, which had been recently sent to Lieutenant-colonel M'Dowell, and was now employed before Maleegâon, made it impossible to undertake the siege this season; and even to invest it so closely as to prevent his per-

sonal entrance or exit, was, in the opinion of the
most experienced officers, impracticable during
the rains.   Again, the recent escape of Apa Saheb,
who had not been retaken, had shown the difficulty of tracing a fugitive, however illustrious or
important, in this wild and rugged tract, and
amongst a friendly population.   Independently,
however, of all these considerations, Sir John
Malcolm was influenced, as he acknowledged, by
a feeling of personal tenderness towards Bajee
Rao, and by a desire of conciliating his adherents,
instead of driving them to desperation.   Such a
course, he thought, would conduce to increase the
credit and reputation of his nation, clemency
and indulgence towards a fallen foe being virtues
of high name amongst the people of India.   It is
but fair to this officer to state these arguments in
favour of the policy by which he was actuated.
The question, however, remains, whether in the
first place personal considerations towards the
individual ought to have been allowed any weight
whatever ; and secondly, whether the disadvantages expected to result from Bajee Rao's remaining at large for a time with broken spirit and
broken fortune, may not have been overrated.
Had he not given himself up, he probably would
have joined Apa Saheb after sustaining another
rout similar to that of Soonee in escaping from
his then position ; and it is doubtful, whether the

two united would have given more trouble, or could have occasioned more expense, than resulted from the ex-Raja's being alone at large. They could never, with all their means, have made head against a British force of the strength of a battalion of infantry, or a regiment of cavalry ; nor could the country in which they must have taken refuge, afford subsistence for greater numbers than were actually cooped up in it with Apa Saheb; so that famine, a principal instrument as it was in the subsequent operations, would have proved a yet more powerful agent for us, had Bajee Rao likewise sought refuge in the same wilds.

Whatever opinion may be entertained of the terms granted, or of the manner of accomplishing the end, no one ever for a moment doubted that there were advantages resulting from the actual possession of the Pêshwa's person. The effect produced on the minds of the native population by his progress in the character of an exile and a prisoner through Malwa, was considerable ; but the knowledge of his present abject situation must necessarily have made even a greater impression on his late subjects in the Dukhun, and have contributed, in no small degree, to their rapid submission.

' Bajee Rao joined the British camp with a force of from four to five thousand horse, and about three thousand infantry, of whom twelve hundred were Arabs, whose numbers were afterwards increased to near two thousand, by the junction of detached parties left to guard the passes in the hills. The Vinshórkur and the widow of Gokla resolved to accompany their late master to Hindoostan. The remainder of his vassals either deserted him immediately upon his submission, or fell off one by one in the course of his march to the Nerbudda, whither he proceeded in company with Brigadier-general Malcolm's division. The General, though not altogether-satisfied with the continued presence of this lawless soldiery, was loth to disturb by harsh interference the last moments of intercourse between a fallen Prince and his yet faithful adherents ; and experience led him to expect that their numbers would gradually diminish on the march. It was not long before the mutinous spirit of these disorderly retainers, and their tumultuous demands for their arrears of pay, compelled the ex-Pêshwa to resort to the protection and friendly mediation of the British commander, who succeeded in satisfying and dismissing them after much trouble. From the banks of the Nerbudda, the captive proceeded with a train reduced to little more than six hundred horse and two hundred infantry, with whom he arrived at

Bithoor, where he still resides ; a British officer being assigned him as an honorary agent, and watch upon his conduct. He is under no further restraint, and amuses himself with making occasional pilgrimages to Mutra, and Bindrabun on the Jumna, when the cold season makes it unpleasant to perform those daily ablutions in the Ganges, which, as a Brahmin resident on its banks, he could not else avoid.

Ram-Deen, who had since the peace of Mundisôr deserted the standard of Holkur, under which he had borne a principal command, and joined the Pêshwa with the wreck of his army, submitted at the same time, upon a promise of pardon for his rebellion. Trimbukjee also was very solicitous to obtain terms ; but found the Brigadier-general inflexible in demanding his surrender as a prisoner, with a bare stipulation that his life should be spared, and some prospect of ultimate pardon at some future period, when tranquillity should have been completely restored. On these terms he refused to submit. Brigadier-general Doveton had, on the 3d of June, sent out a detachment to attack his camp ; but, as it had marched by a route leading under the walls of Aseergurh, and the Kiladar, though written to, refused a free passage, and opened his fire on the troops as they approached, the attack by that route was abandoned ; and, before arrangements, could be made to assail him by another road, he had disappeared with his followers.

Thus was the war in this quarter brought to a happy termination ; for neither Trimbukjee nor any other of the sirdars attempted again to rally the dispersed forces of Bajee Rao, or longer to keep the field.   A few Arabs, however, went off to the eastward in quest of Apa Saheb, and in their way possessed themselves of Mooltaya, after overpowering a detachment of two companies gallantly led against them by Captain Sparkes, as will presently be stated more at length.   The residue of the Mahratta host returned quietly to their homes ; among the rest Trimbukjee, who for some time endeavoured to secrete himself in the villages lately subject to his influence ; but Mr. Elphinstone succeeded in effecting his seizure in the course of the following month, when he was at first remanded to Tannah, the place of his former confinement, but ultimately brought round to Bengal, and lodged in the fort of Chunar, near Bunarus.   To inflict capital punishment on him was deemed an act of unjust and unnecessary rigour, as the escape was no aggravation of the original offence, for which he had only been sentenced to imprisonment for life.   Besides, the subsequent conduct of his then master had afforded pretty strong evidence of his participation in the Shastree's murder.

Throughout the whole of the late dominions of Bajee Rao, there was henceforward not one of his officers who ventured to keep the field in opposition to the British authority. The last vestige of open hostility had been destroyed in the affair of Solapoor. Neither was there, by the close of May, a single fortified place that still held out, excepting a few strong holds in Kandês, obstinately defended by the Arab garrisons. Rygurh, where Bajee Rao had placed his wife for safety, surrendered to Lieutenant-colonel Prother in the course of that month. The wife was treated with every possible consideration, and allowed one of the palaces of the deposed prince for her residence, until an opportunity offered of sending her to rejoin her husband at his place of exile.

The rapidity and apparent ease with which the British rule was established over a country of so much natural strength and difficulty, as that composing the late dominion of the Pêshwas, must excite astonishment in European readers ; more especially when the inimical spirit, testified by all ranks at the opening of the war, is taken into the account. Some of the causes which had produced this important revolution in the minds of the natives of India, have already been hinted at in the relation of the different events as they occurred, and the mode in which they were turned to advantage. It may be useful, however, to give in this place a general summary of the course of policy pursued by Mr. Elphinstone throughout the transactions we have now brought to a close, in order that the merit of his services may be more justly estimated.

At the time when Bajee Rao's concealed enmity broke forth into an open rupture, there was scarcely an individual, from one end of his dominions to the other, that did not confidently reckon upon our being driven entirely out of the country. Even our warmest well-wishers apprehended the probability of this result : consequently, either from hope or from fear, every one assumed the appearance of hostility. The two affairs of Poona, though they had helped to confirm the confidence of our own troops, were not sufficiently decisive to destroy the impression so universally entertained of our relative inferiority. The two succeeding months passed without yielding any more decisive occurrence ; and, though Bajee Rao was all the while little better than a fugitive, still, as that character accorded well enough with the policy and military habits of the Mahrattas, and as the enemy suffered no material loss, our superiority in the field was scarcely yet admitted.

While this feeling was still prevalent, Mr. Elphinstone received instructions to occupy the whole of Bajee Rao's dominions on behalf of the British authorities, and found himself nominated sole commissioner for the execution of this bold measure. Brigadier-general Munro, who had already begun to operate against the southern territories of the Pêshwa, was anxious to expedite the avowal of the intentions of the British government, thinking the assurance of never again experiencing the tyranny of Mahratta misrule would be of the best consequence. And doubtless, in that part of the country adjoining to our own frontier, where the people were in the habit of comparing their relative condition under the two governments, and were familiarised to the estimate of their relative strength, the step would have been attended with great advantage. Mr. Elphinstone, however, feared that our power was not yet sufficiently known and respected in the other and more remote quarters of Bajee Rao's dominions; and that, before the Mahratta population should have good cause to anticipate our ultimate success in the war, the national spirit would probably but take fire at the arrogant presumption of an open declaration of the design to assume the whole sovereignty to ourselves.

Impressed with this conviction, he determined to observe the utmost secrecy, until time and the march of events should have worked a revolution in the prevailing sentiment towards us. The first indication of our real views was exhibited on the fall of Sutara, when Mr. Elphinstone issued the manifesto noticed in the progress of the narrative; but the commissioner, in order more accurately to mark the effect that should be produced by this avowal of our intentions upon the minds of the Mahratta population, at first circulated his *exposé* with great caution, and affected to make the communication a matter of individual confidence. Even after the capture of that fortress, doubt as to the result of the war was still the prevalent feeling, and the explanation of our views was consequently listened to with comparative indifference. The Mahratta prince was still much too powerful for any class to divest itself of apprehension of the consequences of declaring against him, the more especially as he had already made several severe examples.

His defeat at Ashtee, accompanied as that disaster was by the death of Gokla, his only military commander of repute, and followed by the deliverance of the Sutara family, produced at once the desired change in the popular mind. The Pêshwa's approximate downfall was now universally predicted, and all not actively embarked with him looked upon his power as already extinct. The desire of his favour and the fear of his resentment were thenceforward alike discarded; and what was to follow on the establishment of our ascendancy, became the natural object of public curiosity. The manifesto was now sought for and read with avidity: copies were made and circulated by the natives of every class; and the declarations and assurances it contained became the general topic of conversation. This was exactly the disposition that the commissioner had desired to see excited; and he resolved to allow it full swing, in the confidence, that the terms of his *exposé* were calculated to satisfy all ranks of life, and that his own reputation, and that of the government he served, would prevent the least doubt being entertained of its sincerity. The event proved how well this was judged : the immunities held out gave contentment to every one, and the resolution to submit was cheerfully and promptly embraced. The rapidity of our subsequent successes was at once the cause and the effect of the rapid diffusion of this sentiment, for no sooner did the people feel that on one hand nothing could stand against our power, but on the other it was safe to rely on our faith, than they shaped their conduct with a view to the early attainment of this security.

Borne along by the impulse thus excited, the British influence and authority spread over the land with magical celerity. Applications to be received within the pale of our dominion came pouring in faster than civil officers could be provided for the administration of the districts that sued for our sway, and long before the means of military protection could be furnished from our inadequate regular establishments. The most impregnable holds opened their gates as we have already seen, and not unfrequently before they were summoned : nor could the casual possessors urge any claim to consideration for the early surrender, since the submission was so general. It was the commissioner's peculiar merit to have taken advantage of the precise moment, when the tide of popular feeling, which flowed strong against him at the opening of the campaign, had expended its force, and to have made such use of the reflux, as to arrive at the point of his hopes before it had again reached the flood. It will be necessary to trace more minutely the effect of the commissioner's measures on the several classes of Mahratta society, all of which he ultimately succeeded in reconciling to the new form of government.

In India, the terms rent and revenue are so nearly synonimous, that the distinction of payers and receivers of revenue affords a pretty complete classification of the mass of population. The former class throughout the Pêshwa's dominions, though Hindoos by race and in religious tenets, were very partially of the Mahratta nation ; and even where they were so, still as all had equally experienced that most odious form of fiscal extortion, the farming system under the administration of Brahmins* and Mahrattas, they needed only the assurance of future protection to throw off at once the yoke under which they groaned. To change it for any that promised to be lighter, was to them a most desirable occurrence.   Mr. Elphinstone's proclamation gave to this class the guarantee of a direct resort on all occasions to British officers, together with the promise of remissions of tribute on account of military ravage, of protection and equal justice for the future, and, what was a greater boon than all, it contained a guarantee that they should never again be delivered over to Mahratta pillage or extortion.   The effect of these assurances was perceptible in the immediate change of demeanor in the cultivating class, who had no sooner lost all apprehension from the vengeance of Bajee Rao than they with-

* It has frequently been remarked, that a Hindoo is always a more avaricious and pitiless extortioner than a Moosulman. Great subtleness, unwearied patience, and a never satiated desire of accumulation, distinguish the Hindoo all over India; while there is a love of ease and a heedlessness of the future, which give a liberal cast to the character of the Moosulman.   The latter also is fond of popularity, and frequently regards name beyond wealth.

held the revenue from his delegates, expelled his officers, and voluntarily brought the rents and produce of their villages and towns into the British treasuries.

To give confidence and contentment to the payers of revenue, was thus perhaps the easiest part of the commissioner's duties. It was a far more difficult task to procure a recognition of the new order of things from those who enjoyed the benefits of the existing system—men of large hopes and expectations, whose wealth, influence, and education placed superior means of obstruction at their disposal. The receivers of revenue or rent were of two classes; the religious, which, under the Brahminical government of the Pêshwas, had engrossed vast possessions, considerably increased of late, in consequence of the superstitious personal character of the prince; and the military and official, at the head of which stood the jageerdars and ancient Mahratta families.

To conciliate the religious orders was a very material object. Accordingly, the commissioner's manifesto expressly set forth the murder of Gungadhur Shastree, a Brahmin of the highest caste, as the original cause of the breach that had taken place between the British government and the Mahratta sovereign; it besides held out a distinct assurance, that all existing establishments for religious purposes should be maintained, and all endowments, grants, or assignments made before the war, be held inviolate. To increase the effect of these public pròfessions, Mr. Elphinstone took the earliest opportunity, after the battle of Ashtee, to repair in person to Wye, a place of high repute for Hindoo sanctity, whither the principal Brahmins and several moderate men, who desired to stand aloof from the contest, were known to have retired. There he convoked a general assembly, and repeated verbally before them the assurances contained in his *exposé*, so as to leave all minds satisfied of the sincerity of the intentions of the British Government towards them, and content with the concessions made to the interest of the religious orders. A similar meeting was afterwards convened for the same purpose at Poona; and both there and at Wye presents were distributed with a liberality, which was intended as some sort of compensation to the class for the loss of that indiscriminate bounty, with which the Pêshwas were wont to lavish gifts and largesses upon them at festivals and on other occasions of rejoicing. The present expense of this measure was doubtless considerable; but it produced a favourable disposition, or at least served to stifle the jealousy of a powerful body, whose neutrality more than repaid the sacrifice.

The military and official class, which can hardly be considered separately in a Mahratta community, had, in the shape of jageers and military tenures, appropriated upwards of one half of the ordinary revenue of the whole territory. For the most part the jageerdars had proved milder masters than the Pêshwa's fiscal officers and farmers, and their possessions lay in the country peopled by indigenous Mahrattas, amongst whom they had acquired a considerable ascendancy, and enjoyed much popularity. It yet remained, therefore, to reconcile this important body to the new order of things.

The re-establishment of the Sutara Raja, in the very seat of the ancient power and splendour of his race, was well adapted to reconcile the older Mahratta families to the annihilation of the more recent title and authority of Pêshwa. It had the further effect of rendering the cause of Bajee Rao rather a personal than a national one ; more especially as the commissioner's manifesto contained the promise to all, who might submit within two months of its date,* of enjoying in perpetuity, under British guarantee, whatever lands they might at the time be possessed of. No one could doubt the sincerity of the assurance ; consequently the great families very soon saw, that they had themselves nothing at stake, so they did but

* 12th of February. The term expired five days before the rout of Soonee.

stand aloof or withdraw from the scene of action, while Bajee Rao on one hand, and the British on the other, were contending for the mastery· There were amongst the jageerdars, it is to be recollected, many who were indebted to the very guarantee now proffered for what they actually held, and none but what were well able to appreciate the value of the offer, and to set the superior security of property it afforded in comparison with the capricious duration of a despot's favour.   To these motives are to be referred the frequent submissions of the great families, that we have had occasion to record as having been tendered immediately after the battle of Ashtee.   The fear of forfeiting their lands to the victors then began to exceed their apprehension of Bajee Rao's vengeance, and quickened the determination of the generality.   But the indigent of the military class were not to be won over by the same motives ; for they had nothing to lose.   Many of the old families, too, from pride or from principle, resolved still to share the fortunes of their prince.   Wherefore, until the spirit of military adventure should have been subdued by a more lively fear than had yet been created, nothing could be hoped, while every thing was to be apprehended from the jealousy, with which it was natural the new order of things should be regarded by those who suffered in the change.   This object was fortunately ac-

complished to the utmost extent that could be
desired, by the result of the two affairs of Soonee
and Solapoor.   The fugitives from both returned
humbled to their homes, and showed in all their
acts, that their minds were prepared for ever to
abandon their calling with all its ambitious hopes
and vicissitudes, or to be content with the moderate provision allotted to those who accepted
employment in our Sebundee establishment.   As
an act of policy, the levies of men for this force
were carried to a considerable extent, in order to
furnish the means of livelihood to many that must
else have been left wholly destitute.   Nor, indeed,
could their services have been well dispensed
with ; for the regular army was unequal even to
furnish garrisons for the forts reduced, much less
was it in a condition to provide detachments for
the duties of internal administration.   By de-
nouncing and rigorously enforcing the penalty of
instant military execution on all persons guilty of
plundering on their return, and at the same time
by declaring every one's home to be a secure
retreat to such as sought it with peaceable intentions, the late dominions of the Pêshwa were,
immediately on their subjugation, preserved in as
perfect tranquillity, as in a season of profound
peace.   No small credit is due for the complete
attainment of this object, considering the vast
influx of military rabble, that followed the rout of

the Mahratta army at Soonee, and the distressed circumstances in which all returned from the field. Previous orders had been issued to note the names of all who came back, but to leave them unmolested, unless guilty of excess; and proclamation had been made to the same effect. Thus, for their own security, it became a matter of scrupulous caution with the fugitives, to avoid rendering themselves obnoxious to the penalty. It deserves to be recorded, that a comparison of the excesses, which followed the dissolution of the Pêshwa's tumultuous host, and the extinction of his dynasty, with those incident to a large and sudden reduction of the troops of an European state, on the conclusion of a peace or other similar occasion, would have exhibited a result in favour of the Indian executive.

Such were the measures adopted for the reclamation of the military classes; and their minds had been so impressed with awe, as well by the forecast of arrangement with which they had found themselves encountered at every step, as by the astonishing successes obtained from them by mere handfuls of disciplined troops, that, even before the knowledge of Bajee Rao's personal submission, the most sanguine and presumptuous had become sensible of the impotence of their utmost efforts, and were well prepared to take the law from our dictation.

Of the mercantile class, as forming a distinct interest and a constituent part of the population of Bajee Rao's dominions, we have taken no account, because in fact the *bunceas* of India, though many of them absolutely rolling in wealth, are rather a despised caste, little remarkable for public spirit on any occasion, occupied in the exclusive pursuit of sordid and selfish gain, possessed of no influence beyond the walls of the populous towns, and even there generally subservient to the government of the passing hour. The security of property and of public credit, universally attendant on the introduction of the British authority, probably made them rather wish for our establishment, and secured their limited good offices in our favour ; but Bajee Rao also had a strong party amongst them ; as indeed might any one else have had, who possessed but the means of purchasing their services.*

These details of Mr. Elphinstone's general plan for the settlement of the conquered dominions of the Pêshwa, have a very partial application to the province of Kandês. The greater part of this district had been usurped by Arab colonists, who

---

* If ever they rise to consequence, it is when the avarice or poverty of the native princes induces them to assign their revenues for a present supply, a course from which Bajee Rao always kept himself free, influenced probably by the example of the Sindhœa, the Holkur, and several other families which had been ruined by this means.

could hardly be expected to be influenced by the motives of submission, that had operated so extensively upon the Mahratta inhabitants. Fortunately, the Arabs had proved tyrants in the exercise of their usurped authority, and the body of the people were consequently desirous of shaking them off; at the same time, they were not sufficiently numerous to hope successfully to cope single handed with the British power. The condition of submission offered by our policy was, however, nothing short of re-transportation to their native wilds of Arabia; and, as this involved the sacrifice at once of all their past acquisitions, and of all their future prospects, the intrusive race was driven to desperation, and resolved to defend their possession to the last. The Arabs of Kandês were undoubtedly no better than lawless buccaneers, equally incapable of regular military discipline, or of systematic political subordination; their expulsion was therefore a matter of absolute necessity. Accordingly, Captain Briggs, when he commenced the work of reducing the province, declared by proclamation, that such were the only terms upon which the military of the Arab nation could be allowed to capitulate. He offered, however, that the British Government should be at the expense of their transport back to Arabia, and of discharging any actual arrears of pay.

With these views towards the intrusive Arabs,

though guided in respect to the rest of the population by the principles so successfully acted upon by Mr. Elphinstone in other parts of Bajee Rao's dominions, the subjugation of Kandês was undertaken about the middle of May. As the divisions of Brigadier-generals Doveton and Smith were then both employed in the pursuit of Bajee Rao, Lieutenant-colonel M'Dowell's force of about eleven hundred firelocks, and the garrisons of Talnèr and Sindwa, were the only regular troops immediately applicable to the service. The Arabs had concentrated their force at Maleegâon, a fort of more than ordinary strength ; and Captain Briggs, conceiving that he had established an understanding with part of the garrison through Raja Bahadur, (jageerdar of the place, before its forcible occupation by the Arabs, but now held by them in a kind of thraldom,) resolved to make his first attack upon this point. On the 15th of May, Lieutenant-colonel M'Dowell approached within five miles of Maleegâon ; Raja Bahadur now represented that the Arabs in the fort were well disposed, and desired the aid of our troops to overawe those in the Petta, for which purpose he pointed out a position between the two for the detachment to occupy. Captain Briggs was inclined to place confidence in these professions of the Raja ; but Lieutenant-colonel M'Dowell suggested, that, before taking up so hazardous a position, the fidelity of the garrison in the fort should be put to the test, by demanding the admission of a few companies of our troops. The demand was made, and rejected with scorn; as was also the offer of arrears, together with an advance for subsistence until such time as the Arabs might reach their native country. Indeed, it was soon found, that preparations had been made for a most obstinate defence, and that the siege would require the utmost exertion of courage as well as science to ensure success.

The engineers broke ground at night-fall on the 18th of May, Lieutenant-colonel M‘Dowell having disposed two-thirds of his force in working and covering parties, in the hope of completing two batteries in the course of the night. The arrangements for this purpose were, however, no sooner completed, than a vigorous sally was made from the fort. Maleegâon is situated on the Moosee, just above its confluence with the Gyrna. The ground chosen by the engineers was on the opposite bank of the Moosee, and Lieutenant-colonel M‘Dowell gave orders to his covering parties, not to fire a shot until the enemy should have crossed the river. Immediately, therefore, that the firing began, Colonel M‘Dowell, perceiving the determined nature of the attack, ordered down the whole of the troops that remained in camp to support the covering parties.

Major Andrews, with a few men of the Madras European regiment, was the first to arrive on the scene of action. He found the Arabs within twenty paces of the working party, driving our advanced posts in before them. He was fortunate in being able to check their further progress, and ultimately to rally the covering parties and drive the enemy back with considerable loss : the Major, however, himself received a shot through the shoulder ; while Lieutenant Davis, the senior engineer, who hastened forward on the alarm with a party from the trenches, was shot dead by the Arabs in their retreat. In him the service lost one of the most distinguished officers of the Madras establishment : though young in rank, he had seen more desperate service than had fallen to the lot of most colonels.* The besiegers had altogether twenty-one killed and wounded by this sally, chiefly of the European regiment. Notwithstanding this attempt to interrupt their operations, the work was completed according to the original intention ; and, in the course of the

---

* He had accompanied Lieutenant-colonel Gillespie into the fort of Vellore during the mutiny there, and was particularly distinguished for the cool intrepidity with which, from the top of the gateway, he let fall a plummet, to ascertain the exact situation of the fastening, in order to be sure of the direction of his fire, when the galloper should arrive with which it was intended to blow open the gate.

night, two batteries were thrown up within five hundred yards of the fort.

However, after this sample of the opposition he was to expect, Lieutenant-colonel M'Dowell summoned to his aid every reinforcement he could procure, and thus collected from different quarters about six hundred more infantry, and five hundred irregular horse from Hindoostan, who joined before the 23d of May. By the 28th of the month, the breach in the curtain of the fort appeared to be practicable, and the defence, as well of the rampart as of a *fausse-braye* at its foot, seemed for the most part to be destroyed. At the same time, Lieutenant-colonel M'Dowell found ~his ammunition on the point of failing, which determined him to try the chance of an assault. The exact nature of the defences of the ditch and those of the covered way beyond it was not known; but all that was visible above the glacis had been levelled by our fire. Under these circumstances, a few remaining shells, that had been especially reserved to the last for this purpose, were thrown in to clear the breach, and the troops advanced to the assault at daybreak on the 29th of May. They were led by the surviving engineer officer, Ensign Nattes, followed by a party of sappers and miners, each carrying a bundle of wet grass to fill up the ditch if necessary. On arriving at the verge of the outwork beyond the 'ditch, it was found, that the rubbish of a low wall that had stood there had carefully been removed, and that beyond it the Arabs had dug a trench so deep, that it was impossible to descend from the glacis. Ensign Nattes was killed on its verge, while in the act of pronouncing the word " impracticable." The troops were, however, unwilling to desist; but Lieutenant-colonel M'Dowell, finding that the breach had further been cut off from the works on either side, and that loopholed traverses had been erected to bear right upon it from within, while the trench above-described made the attempt to pass forward hopeless, recalled the storming party; but not till Major Greenhill, the officer in command, and three other officers, had been wounded, and the engineer above-mentioned killed. A simultaneous attack, made on the petta by a party led by Lieutenant-colonel Matthew Stewart, was completely successful, the place being carried sword in hand.

Upon this failure, Lieutenant-colonel M'Dowell, having expended all his ammunition, and being determined nevertheless not to move from before the place till its fall, turned the siege into a blockade, and solicited further reinforcements, especially of artillery, from all quarters.

Brigadier-general Smith had by this time returned to Seroor, with the greater part of the light force he had carried eastward in pursuit of Bajee Rao. He immediately ordered off an additional train and a fresh supply of stores from the depôt at Ahmednugur, accompanied by a strong reinforcement of Europeans, and a native battalion, the whole under the command of Major Watson. The convoy arrived on the 9th of June, up to which date little had been done since the failure of the assault, except that three mines had been commenced from the Petta; but, as the fort was built on a rock foundation, that plan of attack was abandoned. By the 11th of June, a battery of five heavy mortars and four howitzers was completed, and opened its fire at day-break. The besiegers had discovered the situation of the principal magazine; and in the course of the day, upwards of three hundred shells were thrown principally in that direction, by which means it was at length fired, and exploded with a tremendous crash, blowing about thirty feet of the curtain outwards into the ditch, and at the same destroying and wounding many of the garrison.

The Arabs now found their situation hopeless. Fearing that a longer resistance would bring on them a similar fate to what their comrades had met with at Talnér, they sent two jemadars on the morning of the 12th of June, to ask on what terms they would be admitted to surrender. Lieutenant-colonel M'Dowell replied, at discretion, for other terms could not now be granted. The jemadars returned; and, on the morning of the 13th, Ubdool Kadir, the principal of the Arab chiefs, came out and declared, that the garrison were prepared to surrender at discretion, but urgently solicited a written assurance that their lives should be spared. These freebooters had no accurate conception of the meaning attached, by the usages of European warfare, to the term surrender at discretion; and the recent occurrence at Talnér had made them yet more suspicious and distrustful than before. Lieutenant-colonel M'Dowell, therefore, out of consideration for this feeling, declared his readiness to give the written assurance of their lives being safe; and, in order further to encourage them, engaged that they should be well treated. By some mistake, however, the Mahratta moonshee, who received orders to write a letter to this effect, used expressions capable of a much more extensive interpretation than was intended; promising to do "whatever was most advantageous for the garrison; that letters should be written regarding the pay; that the British government should be at the expense of feeding and recovering the sick; and that the Arabs should not want any thing till they reached-the places where they wished to go:" this latter expression being a mistake for "where it was intended to send them." Ubdool

Kadir, having obtained this written paper, marched out on the morning of the 14th with the survivors of the garrison, three hundred Arabs and
about sixty Hindoostanees, when the whole laid
down their arms on the glacis, and surrendered
themselves prisoners of war. The Lieutenant-
colonel now wished to transfer his prisoners to the
political agent, Captain Briggs, with a view to
their transportation back to their native country;
but that officer, conceiving the terms of the written
letter not to warrant such treatment of the garrison, declined to take charge of them. Colonel
M'Dowell declared the letter to have conveyed a
mere assurance of clemency after compliance with
his terms, which were, surrender at discretion;
that, consequently, it ought not and was never
intended to limit the right of disposing of the
prisoners according to the original conditions.
The point was, however, referred to Mr. Elphinstone, who determined to allow the Arabs the
utmost advantage they could be entitled to, by
the most favourable construction of the terms of
the letter; and, as there was a kind of promise
of good offices for the recovery of the pay due to
the garrison, as well as an expression admitting
of a construction, that they were to go where they
wished, he ordered the whole arrears to be paid
up to them from the government treasury, and
that they should immediately be released, and

furnished with a safe conduct, and money to supply their wants, till they reached any place.they
might prefer to retire to.

The capture of Maleegâon was the last operation of any consequence in the territories of Bajee
Rao. Umulnêr, the only place that held out,
afterwards was reduced on the last day of the following November. The rest of Kandês submitted
with little resistance ; and the disposition of troops
for the maintenance of order, and for the immediate
punishment of any insurrectionary attempt or other
interruption of the public tranquillity, became
the only remaining requisite for. the complete settlement of the country. The province of Kandês
continued, however, for some time to be the scene
of more disturbance than was experienced in other
parts of the Pêshwa's late dominions; which was
partly owing to the clashing of the various Mahratta authorities anterior to the establishment of
our influence, which had brought the province to
the lowest possible pitch of disorganization, and
partly to Sindheea's continued retention of his
former interest within it.

CHAPTER XXI.

NAGPOOR—ASEERGURH.

July 1818, to April 1819.

Apa Saheb makes head in the Mohadeo hills—joined by Arabs—Captain Sparkes and detachment cut off—Majors Macpherson and Cumming sent—affair at Mooltye—Arabs expelled—sundry affairs with Arabs and Goands in Sept.— Intrigues—operations eastward—Kumpta—Pownee and Ambagurh—Chouragurh attacked by Chyn Sah—Colonel Adams moves into the hills—Apa Saheb expelled—surprise of Chyn Sah, and submission of the Goands—pursuit of Apa Saheb—his escape to Aseergurh—conduct of the Kiladar—fort besieged—its surrender—discovery of Sindheea's duplicity—reasons for retaining Aseergurh—close of the campaign.

It has been stated that Apa Saheb, after his escape from Captain Browne, made for the Mohadeo hills, where he was harboured by the Goand chiefs, and where the Arabs, and loose military of Kandês, and of Bajee Rao's late army sought him out as a leader fitted for their views.

A party of these Arabs were heard of on the. 18th July, 1818, by Captain Sparkes, who was with a small detachment at Bytool, in civil charge of that portion of the territory ceded by Apa Saheb in the preceding January. This officer immediately got together all the troops he could collect, and set off in quest of the intruders. His force consisted of one hundred and seven men of the 2d battalion 10th Bengal native infantry ; and, on the 20th July, on crossing the Taptee, he fell in with the enemy, but found their numbers much larger than his intelligence had led him to expect. He took up in haste the first position that offered, but was surrounded and attacked on all sides by both infantry and cavalry. The post was, nevertheless, made good for some hours, until, having lost half his men, and fired away nearly all his ammunition, Captain Sparkes saw his situation to be desperate, and was induced to display a white flag in the hope of saving the lives of the survivors by negotiation. The signal was wholly disregarded, and served rather to exasperate than to mitigate the ferocity of the enemy. As a last effort, Captain Sparkes resolved to attempt to gain a more defensible eminence at a little distance from his first position, and moved towards it, but on his way was shot dead. The sepahees felt that they had no quarter to expect, and consequently fought on to the last under their native officers, amongst whom a soobadar is mentioned to have been particularly distinguished for desperate valour, until overpowered and slain. Their courage, however, was of little avail, for the enemy, soon after the death of Captain Sparkes, broke in upon the detachment, and cut the whole to pieces, with the exception of nine men left in the rear in charge of the baggage.

After this success, the Arabs took possession of Mooltye, and other places in the Bytool valley, and began exacting the revenue, and levying contributions in the neighbourhood. At Shahpoor, a village between Hoshungabad and Bytool, they surprised and put to death another party of eighteen sepahees, and plundered the place. They also opened a communication with Apa Saheb and the Goands of the Mohadeo hills, and professed to act with the ex-Raja's authority.

Lieutenant-colonel Adams had recently returned to Hoshungabad, when he heard of these transactions. Well knowing the importance, indeed the absolute necessity of nipping in the germ the growing spirit thus excited, he immediately sent a strong detachment of cavalry and infantry under Major M'Pherson, of the second battalion 10th native infantry, to expel the Arabs from the Bytool valley, and revenge the death of the officer and men so cruelly butchered on the 20th July. A second detachment followed two days after, under Captain Newton, with some field artillery; and the force of the enemy being stated to be rapidly on the increase, a further reinforcement, including a second squadron of native cavalry, and some horse artillery, was detached under Major Cumming, of the seventh native cavalry.* The rains had set in with peculiar violence, which rendered these operations the most distressing the troops had yet been engaged in ; nevertheless, they bore their fatigues without a murmur, and in a series of affairs, scarcely of sufficient importance to merit separate detail, effectually revenged the death of their comrades, and drove the Arabs from the cultivated country into the fastnesses of the neighbouring hills and junguls.

Mooltye was the only place at which a stand was attempted : Major Cumming having advanced to Sykura, about six cos distant, sent a troop to reconnoitre their position there on the 16th August. Captain Ker, of the seventh native cavalry, a most meritorious officer, who afterwards fell a victim to the climate, commanded this reconnoisance, and having effected it, contrived, by feigning a retreat, to draw a party of the enemy's cavalry from the town, which he effectually cut up before he retired. On the 20th August, Major Cumming and Major M'Pherson appeared before

* This regiment had relieved the 5th native cavalry immediately on the return of the division to Hoshungabad. The 6th native cavalry had similarly been relieved by the 8th native cavalry.

the place, but found their troops insufficient to invest it closely; at the same time the number of the garrison, and their known character for desperate bravery made these officers determine not to risk a hasty assault. They accordingly sat down before Mooltye, until the means of undertaking a regular siege should be forwarded from Hoshungabad. Colonel Adams, on hearing of this state of things, resolved to take the field with the entire subsidiary force, to reduce this place; but just as he was preparing to carry this resolution into effect, he was informed of its evacuation, which took place on the night of the 22d of August. The want of supplies was the motive for abandoning Mooltye, which was else of a strength to have given much trouble. The garrison separated, and made for the junguls and hills of Mohadeo, in small parties. Captain Newton, who was sent out with one detachment in pursuit, fell in with about three hundred and fifty horse and foot, at day-break on the 24th August, and entirely routed them, destroying more than half the number. Another party was similarly cut up by a detachment sent out in a different direction, under the command of Captain Ker, and for some time after nothing was heard of an enemy in the valley or its immediate neighbourhood.

Early in September a detachment of Madras troops arrived at Bytool, under the command of

Major, afterwards Lieutenant-colonel Munt,* who took the command as senior officer. In the beginning of that month Captain Jones, of the 7th Bengal cavalry, attacked a party of Arabs, who had taken post at Umla. They defended themselves with much bravery during the day, but evacuated the place in the night. On the 18th of the same month, a Madras detachment, under Major Bowen, proceeded from Umla to the attack of Boordye, which was carried with a considerable slaughter of Arabs and Goands, and both these villages were thenceforward occupied as posts of observation. On the 20th of September, Lieutenant Cruickshanks, of the 24th battalion of Bengal N. I. but doing duty with the 2d bat. of the 10th, surprised Dajee, an Arab chief, and Gubha, a leader of Goands, who had ventured out of their fastnesses, in the neighbourhood of Raneepoor. The same officer, with Captain Newton, continued in the field till the close of September, and effected three further surprises on parties of Goands in the hills about Aseer, in one of which a chief of the name of Kulloo was slain. The result of all these affairs was the confinement of the enemy to the central fastnesses most difficult of access, viz. those about Puchmurree and Deo-

* Major Munt was directed on Mooltye by Brigadier-general Deveton, on receipt of the first intelligence of the death of Captain Sparkes.

gurh, which being places of some strength, could not be attacked until the favourable season should allow of a considerable force being carried into the hills with a proper train and equipments.

In the mean time, Apa Saheb was exerting all his influence to raise up fresh enemies against the British power, and to make levies of men and money in all quarters. His agents were discovered to be at work at Oojein and Boorhanpoor, two of Sindheea's principal towns; and besides an active correspondence by letter with Juswunt Rao' Lar, the Kiladar of Aseergurh, several interviews were ascertained to have been contrived by the Kiladar, as well with Apa Saheb himself as with the Pindara Cheetoo, who had become the ex-Raja's confidential adviser.

Intrigues were likewise discovered at Nagpoor, and several individuals, amongst others some members of the family of one of Apa Saheb's wives, were in consequence placed under restraint. Notwithstanding these precautions, however, the strong country east of that capital was raised in insurrection by the influence of a man of the name of Chimna Potêl, who openly declared for the ex-Raja. Against this chief and his associates amongst the jungul Rajas of the tract, a detachment took the field in August, and was out during the whole of the rainy month of September, reducing Kumpta and the strong holds of the Lanjhee hills. On the 7th of October, a more considerable detachment was sent out, under Major Wilson, for the reduction of Pownee and Ambagurh to the south-east, where the standard of rebellion had similarly been unfurled. The Major obtained great credit for the effectual and soldier-like manner in which this important service was accomplished ; and were it our purpose to exhibit the achievements of distinguished officers, instead of a connected political history of the period, the details of some of these affairs would occupy a very conspicuous place ; as it is, they must give way to matters of more direct influence on the general result.

Such reiterated successes, achieved under the worst possible disadvantages of season and situation, produced either by their direct effect, or by the influence of their example, the entire and rapid submission of the country, so that by the close of the rains, that is towards the end of October, the Mohadeo hills, where Apa Saheb had personally found refuge, formed the only tract which still held out. Stations of cavalry and infantry had been established all round these hills, and Colonel Adams waited only for the drying up of the waters in the cold season of the year, to put in execution a combined operation for sweeping the tract in three divisions, so as effectually to quell the insurrection. While he was preparing for this enterprize, Chyn Sah, the principal Goand chief in rebellion, made a bold attempt to recover the fort of Chouragurh for Apa Saheb. This strong hold had, since its reduction in the preceding May, been occupied by a garrison under an European officer; but in October, the place was found so very unhealthy, that Colonel M'Morine urged the advantage of dismantling and leaving it, or at all events, of withdrawing the regular troops. Colonel Adams having referred the point to Nagpoor, obtained through the Resident the sanction of that government to adopt this plan so soon as the projected operations against the Goands should be completed. Accordingly, as a preliminary step to a final evacuation, the regular sepahees were withdrawn, and a party of sebundees left there under a native officer. Chyn Sah, however, being informed of the departure of the garrison, came down from the neighbouring hills and surrounded the fort on the 24th of November with a body of between two and three thousand men. The Goands were, fortunately, despicable soldiers, and unfit for any service but lying in ambush, and firing from behind rocks and bushes; even the. sebundees despised them, and were hence incited by the native officer in command (a soobadar) to exert themselves manfully in the defence of the fort. The assailants were thus beaten off, and the post maintained the whole of the 24th: next

day a detachment of three companies arrived
under Lieutenant Brandon, who, on the first intelligence, was sent by Colonel M'Morine to relieve the garrison. A party of Rohillah horse
arrived also in time to aid in the measures taken
by Lieutenant Brandon to punish Chyn Sah for
the temerity of this attack.

There were one or two other trifling affairs
with detached parties of Goands, prior to the
combined movement projected by Colonel Adams,
whose three columns entered the hills from the
Nerbudda valley, in the early part of February
1819. , Colonel Adams himself moved on Puchmuree, by the direct route from Hoshungabad,
and as he advanced, sent out detachments to
reduce the enemy wherever he heard they were
in force, or otherwise prepared for resistance.
Thus Major Nation surprised Koteegurh, a position occupied by Gubha, on the night of the 7th
of February ; and Major Burgh, also from this
column, was successful against another party
on the 9th of the same month. Colonel Adams
arrived at Puchmuree on the 11th, where he met
Lieutenant-colonel M'Morine, who had advanced
with the second column from Gurawara. Here
he received the submission of the family and followers of Raja Jee, the Goand chief of Raee-
Kheree. Captain (late Lieutenant) Cruickshanks,
had been in correspondence with Raja Jee from

his post at Aseer, and hoped at one time to have been able, by his instrumentality, to seize the person of Apa Saheb, but the plot was detected, and Raja Jee being placed under restraint, was carried off by the ex-Raja on his escape from these hills, which occurred during the advance of Colonel Adams. Before relating the proceedings of Apa Saheb, it will be convenient to bring to a close the operations against the Goands. The flight of the ex-Raja, and arrival of Colonel Adams at his last retreat in the inmost recesses of the hills, convinced these savages at last of the inutility of further resistance, and all the chiefs now hastened to make their submission, with exception to Chyn Sah, and his associate Mohun Singh, who was called the Thakoor, or Lord of Puchmuree. The power of the former lay about Hurye, in which direction the third or left column was to penetrate the hills under Lieutenant-colonel O'Brien, while Colonels Adams and M'Morine made the advance above-described. It fell to the lot of this column to give the finishing blow to the insurrection by the surprise and destruction of Chyn Sah's party, on the 15th of February, and by the capture of two of that chief's nephews. The Nagpoor brigade of the subsidiary force had, in the mean time, taken the field, and occupied Deogurh ; besides which, a double line of posts was established by Colonel

Scot, its commandant, along the southern and eastern boundary of the whole tract, so as to prevent escape or communication by the routes in that direction. These operations effectually reduced the several tribes of Goands to subjection; so that the main body of the Nagpoor subsidiary force returned to Hoshungabad by the middle of March.

It has been stated that Apa Saheb effected his escape from the Hills, as Colonel Adams advanced into them. On the 3d of February he passed Boordye, where there was a troop of the 7th Bengal N. C., and two companies of infantry under Captain Jones. Apa Saheb was mounted and accompanied by Cheetoo Pindara, and a few personal attendants, while a body of about five hundred Arabs and Hindoostanees followed more at leisure. Captain Jones received timely intelligence of the enemy's approach to his post, but was misled into the belief that he had taken the route of Shahpoor; he accordingly marched in that direction, and only discovered his error after Apa Saheb had passed. He counter-marched, however, in time to overtake the party of Arabs and Hindoostanees, who at first drew up to oppose him, but were soon broken, with the loss of about a hundred men. At the Dabur Ghât they again attempted a stand, but with the same ill success; after which they dispersed in the junguls, and Captain Jones hastened after Apa Saheb, whose route was now fully ascertained from the prisoners.

In aid of the operations of Colonel Adams, Colonel Doveton had taken the field with the Nizam's subsidiary force, and, having advanced from Ellichpoor to Warkera, he detached thence Lieutenant-colonel Pollock into the valley of the Taptee ; with orders, after reducing Jilpee Amnér, which had been seized by the adherents of Apa Saheb, to occupy such positions as might seem best calculated to intercept the line of communication between Aseergurh and the Mohadeo hills. Colonel Pollock appeared before Jilpee Amnér on the 6th of January; and, having completed the investment of the place by the 8th, opened next day a battery of 6-pounders on the walls. On the 11th, after having for three days sustained the fire of these guns, and other efforts of the besiegers, the garrison offered to capitulate on condition of being allowed to retire with their arms. This, however, was refused by Colonel Pollock; who had just received some heavier artillery, which he conceived must ensure a surrender at discretion. He was, however, disappointed, for the garrison evacuated the place the same night, and by creeping unperceived along the deep bed of the river, succeeded in eluding the parties stationed to intercept them. Colonel

Pollock, after this, making Jilpee Amnèr his head-quarters, remained on the alert in the valley, waiting the effect of the further operations of Colonel Adams. On the 3d of February he was informed, by express, of the flight of the ex-Raja, and advancing to Peeploud, placed cavalry picquets on every road leading to Aseergurh. These arrangements were completed on the morning of the 4th. Apa Saheb, in the mean time, passed the night of the 3d in Saoleegurh. Late in the evening of the 4th, a small mounted party approached the picquet established by Colonel Pollock, near a village called Yoora, or Joora ; and on its turning out immediately the horsemen dispersed, and five or six were observed to dash into a ravine, by which means, under the experienced guidance of Cheetoo Pindara, the ex-Raja made his way good to Aseergurh. Some foot attendants on the party were made prisoners, and four of them proving to be deserters from Captain Browne's detachment, who had accompanied Apa Saheb in his flight in the preceding May, were brought to trial by order of Brigadier-general Doveton, and blown away from guns for that offence.

In the mean time, Apa Saheb having arrived at Aseergurh, was received there by Juswunt Rao Lar, and from within the fortress opened a correspondence with Sir John Malcolm, in which he professed a desire to treat for submission.

The Kiladar was more scrupulous in his conduct towards the Pindaree companions of the ex-Raja's flight; and Cheetoo being refused admittance, was destroyed by a tiger in the jungul near the fort, as has been mentioned before. Mohummed Punah, the son of Cheetoo, had accompanied his father and Apa Saheb in this flight, until the party came to a place outside the walls, where, by desire of Juswunt Rao Lar, they left the ex-Raja in order that there might be no witnesses to the conference that took place. Separating from his father, he resolved on throwing himself on the clemency of the British government, and made the best of his way to the camp of Sir John Malcolm for that purpose. Here he was well received, and made a full disclosure of the particulars of the flight of the ex-Raja; as well as of the invitation from Juswunt Rao, which had given it this direction. He could not, however, speak to the actual reception of Apa Saheb within the fort, having been sent away as stated above; but this fact was substantiated by other evidence, particularly that of the emissary through whom the ex-Raja sent the proposition to treat.

The instructions of the Supreme Government had directed, that in case Apa Saheb should take refuge in Aseergurh, that fortress should be summoned, and the Kiladar be treated as a rebel.

His misconduct in the preceding May, when
Bajee Rao was in the vicinity, in opening the
guns of his fort on a detachment sent by Brigadier-general Doveton to surprise the camp of the
ex-Pêshwa, had been noticed by the British Resident at Gwalior, and it was then suggested to
Doulut Rao Sindheea that it might conduce to a
better harmony between the two states, were his
Highness to punish Juswunt Rao, and provide
another governor for the fort. Sindheea declared
his intention to summon the offending Kiladar,
and overtly sent orders for him to repair to Gwalior to answer for his misconduct. These were
disobeyed, as was indeed expected. Still Juswunt
Rao placed himself in communication with the
British functionaries, and obtained their guarantee
for his personal security, as if intending eventually
to submit. Prior to the advance of the force
under Colonel Adams into the Mohadeo hills,
Sindheea was distinctly informed, that in case the
ex-Raja took refuge in Aseergurh, that fortress
must be besieged, and he was invited to send
some troops to co-operate, in order that the siege
might have the appearance of a joint undertaking.
The event having occurred exactly as anticipated,
Sindheea sent a Huzoorea, or confidential agent,
to receive charge of the fortress, and repeated the
order for Juswunt Rao to come away and deliver

it up. Sir John Malcolm, through whom this negotiation took place, besides offering to Juswunt Rao full security for his life and property, went so far as to tender him liberty to make over charge of the fortress to some individual of his own family, if he would but obey the order of the Gwalior durbar, and attend in person. Favourable as was this offer, Juswunt Rao nevertheless refused to avail himself of it, or to move from his post; and, in the beginning of March, the arrival of Sindheea's Huzoorea in the British camp, produced no change of his determination, which, it was now evident, was settled—to abide the issue of a siege rather than obey.

In this state of things, the negotiation, which had been open all February, was finally broken off on the 17th March, by which time there was assembled for the siege the entire disposable force of Brigadier-general Doveton, consisting of three regiments of native cavalry, three battalions and a half of European infantry, and seven of native; also the division brought down by Brigadier-general Malcolm from Malwa, composed of a regiment of cavalry, and four battalions of native infantry, together with the horse artillery, and trains of both forces. A further train was on its way from Sagur under the escort of two Bengal battalions, detached from the force under Brigadier-general

Watson. Thus the accumulation of means * exceeded any thing yet brought into the field, if we except the occasion of the siege of Hutras, when, as now, the eyes of the whole population of India being on the issue, it was desirable to strike the blow with an eclât that would redound to our perpetual credit and advantage.

Aseergurh is on a scarped hill, averaging about seven hundred and fifty feet in height from the surrounding plains, and precipitous for about one hundred, except in three points, where the rock failing, the resources of art have been called in to supply the defect. One of those points is on the north face of the west angle, where the natural declivity is not so great as to be inaccessible; another at the head of a ravine to the east; and the third at the south-eastern extremity, where the rock runs away in a ridge of nearly equal eminence. Under the hill to the west is a lower fort called Maleegurh, commanded by the upper, and surrounded by a stone wall of some strength, but of course without any ditch. Beyond this again, on the same side, is the petta, or town, belonging to the fort.

The negotiation having finally closed with the

* There were fifteen 18-pounders, seven 12-pounders, seven mortars, and seventeen howitzers, without the Sagur train, which produced an addition of two 24-pounders, four 18-pounders, eight mortars, and two howitzers.

Kiladar's refusal to give up the place, a column was prepared on the 17th of March for the attack of the petta next morning. It was led by Lieutenant-colonel Fraser, who succeeded in forcing an entrance, and establishing himself in the streets of the town. Dispositions were immediately made for the attack of the lower fort, on the petta side, while Sir John Malcolm amused the enemy to the north. On the 19th, in the evening, the besieged made a vigorous sally on our two most advanced positions in the petta, and getting temporary possession of these, did some injury to the works commenced there. On the 20th, the first heavy gun battery opened on Maleegurh, and by the evening a breach was nearly practicable in the wall. During this day the besieged made a second sally, and gaining the main street of the petta, killed there Lieutenant-colonel Fraser, before they were repulsed. The sally, however, occasioned no interruption in the firing of the battery; and, to secure the breach continuing open, this was kept up every five minutes during the night. Before daylight of the 21st, the enemy had evacuated the lower fort; but unfortunately at seven A. M., while effecting the relief of the covering party at the battery, its magazine of one hundred and thirty barrels of powder blew up from some unknown cause, and destroyed a whole company of the 15th Bengal N. I. The enemy seeing this, came down again and manned the walls of the lower fort, opening also the guns there which had been silenced by our battery. The intermission of fire from this accident was very short: after a very few minutes the battery re-opened with the same effect as before, besides which a mortar battery was got ready in the course of the same day.

Until the 24th, was employed in making a close and minute reconnoissance of the fort on all sides; and, by the advice of the engineers, it was on that day determined to make the principal attack on the upper fort, by the ravine to the east. Brigadier-general Doveton accordingly moved off with his division to occupy ground on that side; while, in order to distract the attention of the enemy, he left General Malcolm to prosecute operations against the lower fort and the north-west angle of the upper. The breach in the walls of Maleegurh had been practicable since the 22d, but no effort was made to storm or get possession, owing probably to its being commanded from above, and to our not having yet the means of silencing the guns of the upper fort. On the 30th of March, after several more batteries had been opened against it, the enemy again evacuated this outwork, whereupon it was seized and converted into a place of arms. Batteries were then raised against the north-western angle of Aseergurh, at

a point where the scarp of the rock had been re-
vetted, to make it more precipitous and difficult of
ascent than it was naturally; and where it was
hoped, that, by bringing down the artificial revetment, a practicable breach might eventually be
made. In the mean time the attack to the east
was advancing; on the 31st March the trenches
there opened, and a heavy fire was commenced on
the defences of the flanks of the ravine before described. The resistance of the garrison was nevertheless obstinate, and the matchlock fire on our
working parties very annoying. On the 3d of
April, the Sagur train arrived, and being immediately made available, the fire kept up thenceforward on both sides of the fort was incessant. On
the 5th of April, the masonry of the north-east
angle, flanking the ravine, was brought down, and
along with it an immense piece of ordnance (140-
pounder) came rolling over the rock. On the 7th
Juswunt Rao Lar having lost his jemadar (chief
officer) of artillery, and seeing the commanding
positions and quick fire of our batteries, began to
despair of his inability to hold out much longer.
At eleven o'clock next day, that is, on the 8th of
April, the batteries ceased firing, in consequence
of his having agreed to an unconditional surrender. Some parley took place in the course
of the day about the manner of the garrison's
delivering up their arms; and to arrange this,

Juswunt Rao Lar had an interview with Sir John
Malcolm in the lower fort. Before day-break, on
the 9th April, he sent to propose that the British
flag should be forwarded to be hoisted on the fort,
and in the course of the morning, twelve hundred
Arabs, Sindees, and Mukranees descended and
piled their arms in a square formed for the purpose
by the troops of Sir John Malcolm's division. The
loss sustained by the garrison during the siege
was only forty-three killed, and ninety-five wounded,
which was owing to the height of the rock being a
protection against any artillery but shells, while
its extent and irregular surface afforded the means
of avoiding these. Notwithstanding that the superior fire of our batteries had, at the points attacked, entirely destroyed the stone ramparts which
crowned the precipitous rock, and besides made
some impression on the artificial revetment before
described, the breaches were still far from practicable,* and Juswunt Rao would probably not have
surrendered so soon but for the failure of his
powder, of which, on our taking possession of his

* Lieutenant Lake, of the Madras engineers, who was at
the siege, and closely examined the fort, is of opinion that a
practicable breach could not have been made at either of the
points attacked, nor indeed at any point, except the south-
east angle above described. Vide Lake's Sieges of the Madras army.

magazines, only about two cwt. remained in store. At his first interview with Sir John Malcolm, on the 8th of April, while arranging the terms of surrender, he expressed apprehension that his master Sindheea would not be satisfied with his defence, and when reminded of that chief's order for the fort's delivery, replied, that "It might be the usage amongst Europeans, but with Mahrattas such forts were not given up upon orders." The total British loss in this siege was one officer, Lieutenant-colonel Fraser, nine Europeans, and thirty-seven sepahees killed : ten officers,* seventy-three Europeans, and one hundred and eighty-one natives wounded.

The fort of Aseergurh was, in the first instance, occupied for Sindheea, whose flag was accordingly hoisted on the ramparts ; but upon questioning Juswunt Rao more closely as to his motive in re-

* Names of officers wounded :—

Major Macleod, Deputy Quarter-master-general.
—— A. Weldon, Madras artillery.
Captain J. H. Frith, ditto, ditto.
—— Burman, 1st battalion, 7th native infantry.
Lieutenant Jas. Bland, H. M. royals.
—— A. D'Estere, Madras European regiment.
—— Gunsell, Bengal artillery.
—— F. W. Lewis, Bombay artillery.
—— T. J. Adair, H. M. 67th regiment.
—— J. Hannah, ditto, ditto.

sisting, he confessed that he had received secret
instructions not to deliver up the fortress, except
on the production of a private token from his
master, which the Huzooria had not brought. A
letter was likewise discovered in a box in the Kiladar's possession, which was in the handwriting
of Doulut Rao himself, and enjoined the Kiladar
to afford to Bajee Rao every aid in his power, and
contained the remarkable expression, " Should
you not do so, I shall be perjured." After this
evidence of the duplicity of the Gwalior durbar, it
was determined to keep the post, and the Marquess
of Hastings caused the original letter, so discovered,
to be returned to Doulut Rao at the time of making
known to him the intention. His Highness was
much relieved by the discovery that this was the
limit of the intentions of the British government,
and that no further chastisement was in reserve.
His mind was yet more completely set at ease by
the assurance that, provided his future conduct
was marked with sincerity and good faith, the
past should be entirely buried in oblivion, and our
best efforts lent to support his dignity and meliorate
the condition of his affairs.

To return to Apa Saheb, it was confidently expected, on the surrender of Aseergurh, that he
would be found there. Strict search was accordingly made for him, but without success. Juswunt
Rao Lar denied that he was in the fort, or had

ever been there, and would give no information respecting him; nor, indeed, has it yet been discovered of a certainty by what means, or when he effected his escape. For several months after this event, no accurate intelligence was obtained regarding the ex-Raja. At last, however, it was ascertained that he was with a few personal attendants in the country of Runjeet Singh, whither he made good his way in the disguise of a fuqeer, and where he was allowed to remain in concealment on a scanty allowance for his support, the Seikh chief not choosing to give him shelter publicly, or to receive him at his durbar in such a manner as to excite the dissatisfaction of the British government.

The obstinacy with which Apa Saheb clung to the phantom of royalty and independence, and refused the liberal offers made by the British government, to induce him to submit, is a phenomenon that can only be accounted for by the supposition that he doubted the sincerity of the offers he received. All the while he was skulking in the Mohadeo hills, and up even to the period of his reception in Aseergurh, he kept open a negotiation through different secret channels, with one or other of the British functionaries, pending which he was frequently assured of a provision of two lakhs per annum, on the terms accepted by Bajee Rao, the ex-Pĕshwa. But his treacherous heart made

him look upon the offer as a snare, and though
naturally a coward and a lover of ease, he preferred travelling the desert as a proscribed out-
law, with a price upon his head, to trusting himself in the hands of an enemy he had twice
offended. He despaired of forgiveness, and knew
not how abhorrent to our policy and disposition
was the gratification of any feeling of personal
revenge or cruelty.

The capture of Aseergurh was the last operation of the Pindaree and Mahratta war. After its
fall, the troops of the three Presidencies returned
every where to cantonments ; and, excepting a
small force sent from Bombay to bring to submission the petty piratical court of Sawuntwaree,
on the Malabar coast, there was not a single
British regiment in the field. It is not our intention to give in detail the proceedings of that
force, neither do we think it necessary to devote
a chapter to the expeditions fitted out likewise
from Bombay, in the succeeding cold season, for
the suppression of piracy on the Arabian coast,
and in the islands of the Persian Gulf. Suffice
it that the objects proposed from all these expeditions were fully attained, and the predatory
system put down by sea as well as by land.
Every where the fleets and armies of Britain
moved triumphant, carrying in their train the
blessings of tranquillity and order ; and these

were ensured as well by the exemplary punishment of those who protected and throve upon the opposite system, as by the arrangements made to substitute for the anarchy of military contention, a permanent, regular, and responsible government.

Having now conducted the reader through the details of the military operations by which this grand consummation was effected in the peninsula of India, it is time to pause and explain the political arrangements consequent upon these successes, or which were simultaneously put in train. It will be necessary also to attempt some general explanation of the conduct and principles assumed by the British government for its guidance in the new position in which it has been placed; as well as the effect of its measures on the wide extent of country subjected to its influence or dominion.

To this object the subsequent chapters will be devoted, and we shall subjoin a brief statement of the financial result, with an explanation of the principal resources of the Presidency immediately under the Supreme Government. A similar review of the two subordinate presidencies would doubtless be essential for the completion of the work, but for this we have neither materials, nor information.

CHAPTER XXII.

POLITICAL REVIEW.

Objects of this chapter—political measures adopted as part of the original plan—arrangements with Bhopál—death of the chief—succession regulated—reasons for extending the protective system to Rajpootana—objections considered—arrangement concluded with Kotá—peculiarity and embarrassment resulting—succession of Moharao Kishwur Singh—Joudhpoor—Oodeepoor—Captain Tod's settlement of its affairs—Boondee—death of its Raja—Bikaneer—Jesulmeer—sundry petty states settled by Sir John Malcolm —Jypoor, Sir D. Ochterlony's proceedings there—death of the Raja—intrigues—a posthumous child succeeds—Regency established—Byreesâl minister—counteracted by the Regent mother—interposition in his favour.

THE relations established with the native powers, under the new order of things, are so various and complicated, that to bring the explanation of them within moderate compass, is by no means easy. In the present chapter we shall commence with stating the political measures adopted as part of the original scheme for the suppression of the predatory associations, giving such particulars of the condition of the several powers

affected by them, as may suffice to show their application in each individual case. We shall reserve for a separate chapter the arrangements
with the Mahratta powers, consequent upon the
success of the war, together with those adopted
towards other princes whose relations with us
continued unbroken ; for it will be necessary to
bring the whole again under review, in order to
explain the new political condition which has resulted to India.

First, therefore, for the political measures
adopted as part of the original plan of Lord
Hastings, and put in train therefore simultaneously with the military operations, of which we have
just concluded the relation. Under this head the
treaties negotiated with Ameer Khan, and with
Doulut Rao Sindheea, and the arrangements made
to enforce their execution, would naturally claim
the first place ; but these were so mixed up with
the movements of the different divisions of the
army, that the mention of them has unavoidably
been incorporated with the general narrative ;
what remains, therefore, to be observed of both
these chieftains, will find its place more appro-
priately amongst the reflections suggested by the
new order of things established.

In like manner, the measures undertaken to
bring the Sagur principality under our influence,
one of the objects contemplated in the original

plan, have already been fully stated in consequence of the misconduct of Bunaeek Rao having
compelled the Governor-general to resort to military coercion.

The arrangements with the Nuwab of Bhopâl,
and those made with the several Rajas and chiefs
of Rajpootana, are thus the first for notice.

It has been mentioned that Nuzur Mohummed
signed the preliminary treaty,* proposed for his acceptance, before the British divisions crossed the
Nerbudda, in November, 1817. It varied in no
particular from the engagement offered to his
father, Wuzeer Mohummed, in the season of
1814-15, as explained at length in the early part of
this work. Seeing the advantage of early choosing
his side, the reigning Nuwab closed with the offer
made him without a moment's hesitation, and entered heartily into the cause, sending his contingent wheresoever directed, in aid of the operations
against the Pindarees, and rendering very important service on several trying occasions. After
the Pindarees had been hunted down, the Nuwab
was made an useful instrument in the negotiation
of the surrender and settlement of several of the
chiefs. Thus Namdar Khan, and other principal
sirdars of the durra of Kureem Khan, were permitted to accept an asylum in the Bhopâl territory.

* See page 38 of this volume.

under the Nuwab's guarantee of their future continuance in peaceful habits. The men, too, of
this durra, after being disarmed, were distributed
amongst the Nuwab's villages, and placed under
the surveillance of his administrative officers, with
small assignments of waste land for each man to
cultivate ; an arrangement that proved most bene-
ficial, and tended to the permanent reform of many
of the vagabonds, while it added to the population
and prosperity of a country that for a century
nearly had been the scene of continual ravage and
violence. As a reward for these services, and for
the cordiality uniformly displayed by the Nuwab,
the Punj Muhal of Ashta Ichawur, &c. along with
some other territory, parcel of the Vinshôrkur's
forfeited jageer, which had long been occupied by
the Pindaree chiefs, was, on their final dislodg-
ment, annexed to Bhopâl, by which addition the
Nuwab's boundary was advanced westward to the
Kalee Sindh. A part of Shujawulpoor was subsequently added, besides which the fort of Islamnugur was obtained from Sindheea by negotiation,
in order to be restored to him. The definitive engagement, fixing the relations of the Nuwab, was
concluded at Bhopâl on the 26th January, 1818,
and ratified by the Governor-general on the 3d of
March following. The contingent, stipulated to be
furnished by Bhopâl, is six hundred horse and four
hundred foot; a low proportion in reference to the

resources of the state, but so fixed expressly to favour the Nuwab. As a more substantial mark of consideration, the obligation of paying tribute in return for the protection afforded is waived in this instance, notwithstanding that the eventual payment of a lakh and twenty-five thousand rupees on this account was an item of the preliminary agreement concluded with Lieutenant-colonel Adams and Sir John Malcolm, in November 1817. Moreover, the entire occupation of the Sâgur territory has rendered it expedient to station the military force required to awe this neighbourhood within the frontier of that province, by which arrangement Bhopâl is relieved from the obligation of furnishing a cantonment with a fort to act as a depôt for a stationary British detachment, which was likewise part of the original contract.

Nuzur Mohummed was not insensible to the value of these benefits; and, while he lived, was grateful in the extreme for the liberality he experienced. From the possessor of a few strong holds, without the walls of which he scarcely dared to venture, he found himself converted into the acknowledged lord of a princely domain ; and his revenue, which, on the death of Wuzeer Mohummed, was little more than a lakh of rupees, realized with great trouble and irregularity, became at once raised to from ten to fifteen lakh, with every prospect of an eventual improvement to near thirty lakh.

In the midst, however, of his prosperity, the life of this young and much-esteemed prince was suddenly terminated on the 12th of November 1819, by the accidental discharge of a pistol in his girdle, while fondling his infant and only daughter. He had no son or other acknowledged heir, so that the choice of a successor from amongst the several branches of the family became the duty of the British Government. It appeared that in the succession to Wuzeer Mohummed, Nuzur Mohummed had himself superseded an elder brother, Ameer Khan ; the principle of *detur digniori* being avowedly recognised in the rules of Mohummedan descent. It further was ascertained that there was a branch of more direct descendants from the original stock of the Bhopâl Nuwabs, of whom Ghâs Mohummed was at the time representative ; but that, although treated by Nuzur Mohummed, as well as by his father before him, with great outward deference, this chief had for many years been allowed no concern in public affairs, and was at this time a mere pageant. Still the widow of Nuzur Mohummed was his daughter ; and the deceased had not only been in the habit of addressing him as a

superior, but did not himself assume the title of
Nuwab * within the Bhopâl territory, although
always considered and addressed as such by the
British Government. This state of things presented considerable embarrassment in the choice
of the successor. The British Government, however, determined to recognize no claim except
as derived from Nuzur Mohummed, with whom
its own engagements had been concluded ;
accordingly an infant nephew of that chief, by
name Mooneer Mohummed, son of the Ameer
Khan, set aside on the death of Wuzeer Mohummed, was seated on the musnud of Bhopâl in
prejudice to the rights of Ghâs Mohummed and
his children. At the same time, in order to
humour the prejudices, and secure the concurrence
of the Putan population, the infant was betrothed
to the daughter of Nuzur Mohummed ; who, as
grand-daughter of Ghâs Mohummed, united also
in her own person the claim of direct descent
from the original parent stock.

The management of the Bhopâl principality
has continued ever since this event in the same
hands in which it was placed by Nuzur Mohummed and his father, and the territory having en-

---

* Wuzeer Mohummed managed the affairs of Bhopâl as
Dewan, and Nuzur Mohummed himself exercised the same
function under the same title.

joyed uniform tranquillity, is fast assuming the appearance of a confirmed and lasting prosperity. Major Henley, the able and upright manager of the British interests in the tract, died in 1823, and his death was regretted by all classes as a second calamity inflicted by Providence on the country. This, however, is the only further event yielded by the even course of its affairs in the succeeding five years.

Before stating the arrangements made with each of the Rajpoot states, it will be necessary to notice an objection urged against the policy of extending our relations by the reception of these at all under protection. It has been maintained, that it would have been a preferable course to have rested satisfied with expelling the Putans and other predatory bands from Rajpootana ; and then to have left the several principalities wholly to themselves, free to pursue their own measures, as well internally for the administration of their respective territories, as externally in their disputes and wars with one another. The establishment of the British supremacy is represented by those who hold this opinion as a needless violation of the independence of the tract, tending to involve us in many intricate disputes ; and adding to the difficulty of managing the complicated system of relations established, without contributing in the least to our strength. On the contrary, it is urged, that as our interference has always been, and must necessarily be, on the unpopular side, the sentiment of the people, which was originally strong for independence, is likely to become more and more confirmed against us, so as to render the connexion a source of perpetual weakness and eventual danger. A further complaint against the system is, that it was ungenerous to confirm in perpetuity, as the price of a constrained protection, tributes yielded to Mahratta violence merely to purchase a temporary exemption from rapine, and of which the native means of the Rajpoots might eventually have enabled them to rid themselves.

Such are the arguments advanced against the policy of these arrangements. Their foundation is evidently in the Utopian principle of leaving each society to manage for itself, under the assurance that the evils of its misrule will produce their own corrective. Admitting this principle, for the sake of argument, it would still by no means follow, that the corrective of one evil did not entail a greater ; and the history of the world bears out the assertion, that there is no end to the mischiefs of misrule from military violence, when once the habit is deeply rooted in a society, except in the depopulation of the country, or its subjugation by some other nation better acquainted with the principles of order, as the foundation of strength and independence. Of all human contrivances for the perpetuation of such misrule, there is none so effectual as to throw together a number of independent tribes, each under a separate patriarchal or feudal government, and urged, therefore, by every motive of passion and policy to seek the destruction of its neighbour for its own aggrandizement. It is this state of things that has kept the interior of Africa in perpetual barbarity, that has depopulated the fertile and flourishing kingdoms of Mawur ool Nehur and Ghiznee, and rendered the once happy and polished Arabia the most savage and inhospitable country on the face of the globe. The only remedy and preventive of such evils consists in the establishment of a general controlling government, to restrain the passions of tribes and individuals, to promote mutual confidence, and teach the population to seek wealth and distinction by cultivating the arts of peace instead of looking on one another, like wild beasts, as legitimate objects of prey. Once or twice at the distance of centuries, the happy fortune and extraordinary qualities of an individual born for empire may cause such a remedy to arise from among the tribes themselves, but ordinarily, unless it comes from without, it comes not at all.

If these considerations have any weight, that is, if any circumstances can warrant an encroachment ·

on the independence of tribes for the purpose of introducing a general government, the state of things in Rajpootana at this period was such as to justify, and indeed imperiously to call for, an interposition by the British Government for that purpose. Independently of quarrels and wars prosecuted from motives of ambition or avarice, there were hereditary feuds and jealousies between the different tribes of Rajpoots, the Kychuhas, for instance, and the Rhatôrs, both these again, and the Chouhans, which must for ever have prevented their living together in harmony without a general sense of the necessity of submitting to the behest of a controlling power.

The expediency of settling Malwa, that is, after expelling the Pindarees from their haunts, of making such arrangements as would offer permanent security against their re-appearance there, is admitted on all hands; but wherein, we may ask, lies the difference between this province and Rajpootana? Both were equally parcelled out amongst chieftains and tribes, whose dissensions and weakness had produced the evil we had been called upon to put down, and the only arrangement offering permanent security in the one case, as in the other, consisted in the establishment of a general controlling government. After effecting this in Malwa, to have left the adjoining provinces of Rajpootana to the chances of perpetual feud

and violence, would have been to leave the object
half completed; with a certainty that sooner or
later the confusion there would re-produce the
mischief, and call for a new series of operations
for its suppression.   In the mean time, this would
have remained the only nook and corner within
the desert, in which tribes might continue to tear
one another to pieces, and to foster the military
spirit, from the evils of which such efforts had
been made to set the rest of India free.

Putting aside, however, the argument against
encroaching on the independence of these petty
states, the question becomes one of mere expediency and convenience to ourselves.   In this
point of view, it must, doubtless, be admitted, that
the establishment of the British influence over
Rajpootana has involved us in a very complicated
system of relations, and thereby somewhat increased the difficulty of managing our Indian
empire.   But this difficulty, when analysed, becomes merely one of finding proper instruments to
be intrusted with the large discretionary powers
necessary for the task.   It is, perhaps, no small evil
to be obliged to create despots for the management of these extensive interests; but, granting
even the impossibilty of devising an adequate
means of controlling the conduct of functionaries
so employed, still the despotism of a well-inten-
tioned and well-educated public officer, whose

fortune, prospects, and character are all at stake, is an arrangement affording greater security for the happiness and good order of the population committed to his charge, than could be hoped from the chance medley of feud and violence in which the tract must else have been left. Of this the people are themselves fully sensible : all their ideas of good government concentrate in the notion of a virtuous despot, and they have been accustomed for centuries to look for such blessing from the influence of a foreign yoke, rather than from their native population. On their part, therefore, there is none of that opposition on principle, and from the abstract love of liberty and independence which, amongst European communities, forms the bond of union and resistance to the domination of a stranger. On the contrary, such is the docility resulting from their habitual subjection, that with common prudence, common honesty, and good intentions, the task of managing the various interests so as to prevent their endangering the public peace, is comparatively easy. It is to be observed, that after the tribute has been once settled, the British Government can seldom have any separate objects of its own to seek of such a nature as to excite a general resistance and dislike. A very moderate portion of intelligence, therefore, must suffice to steer clear of irritation, and to convince the population that their good, and the tranquillity of the country, is the exclusive aim of our interference. The argument against forcing the British protection on parties unwilling to receive it, is thus entitled to weight only as it applies to the princes, feudatory retainers, and military chiefs, amongst whom the measure was necessarily unpopular, as would any other have been that tended to set a limit on their conduct and views by a general pacification of the country. To the lower orders, to all classes engaged in trade or agriculture, that is, to the population at large, our protection came as a blessing great beyond their hopes, and by them it has ever been so regarded.

A very few words will suffice to explain the cause of the tributes being continued. It will be recollected that under the original plan it was intended to make the arrangement palatable to the Mahratta powers, by securing to them the benefit of any revenues their past successes had enabled them to exact from the Rajpoot states. In fairness they were entitled to expect this as the condition of their co-operating in our measures to effect the general pacification. Unless, therefore, we were prepared to make the sacrifice from our own resources, the tribute necessarily became part of the arrangement to be concluded with each state; and the principle having been avowed at the outset of the campaign, the subsequent conduct of the powers entitled to receive the amount at our hands gave no claim to the tributaries to be exempted from the levy.   Such an advantage was, therefore, rightly made the reward of special desert, on which footing it was conceded to several, whereof the case of the Boondee principality is an instance in point.   Even supposing, however, that these claims of the Mahratta powers had not existed as a pretext for continuing the tribute, there were yet strong motives for giving this form to the obligations of fealty and dependence which the system required to be exacted.   In the first place, the protection stipulated to be furnished must necessarily entail on ourselves the expense of an increased military and civil establishment, and it was not reasonable that we should bear the whole burthen of this, while it would have led to suspicion of our ulterior views, had we proffered such protection without the demand of any equivalent at all.   Tribute again was the kind of compensation, and of fealty which the several princes expected to have to furnish, the same having been rendered by them to the Moghul, in whose place they regarded the British power to have now stepped. An engagement, therefore, which limited its amount in perpetuity, was to them as great a boon nearly as could be conferred, and the assurance it conveyed was much more complete than silence on the point, or than a stipulation reserving their contribution to be regulated by state exigency which would have been the expressed or implied alternative. Another very material consideration was, that by the immediate operation of the treaties to be concluded, the several princes would come into the possession of additional revenues, as well from the expulsion of predatory bands, as from the assurance given by the introduction of a regular government to the levy of their just dues from their own dependants. These funds were an available resource, of which it would have been an act of wanton profusion to make a distribution purely gratuitous. Good policy required distinctions, according to the degrees of active friendship and useful service, by which such benefits might be earned ; and, as it was through their tributes only that our new allies could be made to feel they had something to gain and lose, they became in this respect a very useful instrument and means of influence.

Having premised thus much on the general character and policy of these arrangements, it is time to explain them in detail.

Amongst the Rajpoot states, the Rana of Oodeepoor is entitled to the first rank, as being the lineal representative of the Seesodian dynasty that opposed the emperor Ukbur in the field. The other chiefs, even those who owe him no allegiance, regard him with the deference of acknowledged inferiority. Under our new system, however, each Raja was to be recognized as distinct from the rest, and the condition of all to be that of protected dependance. It will hence be most convenient to follow the order in which the several arrangements were concluded.

It was to Mr. Metcalfe, the Resident at Dehlee, that the Governor-general, in the first instance, intrusted the execution of his plans in relation to the Rajpoot states; and the reader has already been apprised, that, at the commencement of the campaign, he addressed a circular letter to them all, calling upon them to send agents to Dehlee if they wished to participate in the advantages of the league about to be formed. None of them failed in obedience to this requisition; and, when the government was administered with efficiency and order, little difficulty was experienced in settling the terms of the alliance to be formed with the British. The conditions were, simply, that any tribute demandable under a fixed agreement with a Mahratta or Putan chief, should be paid directly to the British treasury, leaving us to account for it to the party to whom it might be due, and that our protection should be afforded on the usual condition of abstaining from the contraction of any new relations with other powers, and submitting to our arbitration of external disputes.

The first to conclude a treaty on this basis was Raj-Rana Zalim Singh, who had for near fifty years been the absolute manager of Kota. His agent at Dehlee, Raja Sheeodân Singh, signed an engagement on the 26th of December 1817, which was ratified by the Marquess of Hastings on the 6th of January following. The tribute due from this state to the Mahrattas was three lakhs, reduced by admitted allowances and deductions to two lakh and fifty-seven thousand six hundred Goomanshahee rupees, equal to two lakh and forty-four thousand seven hundred and twenty of the Dehlee currency. To this was to be added twenty thousand Dehlee rupees due from relations and dependants of the family, known by the designation of the seven kotrees or houses; so that the total Kota tribute payable at Dehlee was two lakh and sixty-four thousand seven hundred and twenty Dehlee rupees. This amount has been annually realised with the utmost punctuality, and the adjustment has never given rise to any discussion or dispute. There was, however, a peculiarity in the arrangement for this principality that led eventually to much embarrassment and some bloodshed. The titular chief of Kota was Muha-Rao Omêd Singh, an imbecile, who never meddled in public affairs, and was in fact little better than a prisoner. Nevertheless he was treated with every outward mark

of respect by Zalim Singh, who wielded as Dewan the whole power of the state; and, by his
successful management, brought it, from the
lowest point of decay, to be the most flourishing
and respected in Rajpootana. Conformably to
the principle of regarding occupancy as the rule
of right, the Marquess of Hastings was prepared
to have concluded the treaty for Kota directly
with Zalim Singh, without reference to the rights
of the nominal Raja.   To this, however, the Raj
Rana's negotiators objected, and the treaty was
accordingly executed in the name of Omêd Singh.
Subsequently, however, the point being referred
to Zalim Singh, a supplementary article was
added at his suggestion, by which the Raj was
specially guaranteed to Muha-Râo Omêd Singh
and his heirs for ever; but with a reservation of
the powers of administration to Zalim Singh and
his heirs, as hereditary Dewans.   In like manner, the sunud or grant of the Governor-general
for the four Pergunnas, acquired from Holkur at
the peace of Mundisôr, was, at Zalim Singh's
request, made out in the name of Omêd Singh,
the titular sovereign; although, as the service thus
requited was personal, Zalim Singh would have
been fully justified, even in the eyes of the most
fastidious Rajpoots, had he reserved to himself
the full sovereignty over these new acquisitions.

Zalim Singh, throughout the operations against

the Pindarees, proved a very useful ally ; and the principality was, in order further to reward his zeal, very much favoured in the arrangements subsequently made with Sindheea, of whom the Raj-Rana held several places in farm, and amongst others Shahabad. All this while nothing was heard of the Muha-Rao, or of any other head of the state, but Zalim Singh ; and the affairs of Kota went smoothly on. In December 1819, however, Oméd Singh died, leaving three sons, all grown up to man's estate ; of these, the eldest, Kishwur Singh, succeeded his father as Muha-Rao of Kota, but was not content to hold the titular sovereignty on the same terms. Zalim Singh had two sons, whereof Madhoo Singh, the elder, was the designated successor to the Dewanee. Against him Kishwur Singh conceived a mortal hate ; and, professing to have no desire to interfere with the authority of the Raj Rana while he might live, entered on an intrigue to secure the succession to the Dewanee for Zalim Singh's second son, Govurdhun Das. Madhoo Singh did his best to resist this attempt to supersede him ; and, being backed by his father and by the British political agent, he found himself sufficiently strong to abide the issue of an appeal to arms. In the beginning of 1821, the hasty violence of Kishwur Singh brought matters to this extremity, when the result was the expulsion of

the Muha-Rao and his coadjutor, Govurdhun
from Kota, and their flight to Dehlee, where they
hoped to interest the Resident,* Sir David Ochterlony in their favour. After remaining some
months at Dehlee unacknowledged, the Muha
Rao determined on returning to Kota, under a
vain expectation of being reinstated in the entire
authority of the Raj, so soon as he might arrive
there. On his way he invited all the feudal con-
nexions of the family to assist his enterprise, and
called on the Hara Rajpoots generally to unite in
expelling a rebellious usurper, as he designated
Madhoo Singh, who had dared to turn his arms
against his legitimate sovereign. By this means
he collected together a tumultuous host, which
threatened to disturb the guaranteed arrangement, and seriously to interrupt the public tranquillity. Accordingly the British troops took the
field from the neighbouring cantonments, and in
the course of October 1821, the Muha-Rao having
refused to cause his host to disperse, an action
took place near Kota, which ended in his defeat,

* Mr. Metcalfe, afterwards Sir Charles Metcalfe, was in
1819-20 called down to Calcutta to succeed Mr. Adam as
political and private secretary to Lord Hastings, on the latter
being promoted to council. Sir David Ochterlony succeeded
him as Resident at Dehlee. In December 1820, Sir Charles
Metcalfe was appointed Resident at Hyderabad, in the room
of Mr. Russell, who returned to England.

with the loss of Prithee Singh, his second brother, who was slain by his side. After this he submitted to an arrangement mediated by the British political agent, under which the palaces of the Raj, with an ample revenue, and every outward circumstance of sovereignty, are assured to him; while the power and management of the territory remains with Zalim Singh* and his eldest son. The total revenue of Kota was estimated, at the time this arrangement was completed, at about forty-seven lakh of rupees, of which upwards of four lakh may be set down for the Pergunnas, and other advantages secured by Zalim Singh from the Mahrattas, through the good offices of the British government.

The second in order to sign engagements with the British government was Raja Mân Singh, of Joudhpoor, hereditary chief of the powerful tribe of Rhatôr Rajpoots. Joudhpoor had suffered very severely from the irregular exactions of the Putans, but Sindheea was the only power who had any legitimate claim to tribute or allegiance. The nominal amount due to that durbar was one lakh and eighty thousand rupees per annum ; but the allowed deductions reduced this to ninety-seven thousand

---

* This veteran chief, who was upwards of eighty years of age, died in June 1824 ; and his death occasioned no fresh interruption of the public tranquillity.

Dehlee rupees, at which rate it was fixed by the treaty. It appeared afterwards, however, that a jageer of eleven thousand rupees had been reserved as a personal gratification to the British negotiator; which, though of course declined by the individual, was thrown into the scale, and swelled the amount to one lakh and eight thousand rupees. This has been realised with uniform punctuality. The Raja engaged also to furnish a contingent of fifteen hundred horse. The signed treaty was delivered at Dehlee on the 6th of January 1818, and an immediate benefit resulted to the Raja from the ejection of all the thanas (posts of armed men) placed in the country by Ameer Khan, and other Putan chiefs, with whom all disputes, whether on account of old money demands, or other claims whatsoever, were thus summarily adjusted.

Until lately, very little interference was exercised with the Joudhpoor court. At the time of concluding the treaty, and for about a year after, Raja Mân Singh lived as a recluse, while his son Chutur Singh performed the duties of sovereignty. In 1819, however, the young man died, and the Raja, awakening from his lethargy, resumed the sceptre; but to no good purpose. Several acts of cruelty and injustice perpetrated on the persons of some of the (Thakoors) powerful feudatories of the principality, threatened, in the course of 1822 and 1823, to embroil its affairs in a civil war, and called at length for British interposition. Of the arrangement finally adopted under the mediation of Sir David Ochterlony, we have no sufficient information; indeed the adjustment of the concerns of the state was only recently commenced when the materials were collected for this review.

Of all the Rajpoot princes, the Rana of Oodeepoor had suffered most from the usurpations of rebellious subjects, as well as from the oppressions of the Mahrattas and Putans. This prince had lost nearly the whole of his dominions, and the money exactions of his oppressors were limited only by the extent of his means. Thakoor Ujeet Singh, the chief minister of Oodeepoor, came early to Dehlee to settle the terms on which the principality was to be freed from its present misery; and on the 16th January 1818, an arrangement was concluded, under which four annas in the rupee, that is to say, one quarter of the total revenue, was agreed to be paid into the British treasury, to enable it to answer all just demands against the Oodeepoor state. After five years, when the condition of the territory was expected to improve, the proportion was to be raised to six annas, or three-eighths, and the latter rate was at once promised upon all new acquisitions or ancient possessions recovered by our means. In return, the British government was to lend the aid of its power and influence towards restoring the Rana's affairs,

which, what with external ravage and internal
usurpation, were now at the very lowest ebb.   The
expulsion of the Pindarees, and of Duleel Khan,
a Putan adventurer, who had for some months been
devastating the Oodeepoor territory, was an immediate benefit resulting from the alliance; and,
towards the end of January, the affair with Sindheea's commandant at Jawud placed at our disposal
further means of befriending this state.

With a view more effectually to assist in the
restoration of order, Captain Tod, who had at
first been deputed to Kota to superintend the exertions of Zalim Singh against the Pindarees, and
had since been employed in adjusting our relations
with Boondee, was ordered to proceed to Oodeepoor; and, to increase his influence, he was made
the instrument for bestowing on the Rana the fort
of Kumulnêr, and some other recent acquisitions
from Juswunt Râo Bhâo.   This officer had made
the character and history of the Rajpoots his peculiar study; but found the confusion from the
Rana's weakness, and the jealousies and pretensions of the courtiers and larger feudatories, such
as to afford little prospect of a satisfactory or
speedy adjustment.   At Captain Tod's suggestion, and under his personal guarantee, a general
assembly of the Thakoors was convened for the
settlement of the future constitution of the princi-

pality. After some days of unavailing discussion on points of inferior importance, Captain Tod, perceiving that if left to themselves their mutual jealousies would prevent their coming to any determination, resolved himself to prepare a charter of rights, which the Raja should submit for deliberation and eventual adoption. The sixteen principal Thakoors were accordingly assembled at noon of the 4th May 1818, when the project was laid before them by the Raja ; and after a sitting and warm debate, which lasted without intermission till three next morning, the following articles were agreed to, and the paper containing them was signed by all present.

Article 1. provided, that all usurpations made by individuals upon the Rana, or upon one another, since the Sumbut year 1822, (A. D. 1766) should be mutually restored.

Article 2. No Thakoor to continue to levy the impost known by the name of *Rahwaree Bhoom*, a kind of black mail levied as an immunity from plunder.

Article 3. The *Dhan Biswa*, or rateable impost upon the produce of agriculture, to be the exclusive property of the Rana's government, and to be levied by no other authority.

Article 4. The Thakoors renounce all predatory habits, and engage to harbour or protect no thieves;

but to encourage trade, and leave all caravans un-molested.   (This was a proviso that had become most necessary.)

Article 5. The Thakoors engage to attend on the durbar at Oodeepoor in rotation for four periods, each of three months, with their respective military followers, in order to give strength and respectability to the executive government.

Article 6. At the Dussera of each year, a gene-ral meeting of the Thakoors to be convened for the settlement of all public affairs of magnitude ; the meeting to commence ten days before the Dussera, and not to last more than twenty days after it : but extraordinary meetings to be held on extraordinary emergencies.

Article 7. The immediate feudatories of the prince bound to render immediate service, accord-ing to the terms by which they might respectively hold.

Article 8. All exactions, mutual violence, and fines on dependants, to cease, and every one to be regulated in his conduct by the new order of things to be established.

Article 9. The Thakoors bound to confirm what Ujeet-Singh, the Dehlee negotiator, had agreed to.

Article 10. The Rana vested with the execu-tive authority, for the enforcement of obedience to the new constitution to be established.

To enforce the execution of these articles, particularly the first, was a much more difficult operation than to procure their adoption by the
Thakoors; and the difficulty was much increased
by the easiness of the Rana's disposition, and his
habitual thoughtless liberality to those who immediately surrounded him. Favoritism, partiality,
and corruption in every shape, were continually at
work to prevent his acting on an uniform systematic principle; and thus the constant interposition of
the British political agent became indispensable to
prevent an undue bias in the adjustment of the
relations of the chiefs,* with their sovereign's restored authority.

* The following are the principal feudatories of Oodeepoor :—

The Salumba chief, Rawut Pudum Singh, head of the
Chundawuts, and of the Kishenawut branch.

The Bheendur chief, Muha Raja Zorawur Singh, head of
the Suktawuts. His brother Rawut Futteh Singh is also a
man of consideration.

The Deogurh chief, Rawut Gokul Das, a Sungawut
Chundawut.

The Gogoonda chief, Futteh Singh, of foreign extraction,
being a Jhala by caste.

The Saduree ditto, Raj-Kuleean Singh, ditto.

The chief of Korabur, Rawut Juwan Singh, nephew of
Ujeet Singh, the Dehlee negotiator.

Ditto of Lawah, Rawut Jy Singh, a personal favourite of
the Rana.   Ditto

In no part of Rajpootana were the seeds of jealousy and dissension so deeply sown, or of such long standing, as amongst the Thakoors of this state. They were ranged in two principal factions, as they were of the Chundawut and Suktawut caste; but each of these was again subdivided into several inferior branches, all bearing hereditary hatred to one another; besides which, in the general scramble for territory which had followed the decay of the principality, each had been involved in deadly contention with his neighbour, so as to add the recollection of recent, to the traditionary record of ancient injuries. The extreme jealousy of each other which prevailed, led to a modification of the first of the above articles; for, though content to resign to the state all usurpations from the Rana made since 1822, Sumbut, (A. D. 1766) nothing could reconcile them to

Ditto of Bhudêsur, Rawut Humeer Singh, ditto ditto.

Ditto of Amêt, Rawut Salim Singh, a Jugawut Chundawut.

Ditto of Bednôr, Thakoor Jy Singh, a Rhatôr Rajpoot, descended from Jymul, who defended Cheetôr against Ukbur.

Ditto of Bynsrorgurh, Rawut Rughoonath Singh, a Kishenawut Chundawut, whose family expelled a Suktawut seventy years ago.

Ditto of Shahpoora Raja Omed Singh. In 1818-19, this chief murdered his father; and his estates were confiscated, but restored to the family in 1821.

restore what they had taken from rival chiefs. Such lands, therefore, instead of being given up to the family which had lost them, were retained by the Rana and added to his Khalsa, which made the arrangement much more palatable, and enabled Captain Tod to place the Rana's establishment on a respectable footing. Nevertheless, the expenses of the court, for the five years following the treaty, exceeded considerably the resources and means at its disposal; so that no tribute has yet found its way into the British treasury. That part of the agreement, indeed, which stipulates for the payment of a certain proportion of the revenues of the principality will require to be modified, by commutation for a fixed amount; else the perpetual interference of the British government will be indispensable to secure the full realisation, and to prevent favour or alienations by the Rana,—a form of interposition of all, perhaps, the most galling and intolerable.

A considerable portion, and the most profitable, of the Khalsa lands of Oodeepoor, were leased for five years under an arrangement superintended by Captain Tod, who estimated, that in the last year of the lease the total amount would reach to ten lakh of rupees. Including the profit of these lands, the resources of the state were, in 1822, between twelve and thirteen lakh, and an arrangement for securing the British tribute was then under negotiation.

The Raja of Boondee followed next in order, and signed the engagement proposed for his acceptance on the 10th of February. This chief is the nominal head of the Hara Rajpoots, the Kota family being descended from a younger branch of the same stock. The net annual tribute due to the Mahrattas for Boondee was eighty thousand rupees ; but the chief had established a claim on the gratitude of the British government, by the fidelity and hospitality with which he assisted Colonel Monson in his disastrous retreat through Haraotee in 1804. The rupture with Holkur fortunately afforded the means of bestowing a substantial proof of our grateful recognition of his good offices on that occasion. Not only were all the acquisitions of this family recovered for the Raja, but he was released altogether from tribute, and the restitution of some further encroachments of Sindheea was likewise obtained by negotiation. The town of Patun, an old possession of the Boondee family, was an object of strong desire to the Raja, and he was indulged in the hope of having his wishes in this respect gratified ; but the loss of this place was of too old a date to allow of our calling on the Mahratta chiefs gratuitously to abandon their interest in it ; while, as it lay below the hills forming the southern boundary of Haraotee, the third share enjoyed by Holkur did not fall within the cessions of the treaty of Mundisôr. Sindheea had likewise a third of this town ; and Zalim Singh had claims on it for the Kota state. After much negotiation, an arrangement was at length agreed to, by which the Mahrattas were finally excluded from Patun ; but its restoration to the Boondee Raja was made conditional, on the payment annually to the British government of forty thousand rupees, to enable it to satisfy the claims of the Gwalior durbar. In July 1821, Raja Bishun Singh died, and was succeeded by a minor son, Rao Raja Ram Singh, who was installed by Captain Tod, the political agent for Boondee, on the 3d of August following. Bohara Sumbhoo Ram, the father's minister, was continued in power, and became the responsible regent during the young prince's minority.

The Raja of Beekaneer, lying within the desert, was the next of the Rajpoot princes that came into the league. The treaty with him was signed on the 13th of March 1818. The suppression of the practice of pillage, the restoration of property plundered within his territory, the obligation of rendering military aid on requisition according to his means, and of paying for such as he might require of us, were the terms of this chief's reception to the alliance. He had never paid tribute, and no claim was set up on that score. Bhutnêr the capital of the Bhutee tribe, and the siege of which occupies a conspicuous place in the history of Tymoor-Lung's invasion of Hindoostan, had been conquered by this Raja in 1805 from the Moosulman family* which ruled the Bhutees. Their predatory habits rendered an expedition into the tract necessary in the course of 1819; and it became a question whether, for the sake of a satisfactory adjustment, the restoration of Bhutnêr should not be asked of the Beekaneer Raja. In the end, however, other means were found of satisfying the Moosulman chiefs, and the authority of the Beekaneer Raja over Bhutnêr and the country reduced by his arms in 1805 was not disturbed. Soorut Singh is the name of this chief; and his conduct, since the conclusion of the protective alliance, has been uniformly correct. His revenue is very moderate, but there has yet been no accurate estimate made of its amount.

The state of Jesulmeer is farther within the desert than even Beekaneer, and the same observations will apply to it; the terms of its reception into the league being precisely similar. Raja

* The family is by descent a branch of that of Jesulmeer; but Feeroz Shah compelled the Raja to embrace the Moosulman religion; and his descendants, though still Hindoo in many respects, have since continued in the outward profession of Islam. The three chiefs in 1818 were Khan Buhadur Khan, Zabita Khan, and Gholam Fureed Khan.

Molraj concluded the treaty with the British on the 12th of December 1818, but died in the year following, and was succeeded by his grandson Guj Singh, who has since conducted the affairs of that state; without in any instance giving to the British government the trouble of an interposition.

Arrangements with the Rajas of Doongurpoor and Banswara, and likewise with the chiefs of Purtabgurh, Rutlamnugur, Baglee, and other places of minor importance, were concluded in the course of 1818, under the superintendence of Sir John Malcolm. The two first named were distant branches of the Oodeepoor (Seesodeean) dynasty, and their tribute was due to the Mahratta family of Puwars, settled at Dhar and Dewas. It was arranged, in both cases, that to the extent of 3-8ths (six annas) of their revenue payment should be made to the British government, to enable it to settle the claims of the Puwars. The treaty with Muha Rawut Juswunt Singh of Doongurpoor bears date the 11th of December 1818; that with Omed Singh of Banswara, the 5th of the same month *. Omed Singh died

* A treaty with Banswara was concluded at Dehlee on the 16th of September 1818, to the same effect precisely; but this of the 5th December, having been negotiated directly with the Raja by Captain Caulfield, may be considered as that fixing the relations of the state.

shortly after, and was succeeded by his son Bhuwanee Singh.

The tribute of Purtabgurh, amounting to seventy-five thousand rupees per annum, was due to the government of Holkur; but, under the arrangement concluded with Sawut Singh, the Raja, on the 5th of October 1818, this became payable direct to the British government, and the chief was relieved from dependance on any other authority. His revenues are considerable, amounting to near five lakh of rupees.

In like manner, the tribute claimed by Sindheea from the Raja of Rutlamnugur, Purbut Singh, and from his dependants the chiefs of Silana, Amjera, Kuch Baród, Mooltan, &c., was transferred to the British government; an arrangement the necessity for which was manifested in the course of 1818, when Bapoo Sindheea was about to lead one of the turbulent armies of that family into the tract, in order to enforce the collection of some arrears alleged to be due.

It would lead to a great length of detail, were the terms of the engagements of all these petty chiefs to be minutely explained; and it is particularly unnecessary, after the elaborate work of Sir John Malcolm, in which the history and circumstances of each are given with a precision and weight of authority leaving nothing further to be desired. To this work, therefore, we shall refer the reader, and shall proceed at once to state the arrangements concluded with Jypoor, the most wealthy and important of all the Rajpoot states, and the one likely for some time to give the most trouble. Though nearest in geographical position to Dehlee, this state was one of the last to send negotiators; and, when they did come, they proved the most difficult to treat with. Jypoor, like Oodeepoor, owed no specific money tribute either to Mahrattas or Putans; but the usurpations of both, and of the feudatory Thakoors, had reduced the court to the lowest scale of impoverishment. The remuneration demanded for relief by our means from these evils was proportionally high; for it was considered that the vacillating conduct and indifference displayed by the Raja and his advisers, had left him without claim to favour or indulgence. The Jypoor negotiators made their appearance at Dehlee about the middle of February 1818, that is, not until the successes of the war had shown the Mahratta cause to be desperate; and probably the Raja would not then have treated, had he not felt some alarm at the engagement concluded with Ameer Khan, and at the approach of Sir D. Ochterlony with the reserve to his capital. His apprehensions, were, moreover, quickened by an engagement concluded with the Raja of Kishengurh, and by a show of making terms generally with his feuda-

tories, which would have had the effect of permanently detaching them from his allegiance. Fearing to be left completely in the lurch, the Raja
at last sent his Vakeels, and most of the principal
people of Jypoor hastened to Dehlee, along with
them. After much negotiation, a treaty for the
state was at length concluded on the 2d of April
1818. The amount of tribute to be paid as the
condition of relief from further exaction from the
Putans and other depredators, was, as heretofore,
the main difficulty. Fifteen lakh, with remissions
for the first few years, was the rate demanded by
Mr. Metcalfe, as in the negotiations of 1816. Two
lakh and a half was the amount offered by the
vakeels. In the end, the following scale was
adopted :—For the first year, nothing ; four, five,
six, seven, and eight lakh, for the five succeeding
years respectively; and eight lakh afterwards in
perpetuity, liable to increase by five annas in the
rupee (five-sixteenths) on any excess of the revenues
of the state beyond forty lakh of rupees *. It
was estimated that upon the restoration of order,
the revenue of Jypoor would not fall short of

---

* The tribute actually realised from Jypoor up to 1822-23
was as follows :—

        1818-19. 1819-20. 1820-21. 1821-22. 1822-23.
D. Rs. 2,00,000 2,54,004 2,50,000 5,50,000 12,50,000

The last sum must include the arrears of preceding years :
the payments have never been very punctual.

eighty lakh ; but the necessity of ascertaining its amount, and of interfering in order to prevent alienation, are evils which the British government have for some time been anxious to remedy by commuting the proportion thus stipulated for a fixed and certain payment.

To restore order to the affairs of Jypoor proved a matter of infinite difficulty. The aristocratical faction of Manjee Das had been dismissed in the course of July 1817, for presuming to rid itself of the inconvenient influence of one of the Raja's favourites by putting him to death. The Raja, in a fit of passion, struck his minister in open durbar, and placed him in close confinement for this act ; and the consequence was, that the feudatories of the principality very generally threw off their allegiance; while, within the palace and city of Jypoor, the Raja exercised a capricious authority under the influence of courtezans, eunuchs, and menials ; amongst whom Chutoor Bhoj, a partisan of Ameer Khan, was the most conspicuous.

In May 1818, Sir David Ochterlony proceeded to Jypoor, in order, if possible, to introduce some regularity and system into the administration of its affairs. Under his superintendence a general meeting of the Thakoors was convened, but several proving refractory, it was found necessary to make an example in order to convince them of the fruitlessness of such conduct under the new arrangement about to be introduced. In this view, the strong holds of Kooshalgurh and Madhoorajpoor (or Madhoogurh) were reduced; and the facility with which both enterprizes were effected, quite astonished the Rajpoots, who had seen Ameer Khan's battalions baffled for two years before the latter fort.

In December 1818, before any thing definitive had been arranged, Raja Jugut Singh died, without leaving a son or other acknowledged heir. Two candidates immediately appeared for the succession, and the principality was on the point of experiencing the agitation of a contest in the mitigated form of intrigue and faction, allowed by the British supremacy, when a posthumous child was produced from the Muhul as the son of the deceased Raja, by a wife of the Bhutee race. In order to adjust these matters, Sir David Ochterlony again proceeded to Jypoor; and finding the posthumous infant to be pretty generally acknowledged, he assisted at its inauguration by the title of Sewaee Jy Singh, and gave the sanction of the British government to the establishment of a regency under the Ranee mother, aided by Rawul Byreesâl, as chief minister of the state. The intrigues and confusion arising from the perpetual war of factions in this durbar, obliged government subsequently to appoint a political agent specially to superintend its affairs; and Major Stewart, who had acted some time as Resident at Sindheea's court, was deputed to Jypoor with this commission. He found every thing in the utmost confusion. The authority of Rawul Byreesal was quite superseded by an influence within the Zunana, which thwarted his measures, and annihilated his efforts to restore order in the various departments of administration. It had been one of the points insisted on by Sir David Ochterlony, at the first assembly of Thakoors held under his superintendence, that the affairs of the principality should be restored to the condition in which they stood on the dissolution of the previous alliance with the British government in 1805 ; and in furtherance of this principle, it had been agreed to restore to the Raja's Khalsa, (Exchequer) all usurpations from him, or grants obtained from the state in the period of violence and anarchy which had intervened.* Every attempt, however, of Rawul Byreesal to carry this measure into execution was frustrated by the intrigues of the parties interested, and by the secret influence they were encouraged to resort to

* The Sumbut year 1860 was the date fixed for these resumptions.

amongst the women of the interior of the palace, their eunuchs, and paramours. Presuming on the Dewan's experienced weakness, the Thakoors entered into cabals, and prosecuted their feuds and animosities in the same manner as before the British alliance was contracted. They, moreover, very generally harboured criminals and robbers, so that without a large escort it was utterly impossible to travel through the country; and all commercial intercourse and transit was obstructed by their levy of arbitrary and illicit exactions. Complaints of the anarchy which prevailed came daily to the Presidency from all quarters. This state of things continued till 1822, when the British government found it absolutely necessary to decide whether its support should be given to the sanctioned and responsible minister, or the principality be left, as heretofore, to the chance government of intriguers within the palace walls. The point was specially referred by Major Stewart; and, after some deliberation, the Supreme Government resolved to conquer its repugnance to interfere, and authorised a direct interposition in support of the authority of Rawul Byreesal.

In execution of this resolution, Sir David Ochterlony a third time proceeded to Jypoor, to add weight, by his presence and personal authority, to the representations about to be made to the Regent Rance. He arrived there on the 20th January, 1823, and immediately addressed a serious remonstrance to the court, pointing out in what respects the promises made to himself by the Ranee, or by the deceased Raja, had not been performed, and showing how the country had been brought to the verge of ruin by the system of misgovernment pursued. These evils he attributed to the divided authority which existed, and for their remedy he called upon the Ranee to restore Byreesal to confidence, and vest him with exclusive power in the administration. He required her at the same time to dismiss from her councils and presence Jhola Ram, the most favoured of the minions, by whose influence the minister had been counteracted. The Ranee was not without the support of a number of partisans amongst the Thakoors and principal people of Jypoor ; so much so, that Byreesal, when consulted, was of opinion that it would be necessary to march a British force to Jypoor to support the interposition in his favour. This, however, Sir David Ochterlony was resolved to avoid, except in the last extremity, trusting to the weight of his personal influence, and the known character and power of the British government, to effect the object without a resort to such means. The answer of the Regent to the first remonstrance was controversial, disputing the right of the British government to interfere, and alleging proudly that she held her Regency of God,

to whom only she was accountable. Sir David
Ochterlony replied, that God would find instruments to displace those whose conduct was inju-
rious to the interests of the state, and threatened to
disturb the public tranquillity : and he gave her
to understand that the late Raja had left another
widow of superior family and rank to herself, being
of Rhatôr extraction, and who might, therefore,
conveniently be raised to the Regency in her room.
This lady had before been a candidate for the
office, but Sir David Ochterlony had himself promoted the election of the infant Raja's mother,
and to prevent intrigue, had further caused the
Rhatôrnee to remove from Jypoor.

It was impossible for the Regent to mistake
the hint thus conveyed, and her apprehensions
were greatly excited at the discovery of the decided part the British government were prepared
to take against her. She consulted all the Thakoors, and others whom she considered as attached
to her interest, and made several offers to compromise the matter by nominating some other than
Byreesal to be the responsible minister of the state.
Such an arrangement, however, would have left
the power in her own hands as before, and was
consequently refused ; when at last, seeing no
means of evasion or resistance, she finally adopted
the resolution to submit. Jhola Ram was de-
prived of all his offices, and sent to reside on a

small stipend at Sonagurh, in Bundelkhund ; while the Thakoors most active in her favour retired to their estates, leaving Byreesal to exercise the ministerial functions without further counteraction or intrigue.

Thus, by the effect of our interposition, a party has been made to preponderate, which might else have proved the weaker, and a minister has been maintained in power who without our aid would probably have fallen. Feeling his reliance on the British government, this minister will henceforward be less dependant on any existing faction, and less disposed, therefore, to consult its interests ; indeed, it will naturally become his policy to weaken the power of the aristocracy by enforcing resumptions, and adopting every means to subject the Thakoors to his authority. This state of things is not very different from that produced from nearly the same causes at Hyderabad, and at every other court where the administration has not happened to fall into hands sufficiently vigorous to stand without our help. The tendency of the system is sufficiently obvious ; but if the end be the transfer sooner or later of the entire authority into British hands, there is at least one advantage in the mode, viz. that the result is produced by gradual and insensible steps; and while the odium of the usurpation is removed, the evils of a sudden change are mitigated to the classes most injuriously affected by the revolution. We shall have to recur to this subject in the observations with which it is proposed to close the review of the political condition that has resulted to India from all these measures.

CHAPTER XXIII.

POLITICAL REVIEW.

Arrangements consequent upon the Mahratta war—reduced condition of hostile powers—Sutara Raja—his absolute dependence—Bhoosla—the successor of Apa Saheb, a minor—affairs administered by British officers—Hol-kur—Tanteen Jog's ministry—resources left to the family—dismemberment of Ameer Khan and Ghufoor Khan—Sindheea—British officers introduced into his military establishment—effect in reducing him to dependence —Condition of India generally—classification of native powers—1st. Independent management of their own concerns—2d. British nomination of the minister—examples of this system—3d. Administration by British officers—general reflections—benefit to the country from extension of British influence—Conclusion.

WE come now to state the measures consequent upon the rupture with the Mahratta powers. The result of the campaign of 1817-18, placed the territories and destinies of the three great families, which took the lead in the war, at the absolute disposal of the Governor-general; and although there were circumstances as well in the manner of declaring against us, as in the subsequent submission, which led to shades of diversity in the arrangements concluded in each instance, there is yet so much of similarity as to show the same policy to have dictated the whole. In the place of each of these families there is now established a petty dependant court exercising more or less of authority according to its fitness for rule, but subject to the direct control of the British government.

The greater part of the dominions of Bajee Rao Pêshwa have been quietly occupied and administered by British officers ; and as a substitute for his mischievous authority, a race has been redeemed from captivity, and restored to a nominal sovereignty over the remainder, which, as well from the circumstances of its elevation, as from habit and the inexperience of the world in which its members have been educated, affords so many securities for future subservience.

The case of the Bhoosla family is not very different. The richest provinces of its territory were demanded as the price of forgiveness on the first rupture, and these, like the better part of Bajee Rao's dominions, have been occupied and annexed to the British possessions. On the Raja's second defection, his permanent removal from power was resolved upon ; and expulsion and exile having followed in due course, his place has been supplied by a youth incapable of exercising any real sovereignty. Thus the dissolution of the old government, and the incapacity of the new, have brought the affairs of the state under the direct management of British officers. The policy of the Marquess of Hastings left for the election of the Holkur durbar either hostility, or concert for the suppression of the predatory system, and although, in the first instance, circumstances compelled this court to make choice of the former alternative, still on the issue proving unfortunate, it very soon made its submission ; and having done so, abided faithfully by the terms imposed. The consequence has been, that although circumscribed greatly in its territory and resources, and assimilated in this respect to the Sutara and Nagpoor establishments, the court has since enjoyed much more independence, and stands now much higher in the scale of native powers, than either of the other two. The condition of each will require a little further elucidation.

The motives which induced the Marquess of Hastings to annihilate the name and authority of Pêshwa, and to occupy all Bajee Rao's territories, with exception to the small domain reserved for the Sutara Raja, have already been fully explained. The tract so reserved lies above the western Ghâts, between the Neera and Bheema to the north, and the Kishna and Warna to the south. Eastward it extends as far as Pundurpoor; but the boundary on that side has not been accurately defined. Although the intention of establishing the Raja's authority in this territory was early declared, and the administration was in consequence, from the first, conducted in his name, it was nevertheless deemed politic, in order to ascertain the resources and assimilate the management to that pursued in other parts of Bajee Rao's dominions, to retain the authority for some time in the hands of British officers. Captain James Grant of the Madras establishment was accordingly appointed to administer the affairs of the tract under the control of the commissioner of Poona. The result of his management gave a revenue for the Sutara family of thirteen lakh and seventy-five thousand rupees, besides Jageers and other alienations from the rent-roll, making, in the aggregate, about twenty lakh for the gross revenue of the assigned territory. On the 25th of September 1819, the engagement, fixing the relations of the Raja with the British government, was settled by the same officer. Under its stipulations the territory is to be held " in subordinate co-operation with the British government," and the provisions fixing the Raja's future dependence are more than usually precise. It was particularly agreed, that, for some time to come, the tract should remain under the management of British officers;—that the Jageers should always be under the management of British officers, — that the jageers should always be under our guarantee, and in the event of a tranfer, that the Raja should conform to the British system, in the management of his customs, besides surrendering criminals, excluding Europeans, and the other usual stipulations.

With so many occasions for interference, the Raja's authority can never be looked upon as independent ; indeed, in the interval of our management, revenue settlements and judicial awards have been made, and the interests thence arising will have to be secured from capricious alteration. It will hence always be necessary to hold the Raja in a kind of tutelage, and the permanent residence of a British officer at Sutara, for the general supervision of the affairs of the principality, seems indispensable.

With respect to military establishment, it is not intended to allow the Raja to entertain any troops of his own, and the military services of all the jageerdars, and other retainers of the late Mahratta empire, have been transferred to the British government. In fact, therefore, the Sutara court differs little from the pageant courts of Dehlee, Moorshedabad, and Arcot, and having once been reduced to this footing by our direct assumption of the country, the attempt to retrace our steps will, it is to be feared, only lead to embarrassment and inconvenience. The pledge, however, having been given, its redemption became indispensable, and the territory has accordingly been restored to the Raja's management, but with what success, and under what checks, we are unable at present to state.

The Raja of Kolapoor, the southern neighbour of Sutara, and of the same race with him, is a chief of more consideration than the latter can ever aspire to attain. His territory is very nearly of equal extent, and under an arrangement concluded in 1812 he enjoys absolute independence, and unlimited authority, civil and military, within it. In 1813, when the present Raja came to the Guddee, a resort to British protection was necessary to secure the integrity of the Kolapoor territory from the attacks of some southern jageerdars, fostered underhand by Bajee Rao. Since then nothing has ever occurred to call for interposition of any kind, and pending the subsequent intrigues and distractions of the Mahratta empire, Mr. Elphinstone always looked upon this chief as one of the most favourably disposed towards the British cause.

The piratical conduct of the Sawuntwaree State, situated between Kolapoor and Goa, having, as we have before stated, obliged the Bombay government to fit out an expedition to reduce it to submission, a political agent was left there to control the conduct of the Malwan durbar. Eventually, however, this principality will be placed on the footing of Kolapoor. Its Raja, Khêm Sawunt, of the Bhoosla race, is only just reaching the years of majority, and the intrigues and squabbles of the women, who held the regency pending his minority, were the principal cause of the previous misconduct of the court. Independently of these three principalities, there are likewise six of the larger jageerdars of the Mahratta empire, who, having made their submission in time to save their possessions, enjoy them on the footing of protected independence, thus forming exceptions to the general system under which the whole of Bajee Rao's dominions in the Dukhun have been occupied and administered by the British government. These are the Prithee Nidhee, the Punt Suchem, the Senaputee, and the Punt Ambait, with Apa Desaee of Nipanee, and the Augria family, chiefs of Kolaba. Over these, the Sutara Raja has no authority whatsoever, and their mutual rivalry and jealousies, added to the recollection of the utter failure of Bajee Rao's effort to shake our power with the united energy of the whole Mahratta nation, afford abundant securities against any future mischievous intrigues or combinations amongst them.

With the above reservations, and some few villages and districts held by Sindheea, the entire

Mahratta territory within the Dukhun is directly administered by British officers. The tract above the western Ghâts was formed into five districts, each under a collector, subject to the control of the general Commissioner at Poona. The collectors were stationed at Darwar for the districts southward of the Kishna and Warna, called sometimes the Carnatic districts ; at Sutara* for the reserved domain of that family, and the adjoining territory ; at Poona, for the city and environs ; at Ahmednugur, for the Northern Mahratta territory ; and in Kandês for that province. Mr. Elphinstone continued as Commissioner until 1820, when, in recompense for his services, he was appointed Governor of Bombay, and Mr. Chaplin, of the Madras Civil Service, succeeded him. Up to this period, the Supreme Government had retained the control of affairs over the Commissioner, but the occasion was now taken to transfer the whole territory to the Bombay presidency, for which its situation marked it as an appropriate augmentation. The Konkan, or tract from the sea-shore to the western Ghâts had, from the first establishment of the British authority, been subject to Bombay.

Before leaving Poona, Mr. Elphinstone addressed to the Supreme Government a most com-

---

* Since the transfer to the Sutara Raja in 1822, the officer stationed here has been designated Resident.

prehensive report on the affairs of the country, explaining at length its condition, and that of all classes of its inhabitants, and giving a complete exposé of his mode of administration, as compared on one hand with that of his Mahratta predecessors, and on the other with the systems of the Company's governments. The limit of a work like the present will not admit of any attempt to incorporate the information and opinions of this valuable state paper in the brief review to which we are restricted, and as the report itself has been printed and freely circulated by the Indian governments, it is the less necessary to make the attempt.

Though larger in geographical extent, the reserved territory of the Bhoosla Raja is not much more productive than that of Sutara. By far the greater part of it is unprofitable mountain and jungul, and even what little there is of fertile region, is for the most part imbedded in hills and forests, and occupied by Rajas and petty chiefs of indigenous races, from whom their Mahratta conquerors extorted with much difficulty a very scanty and irregularly paid tribute. It has been seen that Apa Saheb was successful in raising most of these chiefs in insurrection against the government set up in his room. The consequence was, that it became necessary to employ British detachments to reduce them to obedience, and the continuance of Apa Saheb in a condition to excite apprehension, led next to the establishment of posts of troops for the complete military occupation of the country. The transition to the next step was easy and natural. The officers in command of these posts became vested with the entire civil administration in supercession of all native authority within the Bhoosla territory.

In June 1818, Lord Hastings issued his instructions as to the course to be pursued upon the displacement of Apa Saheb. He directed the minor grandson of Raghoojee, by the daughter married to Goojur Apa, to be seated on the vacant Guddee, upon his adoption into the Bhoosla family, by Buka Baee, the surviving widow, which was requisite to perfect his title to the succession.

It was his Lordship's wish that a native administration should be formed from amongst the principal people of the court of Nagpoor, and Nurayun Pundit naturally occurred as a fit instrument for the purpose. After a short experience of his incapacity, however, Buka Baee, the adoptive mother, and regent for the minor, invited Goojaba Dada, who it will be recollected had been driven by Apa Saheb to retire for security to Allahabad,* within the British dominions, to assume

* Vide page 429, vol. 1.

the station of Dewan, and manage the interests of the family. He accordingly was summoned down for the purpose, and upon his arrival, the ceremony of the young Raja's adoption and formal investiture was duly performed. He was proclaimed by the name of Bajee Rao Bhoosla. In the mean time, however, the discovery of further intrigues and designs of Apa Saheb required all the Resident's vigilance and circumspection ; and finding it impossible to trust any Mahratta at the court, it was deemed indispensable, pending the operations against the ex-Raja and his adherents, to place every department at the capital, as well as in the interior, under the direct control of British officers. This extended even to the mint and treasury of Nagpoor, and though adopted as a measure of temporary precaution, the difficulty of withdrawing has led to a continuance of the system even to the present time. Two land revenue settlements have in this interval been made generally for the whole territory, by the direct agency of British officers, acting under the Resident's orders, and in fact the entire administration has been and is still conducted by the Resident, and persons of his selection.

This state of things was much deprecated by the Marquess of Hastings, who, on all occasions, showed his anxiety to prevent unnecessary interposition in the affairs of native governments.—

Though sensible of the necessity of the original assumption of authority, pending the operations against Apa Saheb, his instructions enjoined its confinement to the narrowest possible limits, and directed that there should be no departure from the native system, so that when an efficient and trust-worthy administration could be formed, all might be in a condition to be retransferred without embarrassment or inconvenience.   Again, when the conclusion of the first revenue settlement for three years was reported, it was the special instruction of the Supreme Government, that at the second, which it was resolved should be for five years, the written engagements to be exchanged with the landholders and malgoozars should contain a notice that the Raja's authority would be re-established, and that the ensuing arrangements must therefore be adjusted with his officers.   It remains to see what will be the issue of these measures now that the Raja is attaining the years of majority.   There is so much inconvenience and loss of credit also in withdrawing after having gone so far, that sooner or later some arrangement will probably ensue of the same character as those made heretofore with the Arcot, the Tanjore, and the Moorshedabad families. Howsoever much indeed we may deprecate the tendency of the system, it does not seem possible to stop its course, and to retrace steps once made in advance is always a measure of more than questionable expediency. If the desire of maintaining the old families in splendour and authority weighs on one side, the interests of the population at large, with which such a course appears absolutely incompatible, preponderate on the other, and demand the sacrifice at our hands. The intention of removing the Goand chiefs from their dependance on Nagpoor has been already avowed, and the whole territory nearly is in the same condition with the tract occupied by the Goand tribes, and has therefore an equal claim to be transferred permanently to our direct management. A population, be it observed, that has once been accustomed to an administration conducted on principle by British officers of integrity, acting for the public good, will never yield a ready obedience to the rapacious agents of a native despot; and it is the height of tyranny to deliver them over, bound hand and foot, to become the victims of any vicious system that chance or caprice may substitute for that to which they have been accustomed.

At the same time that the civil administration of the Bhoosla dominions was thus openly assumed and exercised by British functionaries, measures were taken under the more direct sanction of the Supreme Government for permanently securing the military force of the state. All the troops retained on the Raja's establishment, have accordingly been organized on the model of the reformed infantry and cavalry of the Nizam ; that is, have been embodied in corps under the command of British officers of the Company's army. Thus in the scale of native powers the Bhoosla court holds now but a very low grade, and is more absolutely a pageant than even the Sutara Raja. We have no means of stating the footing on which the Raja's personal establishment has been placed, nor whether the charge has been defrayed hitherto from surplus revenue yielded by our management, after paying all the civil and military expenses, or is provided by an annual increase of debt. The matter is well deserving of attention, and doubtless will have received it.

The territories on the Nerbudda, and other tracts acquired from the Bhoosla, and annexed to the British possessions, have been administered on the same principles with the dominions of Bajee Rao. A Commissioner was appointed in 1818 with full powers to superintend the whole, while under him several junior officers performed the local duties. These have been unfettered by the necessity of adhering to any particular set of regulations, and the course of proceeding in every department has been left to be arranged by the Commissioner, under a mere general instruction from the government, gradually to adapt the principles of the settled administration of its old possessions to the habits and feelings of its new subjects. Experience had shown that sudden and abrupt changes of system, even when made from the worst to the best, produced, nevertheless, revolutions of property and extensive misery to particular classes. This was the main evil to be avoided, and the sense of it led the Supreme Government always to prefer leaving the functionaries sent to newly-acquired territories to act on their own responsibility, with only very general instructions for their guidance, and large discretionary powers. The system doubtless required individuals worthy of such high confidence, and in Mr. Charles Arthur Molony*, the Commissioner

---

* In the past rains, that is, in the month of September 1824, this valuable public servant fell a victim to the fever incident to the climate of Jubulpoor at that season, and which had annually attacked him there at the same period of the year. A singular modesty of character and manners prevented his seeking those means of public distinction by which others in his situation might with a small fraction of his talents have made their name generally known to the world. Of his public worth, however, all that have been near the country under his management, or have been brought officially or privately into contact with him, know enough to regret his loss as irreparable, and no one ever left so large a circle of really attached friends. The author was his college cotemporary, and the friendship which arose out of this connexion strengthened with years, and in a long course of similar habits and pursuits, had grown into an affection such as is rarely felt in the short period of human existence. He can trust himself to say no more.

appointed to the Nerbudda districts as in Mr.
Elphinstone, it found an agent peculiarly gifted
for the task, one who will hereafter be cited as a
bright example of the efficiency and success of
this mode of administration.

The court of Mulhar Rao Holkur, which similarly passed through the alembic of a regeneration
by British means, contrived by good conduct to
escape the degradation which befel its associates
in the Mahratta cause. Mulhar Rao, like the
Bhoosla Raja, was still a minor, incapable of
managing the affairs of his family. The oppor- ·
tune death, however, of Toolsee Baee, who it will
be recollected was sacrificed by the Putan military
the night before the battle of Mehudpoor, removed
a source of perpetual intrigue and mischief, and
opened the door for the introduction of a ministry
selected from the most reasonable adherents of
the court. The choice fell upon Tanteea Jog, as
we have before mentioned; and as he possessed
in his own person considerable credit and influence, and was by birth and education a man of
business, he has contrived to make his government work by its native means, without resorting
to British aid or interference in its internal affairs.
It is to be observed, however, that a British political agent has continually resided at the court,
and all its relations with Rajpoot chiefs and feu-

datories or dependants likely to give trouble, as well as all disputes with Doulut Rao Sindheea, or with members of the Puwar family, have been adjusted by his means. The facility of resorting to this mediation on occasions of difficulty has doubtless been felt by Tanteea Jog as a great advantage. Nevertheless he is entitled to much credit for his internal administration, which has not only gone on smoothly without calling for British interposition, but is represented to be in the main good, and to have produced a considerable improvement as well in the resources as in the general prosperity of the country. His system of revenue management seems to be that of farming villages or small districts to middle-men of substance and respectability for considerable periods. Under this plan, the revenue realized from the territory left to the Holkur family by the treaty of Mundisôr, is estimated by Sir John Malcolm to amount now to about twenty-five lakh of rupees, which sum therefore may be assumed as the annual income of the court. The charges of course do not fall much short of the receipts, but this is a matter with which we have no concern at present. Indôr has been fixed upon as the permanent capital and place of residence of the Holkur family, but the territory is still so much interwoven with that of Sindheea as to preclude any attempt to trace its limits. With ex-

ception to the arbitration of some disputed points
with other Mahratta families, and the adjustment
of the Purtab-Gurh and similar tributes, the
treaty of Mundisôr has sufficed for the settlement
of all its relations.

The military contingent to be furnished by
Holkur at our requisition is three thousand horse,
including the quota of Ghufoor Khan. The occasion for calling out this force has not lately arisen,
nor is it likely we shall ever count much upon its
services. The court will thus be saved from one
material source of vexation, by escaping those
efforts to reform and secure efficiency to the contingents which generally end in their being offi-
cered from our own army, and made substantially
British troops. The consummation most to be
wished in respect to all these obligations of military service is, that from desuetude of requisi-
tions, the establishments may be neglected until
they become wholly unmilitary, and are confined
to duties of police and revenue, or other civil functions ; for now that tranquillity has been every
where established, the military character is no
longer suited to the petty states who occupy the
country. The heads of them should therefore be
encouraged to live freely on their incomes, and
improve their territories by beneficence and public
works, while their establishments of horse and foot

fall gradually to decay as the walls of their towns and villages have already been suffered to do. The dismemberment of Ameer Khan, and the establishment of Ghufoor Khan in a guaranteed Jageer from the possessions of the Holkur family, have had the effect of introducing a counterpoise to the predominant influence of the Hindoos in this particular part of India, and the respectable footing on which the Bhopâl Nuwab has been placed, will tend to give weight and consistency to the Moosulman interest so created. No doubt there exists at present very little community of sentiment between the Mahrattas and Rajpoots, or other indigenous races ; still, as there is this common bond of union, it will not be thought an overstrained effort of political foresight to guard against the possibility of revolution by thus consolidating and strengthening an influence unconnected with either. The sacrifice exacted of the Holkur court, in order to effect the arrangements made with these two Putan adventurers, was a revenue of between six and seven lakh of rupees for Ameer Khan, and half that amount for the other chief. Ameer Khan advanced a claim to the lands guaranteed in Jageer to Ghufoor Khan, alleging that chief to have been merely an agent or manager set over them on his behalf, and it is by no means improbable that such was the origin

of the Jageerdar's possession; but as in the settlement with Holkur's court, the present condition of Ghufoor Khan had influenced the stipulation in his favour, it was not deemed advisable
to be over-scrupulous in tracing the origin of his
title, and the claim was therefore rejected, nor
would the British government permit the feudal
allegiance of Ghufoor Khan to be transferred from
Holkur to the Putan, as solicited by Ameer Khan.
In order, however, to console this chief for the disappointment and losses incurred, as well in this
respect as in the abrupt termination of his relations with the Rajpoot states, Rampoora Tonk,
a cession of the treaty of Mundisôr, was conferred
upon him, and he has since been otherwise favoured as well personally as by the grant of an
income to his son.

In all these arrangements, the main consideration has been to guard against any future disturbance of the public peace, and the weakness and
absolute dependance on ourselves, in which all the
chiefs who have heretofore taken the lead amongst
the states of India must now feel themselves,
seems to afford complete assurance against any
repetition of hostile conduct on their part.   Doulut Rao Sindheea is the only one whose power has
not been so reduced, but his character is not the
less changed.   Instead of holding the attitude of
a rival, jealous of our encroaching preponderance,

and ready to head an opposition to our measures, he has thrown himself completely into our arms, and is now endeavouring to avail himself of our name and authority to give system and organization to his own government, which was else on the point of dissolution. It will be recollected that it was a stipulation of the treaty of Gwalior that Sindheea should furnish a contingent of five thousand horse, to be placed under British officers for employment in the Pindaree War. The force was not obtained in time to be made available against the freebooters, and the bad quality of the horse furnished, with other difficulties and delays of the court, led to the greater part being raised directly by the British officers appointed to superintend their movements. The corps was, however, no sooner completed in this way, than Sindheea found his advantage from the power it gave him of controlling his different military commanders,* who had to this time enjoyed almost

* Colonel Baptiste's fate is an example in point. Alarmed at the conclusion of the treaty of Gwalior, he left his troops and hastened thither in Nov. 1818, to ascertain the intentions of the Durbar. He was at first well received and honoured with the title of General ; but no sooner had Sindheea taken his line and come to the resolution of keeping well with the English, at all hazards, than he had both Baptiste and his son confined on the plea of calling them to account for the revenue of the lands assigned for the pay of their troops. A mutiny was at the same time instigated amongst the soldiery,

complete independence ; and at the same time
of consolidating his authority over the heteroge-
neous mass of subjects and feudatories who owned
more or less of dependence on him.   One of the
British officers with a body of these troops was
employed by Sindheea, very soon after the corps
was organized, in settling an arrangement with
the Raghoogurh family, which had heretofore
given so much trouble to Colonel Baptiste. He
effected the object with much skill and success,
and having reduced one branch of the family to
accept an amicable settlement, expelled and dispersed the rest, who still clung to the life of
violence and depredation to which their desperate
circumstances had driven them.   Subsequently
Urjoon Singh, ex-Raja of Gura-Kota, a depen-
dency of Sindheea lying east of Sagur, broke out
into insurrection ; and overpowering the garrison
there, was on the point of recovering the whole
of that territory and setting up in independence.
The contingent was here again made available
to restore the Gwalior authority, and with the aid
of a detachment and train from Sagur, the town

and another commander sent to supersede Baptiste's lieutenants. Mutual violence ensued, and the contingent was then
made use of to awe all parties to submission. Baptiste, after
suffering the torture, not for the first time, was allowed to
retire to Sheeopoor, the only possession left for the maintenance of his family.

itself was besieged and quickly recovered. These
and other services having made the Gwalior Durbar sensible of the value of a force constituted in
this manner, its assent was soon after obtained to
the permanent appropriation of the funds ceded
by the treaty of Gwalior for the maintenance of a
body of two thousand horse, to be commanded
by British officers, and paid from the Resident's
treasury as heretofore. The engagement to this
effect bears date the 6th of February 1820, and
some minor arrangements and exchanges of territory were settled on the same occasion. Feeling
its reliance on this force, the court has since given
way freely to the jealousy with which it viewed
the conduct of its other commanders, and most of
their military establishments have accordingly
been broken up and dismissed. The want of funds
has alone prevented the reductions from being
carried further, and to supply these, it was at one
time in agitation for the British government to
advance a considerable sum to the Durbar on a
territorial mortgage, but the negociation failed,
though the overture came originally from the
ministers of Doulut Rao. The tributes realized
through the British government, along with the
pensions in lieu of Jageers assigned for the payment of the two thousand horse, amount to
10,24,193 Gwalior rupees. Besides this, there
are grants to different sirdars and members of

the family, amounting to 17,14,535 rupees, which being under the British guarantee are equally beyond the control of the court.   Including these items, the gross revenue remaining to Sindheea has been estimated at about one crore and forty lakh, but the cost of collection cannot, under the present system, be assumed at less than twenty-five per cent.   With such a revenue, the Gwalior Durbar still maintains of course a very prominent place among the native powers of Hindoostan, but this court has abdicated altogether its claim to independence, as well by allowing the dissolution of its native military power, as from habitual reliance on the counsels and mediation of the British resident at Gwalior.   The financial resources of the state, moreover, are by no means free, and it will be a long time before Doulut Rao can hope to redeem his territory from the mortgages and assignments made at various periods of distress to native bankers on most ruinous terms, so as to eat up nearly all his income.   When he shall have done so, he will be entitled to rank with the Oudh chief, who has recently assumed the kingly title, and whose revenues are about equal.

From what is above stated, it will be evident that, although Doulut Rao Sindheea has never formally accepted a subsidiary alliance, and engaged to bear the charge of a body of British troops, he is not on that account less dependent, and the arrangement for perpetuating the introduction of British officers into his military establishment, brings him decidedly within the class. All the power his government now possesses is derived from this source, and the arrangement affords a prospect of that degree of tranquillization and prosperity to the country which ordinarily results from a connexion of the kind. Even this will be no inconsiderable gain, when set in comparison with the state of things previously existing ; for the want of organization, or of system of any kind, either in civil or military affairs, had produced a state of anarchy and general distress unheard of among civilized nations, and which had nearly reached its crisis in the absolute depopulation of the country. So sensible are all classes of the advantage which has resulted from the general establishment of the British influence, that even the Mahrattas, and military chiefs of Sindheea's durbar, talk now of the period which terminated in the measures we have related, as the time of trouble, and universally congratulate themselves on having escaped its evils. The prospects of the country, and its population under this system, deserve the severe scrutiny of the statesman.

Of the peninsula of India about two thirds are now under the direct management of the three Presidencies, and these doubtless are by far the best governed regions of Asia. The means of bettering the administration, and of imposing fresh checks on the conduct of the functionaries employed, is the constant study of the most intelligent men in the country, and of many more whose attention is wholly given to the subject in Europe. Hence there is a continual effort at improvement, and the result is, that a system of government has been established which not only affords as complete security of person and property to the natives of the country, as it has been found possible to give, but has promoted an increase of wealth and prosperity and general happiness and contentment such as India never before enjoyed.

The remaining third of the peninsula is in a different state. The traveller cannot enter it without having a guard of armed men. Even the European, whose person is under the eye of a power which all acknowledge and bow to, takes an escort immediately he crosses the British frontier. Still it must not be supposed that there is no improvement. Although the protection from thieves and robbers, and the arrangements for the administration of civil and criminal justice, are incomplete every where, except in the British possessions, this is now the worst that can be said of the remaining districts. A few unlicensed plunderers, single, or in small gangs, form the only interruption to the general peace of the country, for all the native chiefs, amongst whom the tract not directly occupied by the British is parcelled out, have begun to feel the necessity of administering their territory with a view to peace. The obligation to protect travellers, and encourage trade—to render equal justice, and promote the prosperity of the country, is acknowledged by all; but, from their ignorance of the principles of government, their execution is, for the most part, very defective.

The system which prevails throughout is pretty uniform. There is, first, a native family vested with the nominal sovereignty; then there is a military force essentially British, having British officers, or there is a British cantonment at no great distance, and sometimes both, to assure the submission of the population to whatever may be ordained. For the application of this force, and to watch over the conduct of those who originate the administrative measures, there is every where a British Political Agent or Resident, reporting only to his government, and receiving his orders thence, but exercising a large personal discretion as to interference or non-interference with the native local authority.

The administrative function in these states is variously exercised: sometimes the recognised sovereign governs for himself. The Raja of

Mysoor appears, since the death of Poornea, to afford an example of this, and Doulut Rao Sindheea is another of the larger powers who may still be said to reign in person; for although his embarrassments have thrown him into the hands of a banker-minister, Gokul Paruk, who is in fact the principal manager, the choice was Sindheea's own, and the minister was neither imposed by the British, nor does he enjoy our guarantee or sanction.

It was the intention of Lord Hastings to leave the Oudh chief in the same manner independent, but the indolent habits of the prince led him to transfer the power to a designing favourite of low extraction and profligate character, who having a party interest to serve without any assurance of British support to rely upon, has established a very mischievous influence and authority, attended with more ruin and distress to individuals and families whom he has looked upon as personally hostile, than would have resulted from any other system. The confusion and misgovernment that ensued have* recently determined the British

* The determination to urge a reform in the Oudh administration was adopted after the departure of Lord Hastings from India, for his Lordship, though not insensible of the bad character and mischievous results of the minister's conduct, was always averse to interfere otherwise than in the way of mild expostulation.

government to interfere authoritatively for its correction and reform, but in what manner its views of improvement are to be enforced is a question not yet settled, and one that must depend in a great measure on the Resident.

Oudh having fallen into this condition, there are none other of the larger states that can be said to be administered by the prince in person. Of the minor ones Kolapoor and Kota, in the lifetime of Zalim Singh, that is, if he be regarded as its chief, Joudhpoor, and the Rajpoot states within the desert, almost all the petty chiefships of Bundelkhund; Bhopâl also until the death of Nuzur Mohummed; Ameer Khan's possessions; the Rampoor and Elichpoor jageers; Bhurtpoor, Macherree, and the Seikh chiefs beyond the Jumna, and sundry others belong to this class. And it may be observed, that if the chief be well disposed, and the territory small enough to be managed as an estate, the chances of good government are as great under this system as under any other. For the prince or feudatory has a direct interest for his own credit sake in managing well, and he is above the temptations to abuse his authority, which avarice, or the desire of serving party ends, present ordinarily to a casual minister. At the same time there is not much need of system or acquaintance with general principles, when the whole can be personally superintended: character, therefore, is every thing, and its influence is further extended by the despotic form of all the governments from the largest even to the petty chief, whose revenue is but half a lakh. Some check is, however, indispensable, in order to prevent outrageous wrong, and this is afforded by the presence of the British Political Agent. If the conduct of the prince or chief, when left to himself, be radically vicious; if he be an imbecile and the tool of mischievous minions; if again he be a minor, and his guardians fail grossly in their duty, it is the Resident's or Agent's business to report the circumstances to his government, and obtain its sanction to apply a proper remedy. The obligation of interposing in such cases seems to be a necessary consequence of our holding the military power; for we wield it with so strong an arm, as utterly to deprive the population of their natural remedy in rebellion, and the aristocracy of theirs in faction and conspiracy. Unless, therefore, the correction come from the British government there can be no limit to vice and tyranny, howsoever intolerable. The consideration of the remedy brings us to the other forms assumed by the native states under protection.

When the prince is vicious or incapable in such a degree as to require interposition, the British government has a choice of three courses:—First, the reigning prince may be removed, and a successor provided of better disposition, or superior capacity. Secondly, the reigning prince may be placed in tutelage of a native administration; or, thirdly, the country may be administered for him by British officers.

The deposition of the Prince, being an act of extreme violence, is reserved for extreme cases. It has never been resorted to, except on proof of defection from the alliance, which, as the stronger power, we naturally call treachery and rebellion; or of very heinous crimes, such as murder, and the like. The history of British India, from the time of Kasim Ulee Khan of Bengal, to that of Apa Saheb of Nagpoor, affords abundant instances of the former kind. Of princes, or feudatories deposed for murder, without defection or treachery to the alliance, the predecessor of the present Rampoor Jageerdar, who was put aside in the time of Sir John Shore, for assassinating his brother, is a case in point; and a more recent instance has occurred within the past year, in the supercession of the Kurnôl Jageerdar Mohummed Moonuwur Khan, for heinous criminality, and more especially for putting to death one of his wives. Though perhaps justified in such cases, the example would be lost were the same meed to be dealt out to inoffensive imbecility, mischievous only in its consequences, or to mere errors and vices of administration; and yet such are the cases that ordinarily require interpo-

sition. The second course is hence very generally adopted, viz. a ministry, or regency, is established by a direct exertion of British influence,
and the individual, or party, selected for the office
is maintained in the exercise of all power to
the prejudice even of the sovereign's authority.
Under this system less open violence is certainly
done, than by the sovereign's absolute removal;
but the effect is very nearly the same. The remedy, however, may still not be sufficient, and
then there is no alternative but either to take the
country entirely, or to adopt the third and last
course, and directly administer its affairs for and
on behalf of the native state by British officers.
It will be necessary to say a word or two on the
merits of each of these systems.

The administrative power has been exercised
by ministers appointed through British agency
and under British guarantee at Hyderabad, at
Jypoor, and in several other states that might
be named; and the main defect of the system
seems to be, first, that it consolidates all power in
the hands of an irresponsible minister; and, secondly, that the degree of subsequent interposition depends entirely on the personal character of
the British representative, and is wholly beyond
the control of the government. A minister who
owes his elevation to such a source, feels that his
authority and influence depend on his creating the

impression that all his measures have the support of the British government. They must have the appearance, if not the reality, of emanating from close concert and intelligence with the Resident, and the strictest intimacy must therefore be kept up with him. The consequence is, that there is no ascertaining whether a measure is the Resident's, or the minister's. If any thing wrong occurs, the minister is acquitted of responsibility to his court, and the world he acts before, by alleging or giving it to be understood, that the matter was forced on him by his connexion with the British government. On the other hand, if the Resident be called to account, the minister's name is a cloak to cover every thing. Of the consequence of this system, the state of things at Hyderabad affords a notable instance. By the effect of measures originating in an apparent or real concert, a revolution was effected, which destroyed the influence of all the great men of the court, and by the resumption of their military tenures and other possessions, consolidated the whole power and resources of the country in the hands of the minister. Owing his appointment wholly to the British government, and needing its daily support, he avowedly yielded to the influence and suggestions of the Resident in the management and appropriation of the immense resources which thus came to his disposal; but this, instead of tending to the establishment of a frugal and economical system, produced a ruinous accumulation of debt, contracted on most usurious terms to an European mercantile house, establish-ed originally at the residency, and sanctioned at the Resident's intercession by the British go-vernment.

The whole of this subject has been so recently before the public, that it is quite unnecessary to enter into a particular explanation of its details. In so far as the mischief is attributable to the mis-conduct of the British functionaries, the public is the judge of their character and actions, and they have not failed to plead their cause before it. But on the form of native administration, of which the case is an instance, one cannot avoid remark-ing, that these or similar evils seem the necessary consequence of leaving to a single uncontrolled individual the management of such vast and va-rious interests as are involved in the administra-tion of so large a territory. The Nizam's reve-nue is stated at near two millions sterling (Rs. 1,89,33,553), which is much more than the best native steward can look after, although he have in the British Resident the best and most honest adviser ; and when the population also comes to be numbered by millions, some further provision for its interests, than the mere nomination of a steward, seems absolutely indispensable. Although, therefore, with the minor powers, whose territories are mere estates, such an arrangement may ordinarily suffice, we may assume it as a general maxim, that no native minister, ignorant as the best of them are of the principles of government upon system, can ever succeed with a territory meriting the distinction of being ranked as a substantive political interest of the higher order. The limit to which this mode is appropriate, may be assumed at twenty or thirty lakh of rupees.

The last form in which the administrative function appears to be exercised amongst the native powers, is one repugnant, doubtless, to the higher orders, but originating in the obligation felt by the British government to correct glaring and flagrant evils, by sufficiently strong measures. The appointment of British officers directly to superintend the local administration for, and in the name of the native state, is the system alluded to— a system which has been adopted at Nagpoor, and was for some time followed at Sutara, as we have before stated. The disorganization at Oodeepoor obliged a temporary resort to the same plan in that state also; but the most prominent instance of the kind is that of the Nizam's dominions, where, as a necessary remedy for the accumulated evils of the minister's mis-government, British officers have been stationed throughout the country to superintend the revenue settlements, to receive complaints of extortion, and to exercise a general control in all affairs.* These officers, like those employed in the Bhoosla territory, are under the orders of the British Resident at the capital; and as it is impossible for the government to regulate their conduct beforehand, or to establish any effectual check when the functions to be exercised are so ill defined, the powers and discretion necessarily vested in the Residents are extremely large. It depends of course wholly on the personal character of the individuals, whether they are abused or not; but as the Resident is, under this system, directly responsible for all that he does himself, or allows in others, he can no longer avail himself of the minister's name to cloak his measures.

Thus, it appears, that with the British government holding every where the military power, and exercising by the means of political agents stationed throughout such general supervision as is necessary to assure the public tranquillity, there are three forms in which the administrative func-

* This system originated with Sir Charles Metcalfe in 1821, and though disapproved by Lord Hastings, who wished the desired reforms to be effected through influence and advice, rather than by so open a supercession of the minister's authority, was nevertheless maintained by the other members of government to be indispensable, and carried completely into effect after his Lordship's departure.

tion is held by or for the native states now remaining in India. First, the independent, where
the prince manages his own estate with his own
agents; secondly, the ministerial, where the
British government, deeming the prince incompe-
tent from minority, imbecility, confirmed vicious
habit, or other cause of which itself only is the
judge, appoints a native minister, who governs
in his name; and thirdly, the residential, where
the British political functionary in person, and
by officers of his selection, manages the territory
for the native prince.

It must always be the wish of the Supreme
government that the affairs of the native powers
should be so conducted as to give no trouble; that is,
that they should proceed smoothly in the first of
the three forms above mentioned, without calling
for interposition of any kind, direct or indirect,
permanent or temporary. It is only when this is
found impossible, and when matters are so em-
broiled or mismanaged as to threaten the public
peace, that its interposition becomes indispensable,
and ends in giving one of the other two forms to
the state. The last of the three, being the most
violent remedy, is of course the most rare.

Compared with the systems of administration
introduced into the immediate possessions of the
three Presidencies of India, all these plans are of
course very imperfect schemes of government, being

deficient in the first essentials, from the absence of sufficient checks and restraints on the conduct of the individuals employed. The last, however, being the nearest approximation to a direct assumption of the country, seems to afford the population a much better chance of a government on principles with a view to its interests, than the second, which rests on the intervention of a native party at the court, and perhaps even more than the first.

Sooner or later all may possibly come to this stage ; but he must be a shallow politician that would hasten the catastrophe, or attempt the introduction of such a system, until every effort to prop up the native rule, and govern by the agency of the families in existence, had absolutely failed—until the change was acknowledged, by other powers similarly circumstanced, to be indispensable, and was called for by the general voice of the people.

With these observations we shall dismiss this subject : it is scarcely ripe for full discussion yet ; and we ought, perhaps, to offer some apology for touching upon it so imperfectly as we have done.

That the universal extension of the British influence has been attended with advantage to the people of India, is a proposition not likely to be combated at the present day. The different state of Malwa, and of all the provinces recently brought within its range, as viewed now that the system has had five years' trial, compared with the condition of the same countries in 1817-18, establishes the fact incontestably. It would be superfluous to dilate on the evidences of improvement afforded by the return of an expatriated population to resettle the villages they had left desolate, and to reclaim property which in the times of violence and trouble had been thrown up and deserted as valueless. But we may be allowed to observe, that such a result could not have been produced by the simple extirpation of the Pindarees, and suppression of the predatory system ; without the general controlling government established at the same time, the relief must have been but temporary, and the effect would before this have disappeared. The quiet subsiding of all classes into habits of peace, the revival of commerce and agriculture, the general employment of the poor in labour, the contentment of the rich and powerful with the lot in which they are placed, and their abandonment of irregular ambition and views of aggression on their neighbours, are blessings not attributable to the mere present immunity from Pindaree violence ;—they are the effect of a permanent system based on the general conviction felt, that there is a power which has the peace and happiness of the country at heart, and is both able and willing to take the necessary measures to ensure it.

Thus has the first step been gained in the pro-

2 E 2

gress of improvement,—the rest will follow in due course; for, unless checked from causes at present beyond the reach of human foresight, the impulse already given must carry the population forward. Some additional precautions may, perhaps, be required as the machine advances; but those who have set the principle thus in action will, for that at least, have a claim to the lasting gratitude of the large family of the human race which has been brought to feel its influence.

To the British interests there will result from the new order of things established, first, a perpetual immunity from the hostile ravage of our immediate provinces,—an evil against the recurrence of which we could never have had any security, so long as a large portion of India continued to be a hotbed for engendering the instruments of rapine and disorder, and a place of refuge in defeat, or an asylum for the harvest of successful spoliation. The consolidation of the whole peninsula under one uniform system, if that system possess but the stability which experience leads us to expect, will further, while it lessens the occasions of internal alarm, advance the external frontier of the British dominion to the natural barriers of India, the sea, the Heemachul, and the sandy deserts of the Indus. These barriers are assailable at very few points; and the security they afford from external violence must give additional vigour to any effort that may be requisite, whether to suppress local disaffection, or for the resistance of foreign aggression, through any one of the few avenues of approach. In the utter absence of any military power within the barrier, except such as would be equally available with our own against an invader, the strength that can be thrown forward to meet such a danger is almost unlimited; and faulty indeed must that government be, that, with such means at its disposal, should risk the bare possibility of disaster.

The struggle which has thus ended in the universal establishment of the British influence, is particularly important and worthy of attention, as it promises to be the last we shall ever have to maintain with the native powers of India. Henceforward this epoch will be referred to as that whence each of the existing states will date the commencement of its peaceable settlement, and the consolidation of its relations with the controlling power. The dark age of trouble and violence, which so long spread its malign influence over the fertile regions of Central India, has thus ceased from this time ; and a new era has commenced, we trust, with brighter prospects,—an era of peace, prosperity, and wealth at least, if not of political liberty and high moral improvement.

CHAPTER XXIV.

FINANCIAL REVIEW.

1813 TO 1823.

Revenue of India—its character and peculiarities—General statement of receipts and disbursements in Bengal for ten years—explanation of the principal resources of Bengal—land revenue—customs—salt monopoly—Opium ditto—other items—statement for India during the same period —home territorial charges—and London account explained—debt account—cash balances—general results— Measures undertaken for the reduction of debt and relief of the Home Treasury—Conclusion.

IT is usual to close the history of any period or course of events with a statement of the Financial result. This is particularly the case in matters connected with India; and the custom, being a wholesome one, claims our observance. There are, however, some peculiarities in the system of Indian Finance which it will be necessary to explain before submitting the result in a tabular form.

In the first place, it is to be observed that the Revenue of India is, for the most part, if not entirely, an absolute property attaching to the possession of the country. Its amount is not regulated, as in

England and most European countries, by any direct reference to the wants of the state. Instead of determining, in the first instance, the amount required for civil and for military charges, or for other disbursements of the year, and then settling the ways and means by which this specific amount shall be levied, the finance of India begins at the other end. The revenue is fixed and certain ; if the charges can be brought below it, the surplus is net profit to the Company or to the nation. If, on the other hand, a war, or other temporary exigency, demands a larger expenditure than the fixed revenue of the year, the government has not the option of providing for its wants by fresh taxation: the only expedient is to anticipate some of the existing revenue by a loan on the terms of the day. The debt of India is thus a mortgage on the government income, incurred either for its preservation or improvement, or for the acquisition of further income ; and the question, whether any particular measures have been attended with financial benefit, is resolvable by the simple calculation of whether the net revenue produced is worth the outlay. At the same time, the taxation being always the same, whatsoever may be the expenditure, the debt has nothing of the character of an optional alleviation of the burdens of the present generation, by throwing some additional load on futurity, which is the description given of the public debts of most European states.

Another circumstance to be borne in mind is, that the governments of India have none of those facilities which a paper currency and general system of credit offer to the conduct of large transactions in Europe. If a loan is raised or paid off, the whole amount is received or delivered in bullion, and that too silver, the most bulky of the precious metals. With such a currency the public resources cannot speedily be made available in all parts; and the most harassing duty the army has to perform, is that of providing treasure-escorts for the conveyance of cash from place to place. Hence it follows that a large supply in hand is indispensable for the current service of the state, and the amount has been estimated at not less than five or six crore of rupees for the three Presidencies. Unless this amount is exhibited as the balance of the annual accounts remaining in hand, the result is a temporary embarrassment; which means, that the payments of the Government from some of its hundred treasures are less punctual than usual. In England, where all the great payments of the government are made by the Bank, the nation is saved the expense and inconvenience of retaining a fund of this kind. An issue of exchequer bills, at low rates of interest to the Bank, and thence an issue of notes to the public, provides for every exigency; and the cost to the nation is the mere temporary charge of interest on the exchequer bills, until they are redeemed or funded. But if the necessity of holding a large supply thus in hand is a disadvantage we labour under in India, the stability of our currency is a redeeming benefit.

In looking to the state of the debt it is necessary to carry in mind this peculiarity; for it will frequently happen, that the produce of a loan has merely gone to swell the balances ; in which case, as the means of discharging it are in hand, there is no fresh incumbrance laid on the finances. The interest on so much of the debt as is so employed, is the price paid for the increased facility afforded by the possession of the cash to the financial operations of the state, and thus differs only from that paid on exchequer bills for a similar convenience, by being in India, at the same rate as the public stock, of which it is a part; but, in comparing the debt at different periods, the cash balance in hand will require to be deducted, in order to exhibit the true result.

In describing the Indian revenue, as a fixed inalienable property attaching to the government of the country, we by no means meant that the income was certain, and not liable to fluctuation. Putting out of the question its liability to increase or diminution, from the effect of good or bad management, the revenue consists of various items, which, from natural causes, are more or less productive in particular years; and there are some peculiarly variable from their dependence on the course of trade, and the price of articles in foreign markets. We cannot better explain the nature of the resources on which the Indian governments depend, than by passing under review those of the Bengal Presidency,—the largest, richest, and by far the most profitable of all the nation's possessions in the East.

The following is a statement of the receipts and disbursements of Bengal for ten years, commencing with 1813-14, the year in which the Marquess of Hastings assumed the government, and closing with 1822-3, that of his Lordship's return. It has been made up from the Bengal accounts; and most of the items can be verified, by reference to the financial correspondence of the Bengal government, published by order of the Court of Proprietors. The accounts laid before Parliament are made up in a different currency, and on a rather different principle: some little correction would therefore be necessary to show their correspondence.

	1819-20.	1820 21.	1821-22.	1822-23.
Land Revenue........				
Lower Provinces ...	3,17,70,247	3,09,47,025	3,18,27,733	3,18,98,619
Western Provinces...	3,75,68,649	3,81,52,477	3,88,90,770	3,87,63,686
Sagur and Hutta	10,13,440	11,19,115	11,52,256	10,84,806
Collections made by the Bhopâl Political Agent	1,19,530	2,45,228	1,59,588	96,571
Nerbudda distri	....	*58,90,449	23,57,468	19,27,566
Ajmeer	3,85,024	4,57,403	6,11,380	4,27,363
Tributes........	5,48,025	6,72,415	921,203	16,42,686
Charges deducted	— 2,94,194	—16,61,403		
Total Land Revenue, &	7,11,10,721	7,58,22,409	7,59,30,398	7,58,41,297
Customs	65,42,853	73,38,294	75,21,444	72,08,475
Salt monopoly.......	1,63,47,111	1,63,53,921	1,76,59,120	2,04,75,412
Average Price of Sal 100 maunds	(329rs 1as)	(333rs 11as)	(358rs 2as)	(418rs 15as)
Opium (ditto)	68,95,041	1,23,68,041	97,00,631	1,28,70,816
Average Price per Ches	(2,060)	(2,489)	(4,001)	(3,090)
General	28,12,124	28,73,527	28,40,801	27,60,550
Judicial	7,02,893	5,45,378	5,30,848	5,58,751
Marine	3,62,427	3,42,246	3,02,986	2,82,525
Miscellaneous	5,24,680	11,71,919	6,68,353	5,35,267
Total Bengal Receipts	10,52,97,840	11,68,15,835	11,51,54,581	12,05,33,093
Deduct Charges	9,46,38,828	9,40,57,021	9,05,52,964	9,09,89,858
Bengal Surplus	1,06,59,012	2,27,58,807	2,46,01,617	2,95,43,235

N. B. This statemerrinsic value of the coin is about two shillings and a halfpenny (2s. 0,566d.) into 210½ Calcutta Rupees; but as there is a scignorage of 2 per cent. on private bu
The Sonat Rupee is ta Sicca, in being 4½ per cent. less. The current rupee is a nominal one of account,

* The Receipts of ng those of the Nerbudda territory, the realization was as follows—

The Charges—colle reason of their amounting in that year to 16,64,403.
† The Tributes wer

	1821-22.	1822-23.
(	5,50,000	12,50,000
(	2,64,720	2,64,720
(	1,08,000	1,62,000
(	40,000	40,000
	9,62,720	17,16,720
	9,21,203	16,42,686

S.

317-18.	1818-19.	1819-20.	1820-21.	1821-22.	1S22-23.
2,72,023	1,45,85,674*	1,24,48,071*	1,09,29,659*	1,08,00,392*	1,16,84,567*
3,68,130	.78,62,492	79,70,571	79,95,244	82,04,115	80,83,636
2,42,078	23,94,992	24,68,802	27,79,653	26,89,841	28,87,744
1,45,034	70,38,324	70,18,977	76,14,592	70,91,831	76,58,055
				11,69,310	8,19,381
9,07,349	9,08,206	8,97,705	9,22,796	10,26,031	9,52,974
2,06,618	46,59,711	51,65,889	48,83,968	51,48,026	55,53,176
7,69,393	7,66,174	8,54,393	9,63,218	3,40,938	8,95,053
0,10,015	9,99,430	9,81,682	9,60,203	9,90,250	8,90,210
7,35,475	3,89,13,786	3,87,28,210	3,98,35,181	3,50,61,328	3,65,28,309
7,83,415	1,30,74,869	1,55,06,880	1,50,05,207	1,55,97,410	1,26,91,230
3,41,934	16,51,971	25,97,648	20,77,307	19,43,492	23,45,523
5,81,474	9,28,55,629	9,46,38,828	9,40,57,028	9,05,52,964	9,09,89,858

: which grew out of the measures of Lord Hastings, related in this work.

	1818-19.	1819-20.	1820-21.	1821-22.	1822-23.
)	20,81,272	19,77,549	9,39,205	8,80,246	8,86,662
}	2,58,012	20,944	52,522	22,136	34,140
	7,25,947	52,628	....	....	....
	3,23,544	1,04,493	....	....	....
	5,09,731	....	....	....	....
	....	51,037	....	....	....
7	38,97,506	22,09,651	9,91,727	9,08,382	9,20,802

As the most important, and yielding nearly two-thirds of the total receipts, we have placed the land revenue first. Every one knows that this item, instead of being like the land tax in England, a rateable impost on the income derived from the rents of land, is in India the better part, and sometimes nearly the whole, of the rent portion of the produce. The government does not claim to be proprietor of the soil, but acknowledges this right to be in the possessors, who may do what they please with the land. The adjustment of the government dues, however, is the condition of their possession ; and the remainder only of the rents, after these shall be satisfied, is the property of the occupants. Subject to this condition, the land is inherited, sold, mortgaged, or given away; and into whosesoever hands it passes, the government portion must first be set apart from the produce, for nothing but the act of the government can alienate its indefeasible right thereto. Such being the recognised state of landed property in India, one cannot wonder at the avidity with which schemes of conquest have been pursued there in all ages. The subjugation of any European state would give the power, and perhaps the right, of imposing contributions and taxes to support the conquering army ; but their amount is limited to the pay of that army, or to some other special object; and each requisition for a supply being felt as a new and grievous impost, the yoke which is attended with such a consequence is always galling and insupportable to the conquered. In India, however, the thing is ready done to hand. The displacement of the old government leaves the new in possession of its land rents : these, being no one else's property, fall naturally as the conqueror's prize.

The land revenues of Bengal and Buhar were in 1790 settled in perpetuity by Lord Cornwallis ; that is, a perpetual composition was then made with the individuals through whom this branch of revenue was then paid ; limiting the government rateable demand, on account of the lands in their management or occupancy, to a certain fixed amount by the year. That settlement exists to the present day, and the amount annually brought to credit for these two provinces (called the Lower, from their situation relatively to the Ganges,) will accordingly be observed to stand at a rate nearly uniform. In 1813-14, the land revenue of Bengal and Buhar was sicca rupees 2,99,81,588, including Sayer, 4,46,295, and Abkaree, 9,35,902. In 1822-23, it was 3,18,98,619, including, under the same heads respectively, 6,48,628 and 16,88,280. Upon the land, therefore, the increase in ten years was not ten lakh, or about 3 per cent. ; and this has been occasioned by the lapse of Jageers and other temporary alienations, or by the resumption of invalid grants, the resettlement of farms, and the like.

The reason for annexing the Sayer and Abkaree to the land revenue, in statements of this description, is, that the realisation of these items is effected through the same officers, the land revenue collectors. Originally these imposts were levied through the Malgoozars, or payers of the land revenue, and the settlement with them included their receipts on all accounts. The separation was, however, made by Lord Cornwallis in 1790; and both the Sayer and Abkaree have since been levied by the direct agency of the government officers. The former * consists of sundry petty receipts from Bazars, Gunjes, or the like, the property of government. The Abkaree is a general tax on spirits, raised by licensing houses of retail; the land revenue collectors are paid for the trouble of managing it by a commission of ten per cent. on the proceeds.

The land revenue of the western provinces, the second head of the statement, includes Bunarus, which was settled in perpetuity in 1795, on the same principles with Bengal and Buhar, and which has since yielded a gradual increase in the same proportion, and from the same causes. The total

---

* The transit duties generally bore the name of Sayer, and were levied also through the Zemindars, until separated and abolished by Lord Cornwallis, who substituted the inland customs in their place. They still exist at Madras.

amount levied under this head for the province of Bunarus, may be taken at from forty-five to forty-eight lakh of Calcutta rupees.—The bulk of the item, however, consists of the revenues of the territories obtained by cession from the Nuwab Vizeer in 1801, or conquered from the Mahrattas between 1803 and 1806; that is, of acquisitions made during the government of the Marquis Wellesley. The settlements are here periodical; and although Lord Wellesley, in the excess of his admiration of the system of Lord Cornwallis, promised by proclamation that a perpetual settlement should be made at the end of ten years, the pledge has not yet been redeemed; which is owing partly to the change of sentiment which has taken place as to the advantage of that system, and partly to the difficulty of determining with what classes to conclude engagements of the kind, and of devising sufficient securities for the various interests that would be directly or indirectly affected by such a measure. In the mean time, each periodical new settlement leads ordinarily to an increase of revenue; and hence it will be observed that the entry under the head Western Provinces, gives for the year 1813-14, 3,39,47,291, and for 1822-23, 3,87,63,686. Allowing for the proportion of this increase borne by the Sayer*

	1813-14.	1822-23.
*		
Sayer,	3,85,600.	8,62,054.
Abkaree,	9,65,300.	13,69,188.

and Abkaree included in both items, there is yet an advance of forty lakh on the land revenue; which is upwards of ten per cent. without making any allowance for Bunarus, where the increase has, of course, been in a lower ratio.

We have entered separately, in the statement, the revenue realized from the districts acquired in 1817-18, or subsequently, and annexed to the Bengal Presidency. This is rather to gratify curiosity, than for the purpose of exhibiting the financial advantage resulting from the measures then undertaken ; for the great gain was on the side of Bombay, where all the territories of Bajee Rao, and all other acquisitions made in Kandês and Goozerat, are brought to account. Of this, however, more hereafter. Including the acquisitions mentioned in the statement, and likewise the tributes, which are similarly stated separately, it will be seen that the total improvement of the land revenue, on the side of Bengal, has not been less than a crore of rupees in the ten years under review. This increase may be deemed permanent, as it is not likely any thing should occur either to deprive us of the demand, or to affect its realization. To explain the causes of the improvement more particularly would require a detail quite inconsistent with our present object, which is merely to show the nature of the principal sources of the revenue of the Indian governments, and the footing on which they are held.   We shall pass, therefore, to the next head.

The customs of Bengal consist partly of duties levied on the import and export trade of the country, and partly of an inland transit duty substituted for the abolished Sayer.   The former have been regulated from England, on the principle, of course, of favouring British manufactures as much as possible.   They are levied entirely at Calcutta*, which city has become, from its advantages as a port, and from its command of the navigation of the Ganges, the entrepôt of the whole foreign trade of Hindoostan.   The transit duties are levied on all goods, the manufacture of the country, or imported by land into the British possessions.   Heretofore the goods were made to pay a separate duty at each of the custom-houses they passed ; so that, according to the length of the journey, they reached the consumer, taxed with a single, double, or treble impost.   In 1810 this system was abolished, and the present introduced.   The pass, or receipt for duty (ruwana), given at one custom-house, will now carry the goods free from Dehlee to Chittagong.   The system, however, is still imperfect, and its further revision has been for some time in hand.   It is to

---

* There are custom-houses at Chittagong and Balasore ; but the exports and imports at both places are too insignificant to be mentioned.

be observed, that the salt-tax of the western provinces is levied in this form, and constitutes the
larger portion of the amount brought to credit, as
the produce of the customs in that division of the
Bengal territory.   This is owing to the salt being
there an article of inland importation from the
Jypoor and Lahore countries, or generally from
the salt lakes on the borders of the desert.   None
is produced in the part of Hindoostan under the
direct administration of the Bengal government.
The duty on import is one rupee per maund,
which may be assumed ordinarily to double the
market price to the consumer.   The total receipt
under the head customs will be observed to have
increased from Sicca Rs. 60,62,452 to 72,08,475;
and as in the course of the period comprehended
in the statement, the rates of duty have in several
instances been reduced, and in none increased,
the rise affords a satisfactory evidence of the increasing activity of commerce.

The salt-tax of Bengal is a peculiar impost, requiring some explanation.   Under the old Moghul government, this necessary of life was taxed
partly by a high transit duty, and partly by leas-
ing out, for an annual consideration, the right of
manufacture, which was else prohibited.   After
the battle of Plassee, most of the salt districts
having come into the hands of the Company's
servants, their endeavour to carry the article under

2 F

the free privilege obtained for the Company's
European goods, was a source of eternal dispute
with Meer Jafur, and produced the rupture with
his son-in-law Kasim Ulee.   Upon the acquisition of the Dewanee, and assumption of the administration of Bengal, Lord Clive re-established
the public dues on salt, by imposing a heavy transit duty on the article ; but he reserved the monopoly of its production, that the profits might
furnish himself and the other members of the
council with sufficient salaries, which they else
had not.   This system was abolished by orders
from England, and for some years the salt revenue was confined to a transit duty of thirty Rs.
per hundred maunds, and a Khularee duty on the
salt works levied in various ways, and credited in
the land revenue accounts.   In 1772 Mr. Verelst
attempted to revive the monopoly on account of
government, by the agency of contractors, who
were to buy from the manufacturers, and furnish
all they obtained to government at a small advance.   Government again, by reserving the exclusive privilege of giving the article out for consumption, were to realize a profit on the resale.
The plan failed from the want of sufficient means
of securing to government the exclusive market ;
accordingly, in 1776, Mr. Hastings adopted a
new scheme, and leased out the privilege both of
manufacture and sale to the individuals who en-

gaged for the land revenue. The production was now left so nearly free, that the price in the market fell almost to the natural rate, and those who had taken the leases, finding it impossible to realise the profit they expected from the privilege, very generally threw them up.   Upon this failure Mr. Hastings finally, in 1780, assumed the exclusive manufacture to the government, and undertook its management by agents established throughout the Sundurbuns and tideways of the mouths of the Ganges, where only salt can be produced in Bengal.   The manufacture was prohibited, except on account of government, and all the salt produced was lodged in public store-houses (Golas), whence it was to be given out for retail at a price fixed annually by the council at Calcutta.   The same system still prevails, except that Lord Cornwallis, in lieu of fixing the price by an order of council, instituted public sales to regulate the price by open competition, and the free speculation of bidders on the declared total supply of the year compared with the known demand.   All subsequent improvements have been directed to the prevention of illicit dealing and interference with the monopoly thus established; the system remains in other respects unaltered.   Under it the revenue realised in Bengal will be seen to have risen between 1813-14 and 1822-23 from a crore and a half to two crore of rupees, while the total charge of manufacturing the salt, and of maintaining the establishments necessary to secure the monopoly, amounted to between forty and sixty lakh per annum, including four lakh paid annually to the French, since the peace of 1815, to buy off their privilege of manufacturing salt at Balasore. The importance of this article of revenue will hence be manifest. In order to show the rate of taxation, the average price per hundred maunds at the Company's sales is noted for each year; the cost to the Company will be highly estimated at one hundred rupees the hundred maunds.

Next to the salt is the opium revenue, managed also as a monopoly, but forming one of the most extraordinary resources ever made available for a public purpose. The provinces of Buhar and Bunarus seem to possess advantages for the production of opium, which place them above the competition of the rest of the world. All that is produced, is taken by the government; and the cultivation of the poppy is prohibited, except under engagements to deliver the opium to the government agents. There is no difficulty in enforcing this prohibition, for it is impossible to grow the poppy by stealth. The agents receive and prepare the opium, and send it to Calcutta in chests. There it is sold by public sale; not for consumption in the country, the transit into the interior being absolutely prohibited, but for exportation by sea to China and the Malay Islands. The price at Canton regulates the bidding at Calcutta ; and notwithstanding that the article is there also contraband of import, still, such is the competition to engage in the trade, and such the facility of evading the Chinese prohibitory laws, that the price at the Company's sales reaches ordinarily ten times the original cost of the article. The Chinese, who are the consumers, pay the tax, and the sacrifice to the people of India is merely the loss of so much additional gain as might be made by a more extensive production and export of the article. The opium consumed in India is likewise taxed, but the impost is levied along with that on spirits, and is brought to account under the head Abkaree, so as to form no part of this item. Bengal draws no supply from China equivalent to the opium thus furnished. England again has no equivalent to give for the teas it obtains from them. The Company's cargoes are consequently paid for in a great measure by bills on Bengal, which bills form the returns of the opium trade. Thus a large portion of the remittance required to meet the home territorial charges finds its way to England through this channel.

The increase observable in the statement in the proceeds of this branch of revenue since 1813-14, is not an asset to be relied upon as permanent. Any fluctuation in the China market affects, of course, the Calcutta sales; and the measures which have ended in the pacification of India, have produced a result likely seriously to interfere with the profit derived from this source. The province of Malwa yields an opium not indeed equal in quality to that of Buhar and Bunarus, but in quantity rather abundant; and the developement of its resources, consequent upon the return of tranquillity, threatened very soon to create an active rivalry and consequent abatement of the price in China. In order to prevent the serious loss of revenue that would ensue from such a competition, Government resolved to establish a branch of its monopoly in Malwa, and entered the market there as purchaser of the article at the first hand. A considerable expense has been incurred in the outlay for this purpose; and as the returns do not appear till the second year after, a superficial observer might suppose the measure to have been attended with much greater loss than the reality. The system, however, is not yet complete, and it would be premature therefore to say more upon the subject: the circumstance has only been noticed at all because of its probable effect on the receipts of the Bengal government.

The exclusive privilege of dealing in opium, is one of the resources derived from the old Moghul government. It used to be farmed out yearly, and until 1772 was a great source of emolument to the members of the Patna provincial council. In that year Mr. Hastings introduced the system of procuring the article for government by contract, with a view to resale at Calcutta for exportation to the eastward. This plan continued until the time of Lord Cornwallis, who assimilated the management to that found so efficacious in the salt department; and the opium has since been provided by government agents, paid by a commission on the profit made on the resale. The receipts under this head have necessarily fluctuated greatly; but they have more than once reached a crore of net revenue, and hence are justly an object of consideration. The average price at the Calcutta sales for the chest of two maunds, is noted in the statement, in order to show more accurately the extent of fluctuation. The time of sale occasions the proceeds to be brought to account frequently in the following year, so that the revenue realised in any given year, bears no direct ratio to the price: moreover, the quantity brought to sale is not uniform.

The land revenue and customs, with the salt and opium monopolies, are the main articles of receipt in Bengal; and the two latter, in particular, produce the surplus which so much distinguishes this from the other presidencies. We have dwelt so long upon these resources, that the rest must be dismissed with a few words. The remaining heads of receipt are General, Judicial, Marine, and Miscellaneous.

The first includes all sums realized by the sale of presents to the Governor-general or public officers—Some fines levied at Dehlee—The mint duty, consisting of a seignorage of two per cent. on private bullion brought to be coined, and which, though fluctuating necessarily with the course of exchange, has occasionally yielded seven lakh of rupees—The post office, which has gradually risen, between 1813-14 and 1822-23, from three lakh and a half to five lakh of rupees ; and lastly, the stamp duty on deeds and law papers, which may be set down at eighteen lakh for the latter years of the statement. This last is the only impost entirely of European origin ; it was established by Lord Cornwallis in 1793-94, to meet the expense of the police establishment. In 1814, the institution fee on civil suits was transferred to this head, which is the cause of the sudden defalcation apparent in the judicial receipts after that year. It may not be out of place to notice, that while this tax is generally enforced throughout the provinces, and has been extended even to Dehlee, Calcutta enjoys a very unfair immunity from the impost. Neither deeds nor law papers, executed within the city, require a stamp, except they relate to property in the interior, and are intended for production in the native courts. Another fault of the present system is, that although the impost is light, it is the same on common receipts and bills of exchange, as on bonds, deeds of sale and mortgage, or other permanent securities. All are taxed with the same per centage on the amount affected by the transaction they record. This defect has not failed to attract the notice of the local government ; but by the act of 1813, the power of meddling with the taxation of India has been transferred to other hands.

The judicial receipts need no explanation; they can only mean what the name implies,—fees, fines, and the like, realised through the courts, or judicial establishments. The spirit duty of Calcutta being levied by the magistrates, is comprehended under this head.

Marine consists of the pilotage duties, and rents of mooring-chains laid down by government in the river Hoogley. The charges of the marine establishments exceed greatly these receipts ; but this is no test of the advantage of maintaining them on their present scale. Miscellaneous is a head which admits of no explanation, and the total amount of the items brought to credit under it is not such as to deserve more specific detail.

The Charges of the Bengal presidency will be observed in the statement to be arranged under heads corresponding, for the most part, with those on the opposite side; very few therefore require notice. With respect to the head General, this comprehends, besides the charges of the mint, post office, and stamp departments, of which the receipts are credited per contra, the salaries of the members of government ; the secretariat, in all its branches ; all the political residencies, and the expense of permanent or temporary missions. Also, the stipends of native princes, or nobles, with whom political arrangements have at different times been made ; and all donations to them, or disbursements of a similar nature. The largeness and variable amount of the item must not therefore excite surprise.

The registered debt of the other presidencies having been transferred to Bengal, the charge under the head Interest includes nearly the whole amount paid in India on that account. In like manner the head Miscellaneous includes the expense of maintaining the subordinate settlements of Bencoolen, Penang, Singapoor, and St. Helena, which is likewise borne by Bengal. The large surplus exhibited in the statement, is the excess of the receipts of this presidency, after providing for all these charges.

Having given thus in detail the receipts and disbursements of the Bengal presidency, we shall proceed to exhibit the financial result for the whole of India for the same period, and we shall adopt the same course; first giving the statement, and then subjoining the explanations necessary to make it intelligible. This statement is also in the sicca rupee of the Bengal accounts, and in comparing it with the accounts laid before Parliament, or with those of the other presidencies, it will be necessary to observe in what currency they are made out, and to make the conversion accordingly.

The circumstance first to be noted in this statement is, the result of the general comparison between the receipts and disbursements of India. In 1813-14, which was a year of perfect peace, there was a surplus of a crore and forty-five lakh. The operations of the Nipal war, and the attitude of preparation maintained during it towards the rest of India, trenched greatly on this surplus, in the following years, but did not absolutely consume it. The great effort of 1817-18, which was extended in its consequences into the two subsequent years, required the whole surplus of that period ; but no sooner was tranquillity restored, so as to allow the system established to produce its effect on the finances of the country, than the surplus returned, and was in the two last years brought to a higher rate than before, the result being considerably more favourable than was anticipated by the most sanguine. The great excess of receipt is on the side of Bengal, and it will have been seen from the statement before given, that fifty lakh of that is a clear addition to the rent-roll of this presidency, from the effect of the political measures of 1817-18. On the side of Bombay, however, the revenue has been increased by more than two crore of rupees; and although the charges have risen in nearly the same proportion, many of these are only temporary, as the life-stipend of Bajee Rao, and other political payments: moreover, the disbursements of the last two years in particular, include a large outlay of funds to establish the opium agency in Malwa, the returns of which will hereafter appear. Upon India only, putting out of the question the charges of the Burmese war, in which the government subsequently became involved, and which of course have no connexion with the political measures, the effect of which we are now examining, there can be no doubt that the surplus was fully ré-established at the time of Lord Hastings' leaving India, and with every prospect also of its permanently exceeding all demands upon it, and yielding a fund for the reduction of debt. The result has thus more than fulfilled the anticipation we ventured to hold out to the public in 1820. We then assumed that the net surplus of India would be raised to about a crore and ninety lakh. The average of the two last years gives a considerably higher rate, and were it necessary to enter into details, there are further funds that might be claimed to swell the surplus beyond the amount exhibited. The consequent reduction of debt had commenced as we shall presently explain more fully.

But the revenues of India cannot be said to yield a surplus, unless, besides the disbursements in the country, they provide the means of defraying all the charges incurred in England under the present system of administration. The legislature has provided that these shall constitute a demand on the resources of India to be discharged *pari passu*, with the pay of the civil establishments and other civil expenses in India; and the mode of payment has been thus regulated by the same high authority. For all territorial payments made in England the Company in its commercial capacity is to have a credit on the treasuries of India, at the rate of 2s. 3d. $\frac{84}{100}$ for the Calcutta sicca rupee. The profit or loss on the remittance is the concern of the Company, who issue their instructions as to the time and manner of investing the funds, the governments in India being merely their agents in the transaction. The rate was fixed at a time when the British currency was much depreciated, and was then doubtless very favourable; but as the restoration of cash payments has increased the value of the shilling, and altered the exchange one-fifth, it is now a losing rate to the Company. In order to show the state of this account, the several entries which follow the general comparison of the receipts and disbursements of India have been subjoined to the statement, and we shall now proceed to explain them.

First, the net debt annually incurred. So long of course as the revenues were not sufficient to meet the home as well as the Indian charges, it was necessary to provide the means by borrowing. The entries under this head include, as well all sums taken up from the public as the funds obtained by Lord Hastings from the Nuwab Vizeer; and the amount which came into the possession of Government upon the death of the Fyzabad Begum, widow of Shooja-ood-Doula. The payment of six per cent. interest was the condition upon which all these funds were obtained, and though, as mentioned in the body of this Work, the second crore obtained from the Nuwab Vizeer was cancelled by a cession of territory, that circumstance did not alter the character of the original transaction. The amount is therefore included in the entry for 1815-16, as part of the debt incurred. Again, in 1816-17, the entry is less, from the same amount being deducted as paid off. It is to be observed, that deposits and other non-interest debts are included under this head ; so that the amount entered for each year will not be found to correspond with the annual difference in the state of the registered and interest debts of India, the amount of which is likewise inserted for the years we have been able to ascertain it.

Besides the debt incurred, other funds have occasionally been made available for the wants of the public service in India, and the statement of the financial result would not be complete without inserting them. Of these the supplies from London are the most material item, and we shall endeavour to explain how this has arisen, and why the account is kept distinct from that between the territory and the commerce for the home territorial charges. Payments on account of his Majesty's government, bullion remittances to and from India, and bills of exchange negotiated on either side, form the basis of this account. In the first two years it will be observed that the result was against India, which had to furnish for Java and the Mauritius, for his Majesty's navy, or in payment of bills from England, more than it received from thence. In every other year, however, till 1820-21, the balance was considerably on the other side, so as to exhibit India indebted to England, in the whole account under this head, in a sum exceeding two crore of rupees. This has been owing to several causes. In the first place, the entire Indian debt was held on terms which entitled the creditor at his option to take the interest in cash, or to require bills for the amount on England at two shillings and sixpence the rupee. In the earlier years of the statement, the exchange with England being ordinarily at two shillings and eight pence, and sometimes two shillings and ten pence for the rupee, none availed themselves of this option; but the exchange was no sooner brought down below two shillings and sixpence, by the financial measures of the British legislature, than, instead of taking cash, bills were universally demanded, as well by residents in India as in Europe, for they were always saleable at a high premium in Calcutta. The relief purchased for the Indian treasuries at this ruinous rate, appears under this head of the account. Again, the British legislature, besides providing for the appropriation of the territorial funds under the Company's management, has enacted, that any commercial profit made by the China and Indian trade, in excess of what may suffice for a dividend of ten and a half per cent. on the stock, shall go to the reduction of debt. Such profit in excess appears to have been made in the early years of the period comprised in the statement; for, between September 1818 and April 1819, half a million sterling was transmitted to Bengal in bullion, and a like sum was dispatched towards the end of 1819, with special injunctions that the whole should be applied as a sinking fund to reduce the Indian debt, to which purpose, as being a commercial profit of the kind above described, it was exclusively applicable under the provisions of the Company's charter. By June 1821, a further sum of a million and a half became available for the same object; but this was effected by a mere transfer of account, no remittance of bullion being made in that year. Besides the transactions on these two accounts which form the principal part of the supplies from London, his Majesty's government sent out bullion to meet the charges of the public service in India; but since the restoration of Java to the Dutch, and the reduction of the navy to a peace establishment, the advances on either side, on this account, have ceased to produce any material effect on the general balance.

The aid afforded to the Indian treasuries by the effect of such operations, was doubtless in some respects opportune; but it was not wanted, and could not be reckoned upon; and hence, in making provision for the exigencies of each year, the expectation of such a supply had very seldom any influence in preventing a resort to loans. The circumstance, however, contributed to produce the inordinate augmentation of the cash balances which the statement exhibits, and thus enabled the Supreme Government to undertake the financial measures for the reduction of debt, and relief of the home treasury, which we shall presently mention.

The only other addition to the annual assets noted in the statement, is an entry in the Bengal accounts, of sums raised by the sale of stores belonging to the Company, and hence not an ordinary receipt of revenue : the item is not of sufficient magnitude to deserve further mention.

Under the assets of each year the supplies to commerce are given in the statement ; and it may at first sight strike the reader, that the excess or deficit of the assets, compared with these supplies, ought to equal the annual difference in the amount of the cash balances on the last day of the official year. That this correspondence does not exist, is owing to an amount of floating unadjusted debits and credits between the different presidencies —an item it is obviously unnecessary to exhibit in an account of this description, but which, nevertheless, cannot be thrown out of the statement of the annual balances. The nature of the item, and the impossibility of making the result exactly correspond in this respect, will be evident, when it is recollected, that all the accounts throughout India are made up to the same day (the 30th of April). If Bombay, therefore, has received money for a bill on Bengal a few days antecedently, the amount will be credited to Bengal, and added to the cash balances of the Bom-

bay presidency from that day ; but the corresponding debit to Bombay, and deduction from the
cash balances of Bengal, will not be made until
after the day of general account, when the bill so
drawn may be paid. The statement of the cash
balances in hand consists of a general return from
the several treasuries, and hence cannot exactly
correspond with an account of receipts and disbursements from which such items are excluded.

We shall now hasten to the general result. It
will be seen that, during the whole period comprised in the statement, the supplies to commerce
were never suspended; and although in the first
years they did not quite equal the demand on
account of the home territorial charges, the debt
incurred to commerce on that account was by the
year 1820-21 wholly redeemed, leaving the balance of the London account only to be thereafter
adjusted. It will be seen further, that the registered and other interest debt of India, which on
the 30th of April 1814, stood at 21,31,92,502 was,
on the corresponding date of 1821, 25,85,06,540,
or about four crore and a half in excess; but the
cash balances were in the same period augmented
by nearly five crore; so that, in fact, the amount
borrowed was still in hand, and the financial condition of India considered merely with reference
to the Indian debt, was much the same in 1821
as it was in 1814. For this result the country

was indebted to the supply of somewhat more than two crore, received from London in the interval, and a corresponding increase of the debt for its repayment would have been indispensable; but this item was counterbalanced by the profits of the China trade, which the legislature had made applicable to the reduction of the territorial debt, and which appear to have exceeded the supply in question.

Assuming, however, that the political measures had been found, on closing the account in 1820-21, to have added five crore to the debt of the country, we are still prepared to show that the financial condition and prospects of that period were worth the purchase. In the first place, the gross revenue of India was increased four crore; and although the charges had been increased in a similar amount, these had reached their limit, and were in the course of diminution,* while the revenue was obviously further on the increase, so as to afford the certainty of an annual surplus not only sufficient to meet the interest of the additional debt, for that item was provided for in the

* Bombay is the only presidency in which there was not subsequently a diminution of charge, and that was owing to the outlay to establish an opium agency in Malwa. The military charges of this presidency were reduced from 1,89,60,880 rupees, which amount they stood at in 1820-21 to 1,57,52,599, the amount in 1822-23.

charges, but yielding a fund applicable to reduce the debt, or otherwise improve the resources of the country, after providing for all demands, as well in Europe as in Asia.

Confident in the prospects of that period, the Supreme Government immediately commenced a series of operations, directed to the reduction of its burthens, and combining with this object the permanent relief of the home treasury. The notice of some of these measures will best show the financial prosperity under which only they could have been attempted.

The public debt of India consisted in 1820-21 of two descriptions of stock. First, the six per cent. loan of 1811-12, into which the bulk of all the previous debts of the government had been transferred. The terms were, that the interest should be payable half-yearly, either in cash, or by bills on England, at two shillings and sixpence the rupee, at the option of the stock-holder. Payment of the principal was assured in the order of inscription in the register, and three months notice was to be given before payment. The amount of this debt was 13,36,99,346 rs. Secondly, the loan of 1812-13, and all subsequent, which were likewise at six per cent. and with a like condition as to the payment of the interest; but containing the further stipulation, that, in the event of repayment, it should be at the option of the stock-holder to receive his principal in cash in India, or by bills at two shillings and sixpence the rupee, on the court of directors in England. The total amount of stock held on these terms was 11,50,63,494. The first loan from the Nuwab Vizeer, and the sum of fifty-six lakh obtained on the death of the Fyzabad Begum, were the only public debts not of one or other of the above two descriptions. The interest of both these debts having been assigned by special arrangements of a political nature for the provision of certain stipends, the power of redemption was virtually resigned by the government, though no formal stipulation to that effect was at the time recorded.

The first object which engaged the attention of the Supreme Government was, to relieve the Company from the necessity of providing a remittance at two shillings and sixpence for the interest of the loan of 1811-12, which, as the exchange was now at its par of from two shillings to two shillings and a penny, had proved a serious burthen on the home treasury. On the 1st of May 1821, a loan was opened at six per cent., of which both the interest and principal were to be payable in India only. The first numbers of the loan of 1811-12, were at the same time advertised for peremptory payment, and a transfer into the new loan was allowed at par. The measure was completely successful; 11,75,33,300 sicca rupees were transferred, and the remainder, including about twenty-four lakh held by the sinking fund committee, was absolutely paid off.

The next measure undertaken was to effect a similar relief to the home treasury for the interest on the loans of the second description. Here, however, the option of demanding bills at two shillings and sixpence for the principal was an advantage, requiring to be purchased of the creditor by the offer of some equivalent benefit in the new loan, to which it was intended to invite a transfer. Not deterred by this consideration, the Supreme Government opened a new loan in 1822, on the following terms. First, that the principal should be absolutely irredeemable during the period of the existing charter; and, if paid off afterwards, fifteen months' notice should be given; and it should be at the holder's option to receive cash, or bills on England at two shillings and sixpence for the principal, payable at twelve months' date. Secondly, that the interest at six per cent. should be payable half-yearly in India only, if the proprietor were resident in India; but, if resident in Europe, it should be at his option to receive bills for the interest at two shillings and a penny.

A loan on these terms was advertised on the 1st of May 1822, at a time when the remittable paper bore a premium of twenty-seven and thirty per cent. On the account being closed on the 30th of June, the following was found to be the result. The Oudh loan, amounting to 1,03,82,094, stood on the register as part of the debt incurred on these terms. This amount being set apart, together with 21,98,300 sicca rupees, stock purchased by the operations of the sinking fund, which was, of course, cancelled, there remained of the eleven crore and a half 7,51,26,900 transferred, and about two crore and seventy lakh taken out in bills on England at two shillings and sixpence. Provision was made by large remittances of bullion, in addition to the ordinary supplies to commerce, to enable the court of directors to liquidate these bills. It was at their option, however, either to pay them as they fell due, or to defer the payment of the whole, or of any part, for one, two, or three years, on the condition of paying interest at five per cent. on the amount. We have not the means of filling up the heads of the statement for the two last years, so as to show the result of these operations. The amount of the interest debt of India will, however, be observed to have suffered a great diminution between the years 1821-22 and 1822-23, which was owing to the conversion of so large a portion of the remittable loan into bills within that period.

Not content with effecting the important permanent relief to the Home Treasury, resulting from these two operations, and relying confidently on the still improving condition of the Financial prospects of India, the Supreme Government resolved, in 1823, to pay off a considerable portion of the six per cent. loan of 1821, and to reduce the interest on the remainder from six to five per cent. The stock of this loan was at a premium which showed the practicability of such a measure; and had the government been disposed to avail itself of the effect of its own measures in sending fresh capital into the market, a much harder bargain might have been made than the simple reduction of one per cent. of the interest. Consideration for the public creditor, however, prevailed over the motives of cupidity which urged a further saving; moreover, as it was a hardship to receive payment of any part of the principal in the then state of the money market, means were devised of distributing the disadvantage equally amongst the holders of the stock of the loan. The intention of paying off two crore and fifty lakh of rupees was formally notified to the public, and the stockholders were invited to tender their stock for transfer into the five per cent. loan, opened at the same time, upon the condition that on a given date the transfer should close; and if, as was expected, the amount remaining untendered fell short of two crore and a half, the complement of that sum should be made up by a proportionate deduction from the principal of all the tenders, which being paid in cash, obligations of the new loan would be granted for the remainder. There was a further provision, securing to the earliest obligations the latest eventual repayment, and apportioning the total amount of the loan in instalments, which government were to be free to pay off at different periods, so fixed as to clear the whole debt on the expiration of the term of the present charter of the company.

On closing the transaction, the principal of the new five per cent. loan stood at nine crore and eighteen lakh, which was a deduction of more than two crore and a half from the loan of 1821 ; thus relieving the revenues of India from the entire burthen of interest at six per cent. on this sum, besides one per cent. on the remainder,—a relief amounting in the whole to upwards of twenty-four lakh per annum.

The above are a part only of the operations which the improved financial prospects of India at this period gave the means of undertaking. The Madras presidency paid to the Nizam an annual peshkush of seven lakh of rupees for the northern Sirkars (Chikakôl, &c.) The redemption of this was negotiated in 1823, for a prompt payment equal to its fair value, calculated at six per cent. which was in effect the same thing exactly as if debt chargeable with this amount of interest had been put in liquidation. But a yet more important burthen was removed from the growing income of India, by an arrangement which the superfluity of funds gave the Company the means of concluding with his Majesty's government in England. In the year 1812, the Company being under considerable embarrassment from a drain on the home treasury, consequent upon the measures for reducing the interest on the Indian debt from eight to six per cent. were compelled to apply to the public for aid, and obtained two millions and a half sterling in three per cents. negotiated at the price of the day. Besides the interest, a proportionate sinking-fund was to be paid annually, and both were to form a territorial charge on the revenues, until the whole should be redeemed. Considerable sums, however, having been advanced in India for the expenses of Java and other possessions of the crown, and for the navy, &c., the account of these was finally adjusted on the 30th of April 1823, when the debt due to the Company was found to be 1,300,000*l.* The opportunity was accordingly taken of cancelling the loan of 1812, by paying in cash the further sum of 508,617*l.* which formed the complement of the amount remaining unredeemed up to that day. The territorial demand to be made good by advances to the commercial department in India, will henceforth be diminished in the amount of the interest and sinking fund of this loan.

All these operations were the result of the flourishing condition into which the finances of India were brought towards the close of the administration of the Marquess of Hastings, that is, after the resources acquired or improved by the political exertions we have attempted to record had begun to be fully developed. After this detail, it surely will not be maintained that the concern is necessarily a losing one, that cannot be carried on without an annual increase of the debt, or the aid of large supplies from England. So long, doubtless, as the struggle for existence lasted, or as the nation had to contend with jealous rivals aiming, like itself, at the mastery ; so long, in short, as further outlay was requisite to acquire the entire estate, and secure the full benefit of which it could be made productive, the debt of course went on accumulating, for it was the price paid for the possession. But the tables were turned by the establishment of the British supremacy over the whole country ; and the rapid diminution of the incumbrances laid on the vast income which then became the nation's prize, is both a consequence of the completeness of our possession, and an irrefragable proof of its value.

The Burmese war has since supervened, and

has brought with it a load of expense, that must for some years impede the action of these financial results; but we do not on that account think them less certain or permanent; and when the objects of that war shall have been accomplished in the punishment of past insults, and the creation of such an impression of our power as shall give assurance against their repetition, we shall not despair of again seeing the local government occupied, as before the war broke out, with the consideration of how best to dispose of its superfluous income, instead of seeking either from Europe, or in loans from the public of India, for the means of supplying the current expenses of the year.

With this summary of the financial condition in which India was left by the Marquess of Hastings, we shall take leave of the reader, whom curiosity or past recollections may have conducted thus far. We have done little more than simply relate such facts as it seemed of importance to place permanently on record before the public; and if they prove wanting in interest to the generality of European readers, the fault may perhaps be ours; but it will entail no disappointment, for success in this respect was always beyond our hopes. But though we have not the art of clothing our subject with all the interest of which it is capable, this would have been no sufficient reason for leaving it untouched. Our work will mostly fall into hands of those who seek profit rather than amusement from its pages; and if readers of this class rise from the perusal tolerably satisfied with the insight it has given them into the events of the period, we trust we shall not be thought to have thrown away our labour. It is not fit that measures of such incalculable influence over the wealth and happiness of millions, should be left to be gathered from occasional party statements, or from correspondence published without method or arrangement, to suit the views of some particular public man, and all for the want of any connected account of them to which those who sought the information might refer. Such a record, therefore, it has been our aim to supply; and we have not hesitated to place the conduct of the British functionaries in the East, without any reserve or concealment, before their fellow countrymen; claiming for them to be judged by British feelings and principles, tempered only by a due regard to the peculiar circumstances under which the Indian dependencies of the empire were first acquired, and the moral duties entailed by the possession.

INDEX.

A.

G.

INDEX. 479

Nagpoor, capital of the Bhoosla family, subsidiary alliance concluded there with Apa Saheb, vol. i. 365—further proceedings there, 385. 422 to 430. also 66 to 103. vol. ii. —first battle of, vol. ii. 71 to 80—second do. 91 to 92— siege of the fort, 93 to 95—See heads Apa Saheb and Bhoosla.

Nahn, occupied by General Martindell, vol. i. 96.

Nalapanee, General Gillespie's attack of, vol. i. 87—second assault by Col. Mawbey, 91—evacuation, 93—fort dismantled, 94.

Namdar Khan, nephew and Lieutenant of Kureem Khan Pindara, vol. i. 44—his surrender, vol. ii. 149—See Pindarees.

Nana Furnavees, his policy, and ruin by Bajee Rao, vol i. 267.

Nana Govind Rao, of Jaloun and Sagur, vol. i. 239—arrangements with him consequent on the treaty of Poona, vol. ii. 38—his rights considered on the occupation of Sâgur, 204, 205.

Naroba Chitnavees (secretary) minister of Raghoojee Bhoosla, vol. i. 357—his intrigues, &c., 358, 359.

Negotiations with Nipâl, vol. i. 179. 193—with Bhopâl and Sâgur, 238 to 240—with Nagpoor, 360 to 365—with Jypoor, 376 to 382—with Bajee Rao, prior to treaty of Poona, 443 to 450—with the Gykwar, vol. ii. 6 to 9—with Sindheea, 25 to 32—with Ameer Khan, 34 to 37—with Holkur, 135 to 139—with Bajee Rao, prior to surrender, 273 to 277—with the Rajpoot states, 352 to 380.

Nicol, Colonel, H. M. 66th Foot, commands under General Ochterlony in the 2nd campaign of the Nipâl war, vol. i. 195—penetrates to Etounda, 201.

Nicolls, Colonel *Jasper*, commands a brigade employed against Kumaon, 1st campaign Nipâl war, vol. i. 151— his proceedings, 152 to 156—reduces Almora, 157.

Nipâl, condition of, and origin of the war, vol. i. 54 to 80— first campaign against, 81 to 176—second campaign, 194 to 205—peace concluded, 206—relations with China, 208 to 213—mission from, received at Patna, vol. ii. 17—intrigues at commencement of the Pindaree war, 32.

Nizam, his condition in 1814, vol. i. 8 to 13—disturbances raised by his sons, 261 to 266—condition after the Pindaree and Mahratta war, vol. ii. 413, 414, 416.

Nizam-Ulee, his relations with the British, and death, vol. i. 9, 10.

Nurayun Pundit, minister of the Bhoosla, vol. i. 360—negotiates a subsidiary alliance, 361 to 364—subsequent

vol. i. 189—discovers a route to turn the Choorea Ghatee defences, 195—activity at Mundela, vol. ii. 207.

Pindarees, their rise and condition in 1814, vol. i. 32 to 48 —reference to England regarding, 229—second more urgent reference, 327—expeditions sent out by them, 328—Guntoor plundered, 331—further proceedings, 395 —expeditions of 1816, 398 to 406—preparations of 1817, vol. ii. 40, 41—proceedings on British advance, 46—dispersion of two durras, 114, 115—surprises, 117, 147, 151 —distress, 149—general submission and settlement of the chiefs, 150 to 153.

Political review, vol. ii. 336 to 420.

Poona, affairs of---See Bajee Rao.—Treaty of, vol. i. 450— battle of, vol. ii. 59, 60—second ditto, 64.

Poornea, dewan of Mysore, notice of his death, vol. i. 16.

Poorundur, guarantee fort, surrendered by Bajee Rao, vol. i. 445—restored, vol. ii. 2—siege and capture by Brigadier-general Pritzler, 184.

Post Office Revenue, vol. ii. 440.

Prithee Nurayun Sah, first Goorkha Raja of Nipâl, vol. i. 56.

Pritzler, Brigadier-general, in command of the reserve of the Dukhun army, vol. ii. 14---his march to Poona, and pursuit of Bajee Rao, 167---reduces Wusota and other forts, 249 to 251---engaged in the battle of Selapoor, 254.

Pundurpoor, Gungadhur Shastree murdered there, vol. i. 292 ---Bajee Rao retires there after treaty of Poona, vol. ii. 4---limit of the Sutara dominions east, 383.

Pursa, detachment cut off there by the Nipalese, vol. i. 124.

Pursajee Bhoosla---See Bhoosla.

Pursaram Rao, his intrigues at Nagpoor, vol. i. 358. 428.

Putans, force organized by chiefs of this class, vol. i. 48. 50 ---See Ameer Khan, &c.---Dissolution of the force arranged by Sir David Ochterlony, vol. ii. 192 to 196---chiefs established in Malwa, policy of the measure, vol. ii. 399, 400.

—— *Punnee Putans,* notice of their guaranty, vol. i. 354.

—— of Rohilkhund, raised for service in Kumaon, vol. i. 143—insurrection amongst quelled, vol. i. 417.

R.

Raghoojee Bhoosla---See Bhoosla.

Raja of Nipâl, of Rewa, &c.---See Nipal, Rewa, &c.

Rajas and Chiefs, restored in the western hills on their conquest, vol. i. 177.

Rajpootana and *Rajpoots,* their condition in 1814, vol. i. 49---